REFUGEES, CITIZENSHIP AND SOCIAL POLICY IN EUROPE

First published in Great Britain 1999 by
MACMILLAN PRESS LTD
Houndmills, Basingstoke, Hampshire RG21 6XS and London
Companies and representatives throughout the world

A catalogue record for this book is available from the British Library.

ISBN 0–333–71910–7

First published in the United States of America 1999 by
ST. MARTIN'S PRESS, INC.,
Scholarly and Reference Division,
175 Fifth Avenue, New York, N.Y. 10010

ISBN 0–312–21724–2

Library of Congress Cataloging-in-Publication Data
Refugees, citizenship, and social policy in Europe / edited by Alice
Bloch and Carl Levy.
p. cm.
Includes bibliographical references and index.
ISBN 0–312–21724–2 (cloth)
1. Refugees—Government policy—Europe. 2. Asylum, Right of–
–Europe. I. Bloch, Alice, 1964– . II. Levy, Carl, 1951– .
JV7590.R44 1998
325'.21'094—dc21   98–35605
                                                        CIP

This book is printed on paper suitable for recycling and made from fully managed and sustained forest sources.

10   9   8   7   6   5   4   3
08   07   06   05   04   03   02   01   00

Printed and bound in Great Britain by
Antony Rowe Ltd, Chippenham, Wiltshire

Contents

Notes on contributors

Alice Bloch is a Senior Lecturer in the Department of Sociology and Anthropology at the University of East London

Claudio Bolzman is a Professor in the Centre for Social Research at the Institute of Social Studies, Geneva

Karen Duke is a Research Fellow in the School of Social Science at the University of Middlesex

Jeanne Gregory is a visiting Professor and Head of Gender Research Centre at the University of Middlesex

Carl Levy is a Lecturer in European Politics in the Department of Social Policy and Politics at Goldsmiths College, University of London

Paul E. Minderhoud is a Senior Researcher at the Institute for Sociology of Law at the University of Nijmegen

Rosemary Sales is a Principal Lecturer in the School of Social Science at the University of Middlesex

Karen Schönwälder is a political scientist at the Justus Liebig Universität in Giessen, Germany.

Liza Schuster is a research assistant at South Bank University.

Helena Scott is a European Development Officer at Age Concern Scotland

John Solomos is a Professor of Sociology at South Bank University

Patricia Tuitt is a Senior Lecturer in the School of Law at the University of East London

Louise Williamson is a research student at Queen Mary and Westfield College, University of London and was formally Director of the Children's Division at the Refugee Council

List of tables

List of figures

1 Introduction
Alice Bloch

BACKGROUND: REFUGEES AND SOCIAL POLICY

Refugee migration has become a key policy concern of European countries in the late twentieth century. The reasons for the concern about refugee migration include: increasing numbers of refugees arriving in Western Europe from Africa, Asia and Latin America; the dissolution of European borders; economic downturns and high levels of unemployment across Europe and increasing levels of xenophobia from the media and the general public.

Prior to the 1970s, most refugee migration to Europe was inter-European and this was reflected in the first international legislation, the 1951 Geneva Convention which concerned refugees and asylum seekers in post-war Europe. The Geneva Convention defined refugees as 'persons who are outside their country because of a well-founded fear of persecution for reasons of race, religion, nationality, membership of a particular social group or political opinion'. The Bellagio Protocol, signed by nearly 100 countries in 1967, adopted the Geneva Convention's definition of a refugee but removed some of the limitations of the Convention by giving the United Nations High Commissioner for Refugees responsibility for refugees from all over the world which reflected international changes as refugees were no longer just a European phenomenon; instead refugee migration was occurring from conflicts all over the world.

The 1970s saw an increase in the numbers of refugees and asylum seekers arriving in industrial countries from Asia, Africa and Latin America. This coincided with attempts to reduce the number of primary economic labour migrants entering, and in some cases staying in Europe, as an economic recession took hold. Many European countries had experienced labour shortages in the post-war period and recruited what they thought was temporary labour, often from displaced persons camps in Europe. However, Britain, like other European countries, actively recruited workers from countries with which it had a colonial link. Many of the new labour recruits were

1

from less developed countries in Africa, Asia and the Caribbean and immigration, especially immigration control, became a feature on the political agenda. Entry to Europe became increasingly restricted and so there was little primary migration, except among refugees and asylum seekers and on the basis of family reunion.

An atmosphere of suspicion has emerged around refugees and asylum seekers. Refugees are those who have had their refugee status recognized by the host or receiving country. An asylum seeker is a person who is seeking asylum on the basis of his or her claim to be a refugee. People who are waiting for their cases to be considered are know as asylum seekers, whether or not their claims will be eventually accepted as legitimate. Asylum seekers who are not recognized as refugees are not always deported. In some cases it is recognized that they cannot return to their country of origin and they are granted leave to remain on humanitarian grounds.

Different rights are afforded to different statuses, in receiving countries across Europe. People with full refugee status have the same citizenship rights as nationals of the host society while those with leave to remain have less rights and asylum seekers have the least rights and in some cases are excluded from employment, welfare entitlements and freedom of movement.

The trend across Europe has been to try and curb the migration of asylum seekers. In their efforts to discourage asylum seekers, governments have put legislation in place which makes it increasingly difficult for asylum seekers to find a safe haven in Europe. Discourse in the media has often emphasized the notion of 'bogus' or 'undeserving' asylum seekers who are portrayed as economic migrants exercising their right to asylum as the only means of migrating to Europe in order to increase economic opportunities. However, this discourse ignores two key facts. First, across much of Europe restrictions on access to employment and social security benefits often leaves asylum seekers in situations of extreme hardship rather than benefiting from economic gain. Secondly, the situation and the experiences of refugees and asylum seekers differ quite markedly from that of voluntary economic migrants.

REFUGEES: A SPECIAL GROUP OF MIGRANTS

What makes a refugee a refugee as opposed to an economic migrant is something which has been subject to much debate. Collinson (1993) devised a matrix which revolves around two key concepts: political versus economic and voluntary versus involuntary. Migration which is political and involuntary represents classic refugee flows while migration which is economic and involuntary would be refugees from famine and ecological disaster. It is the latter type of refugee who is often thought to be an economic migrant.

Some refugees flee their homeland in acute circumstances and are not able to plan for their flight while others anticipate the need to depart and plan their flight before the situation mitigates against an orderly departure. What Kunz (1973) terms anticipatory refugees are sometimes mistaken as voluntary migrants and so the historical background to a refugee producing situation is vital. The main thing that differentiates a refugee from other migrants is that refugees are involuntary migrants; they did not want to leave their country of origin. According to Kunz,

It is the reluctance to uproot oneself, and the absence of positive original motivations to settle elsewhere, which characterizes all refugee decisions and distinguishes the refugee from the voluntary migrants (1973: 130).

Given the forced nature of the departure of refugees and in some cases, their experiences of war, civil unrest, political disturbance, violence, death of family members, torture and poverty it should be clear that their migration situation and relationship to their homeland would differ markedly from that of voluntary migrants.

Refugees and asylum seekers often arrive in the host society without previous contacts or links with the host society and many have left behind family members and friends. This is in contrast to voluntary migrants who, in many instances, follow a pattern of 'chain migration' and migrate to countries where there is a connection which is often based on a colonial past and kinship ties (Castles and Miller, 1993). These factors will affect the migration experience, aspirations for the migration and the resultant experience of settlement among migrants (Kunz, 1981).

Factors which affect settlement in the host society tend to fall into two broad areas: the characteristics of the refugee themselves, such as educational background, age and gender, and national policies or what Weiner (1996) terms as 'immigrant policies'. Immigrant policies are those which are associated with the receiving country and their attitudes towards the settlement of migrants. Moreover, it is concerned with the extent to which migrants are granted full citizenship rights and as we have seen, there is a tendency, throughout Europe, to place restrictions on the rights and freedom of asylum seekers which will impact on settlement.

Given the differences between forced and voluntary migrants it is surprising that there has been so little work which addresses the situation of refugees as a separate and distinct category from other migrants. Indeed, Joly (1996) notes that much of the theoretical work on migration does not consider the situation of refugees which is clearly an area which needs to be addressed.

THEMES

This book assesses the situation of refugees and asylum seekers across Europe from the perspective of social policy. Policy decisions ranging from the way in which borders are controlled and asylum claims are processed to benefit entitlement and care provided for unaccompanied children, all affect the lives of refugees in the host society. The book is topical given the increasingly high profile that refugees and asylum seekers have in both domestic policy and the policies of the European Union.

Many themes clearly emerge from the collection of essays. First, there is the increased focus of European governments on policies which specifically target asylum seekers within the law with the aim of curtailing and discouraging their migration to Europe. These issues are explored from a European perspective by Levy, from a British perspective by Schuster and Solomos while Schönwälder explores German policy.

The second theme to emerge concerns the role of local government in the reception and resettlement of refugees and asylum seekers. The tension between central and local governments is apparent. Minderhoud examines issues around social security and highlights some of the legal proceedings that local authorities have instigated against central governments. Williamson looks at the tensions between central and local government in the UK with regard to statutory provision for children. More generally Duke, Sales and Gregory consider the role of statutory and voluntary sector organizations in the reception and resettlement of refugees.

The third theme which runs through the chapters is the impact of reduced citizenship rights, such as limited access to welfare and employment, and the resultant disadvantage experienced by asylum seekers. Minderhoud explores welfare entitlements in four European countries and argues that, in some cases, the limited access to welfare does in fact contravene basic human rights. Bloch examines the position of refugees and asylum seekers in the labour market and shows that as a group, refugees and asylum seekers experience higher levels of unemployment than any other group. Moreover, the minority who are in paid employment are in the poorest paid jobs and are working in areas which do not reflect their previous skills and experience.

Finally, the general exclusion and marginalization of refugees and asylum seekers from the host society is a theme which is apparent throughout the book. For example, Scott and Bolzman examine the case of older refugees and show that they can be excluded and that their needs are not being met by statutory agencies. Indeed, a lack of understanding about the experiences and needs of refugees becomes evident when specific policies and groups are examined.

THE REST OF THE BOOK

In Chapter 2, Levy charts the migration of refugees and asylum seekers to Europe and shows the way in which individual members states have, for the most part, adopted increasingly restrictive policies towards refugees and asylum seekers although there are variations across Europe. Variations in refugee policy are explored through a case study of responses to the crisis in the former Yugoslavia.

Levy also examines the changes in European Union policy from the mid-1980s and shows the gradual harmonization of European policy during this period. However, the tensions between the policies of the individual member states and the policies of the European Union are highlighted and examples demonstrate the incidences where some members states have asserted their own domestic sovereignty by opting out of European agreements. Finally, the 1997 Treaty of Amsterdam is explored along with the inherent tension between its concern for human rights and the exclusion of asylum seekers.

Schuster and Solomos, in Chapter 3, document immigration policy from its inception in 1905 and especially the development of a specific asylum policy in Britain. The chapter shows that despite Britain's perception of itself as a liberal and tolerant country, the reality is somewhat different. Even the persecution of the Jews in Nazi Germany demonstrates the selectivity of asylum policy, where entry was limited to those who would not require the support of the state and those who were prominent in their fields and could therefore enhance aspects of research and cultural life in Britain.

The selective approach to refugee migration continued and the authors demonstrate this by comparing the response to Chilean refugees with refugees from Vietnam. The Chileans, who fled the overthrow of the Allende government, were admitted to Britain as quota refugees and their cause was championed by the then Labour government who were sympathetic to the overthrow of Allende. The attitude towards refugees from Vietnam was very different. Indeed, it took pressure from the United Nations before Britain would agree to accept a quota of 'boat people'.

The 1980s and 1990s have seen an explosion in legislation concerned with controlling the migration of asylum seekers to Britain. This has included the 1987 Carriers Liability Act, the imposition of visas for some foreign nationals, who were entering Britain from refugee producing countries like Sri Lanka, and the two pieces of legislation in the 1990s concerned exclusively with asylum seekers. The Acts were justified by the agreement that it was to prevent 'bogus' asylum seekers and the exploitation of asylum rules for migrants seeking entry to Britain. The authors argue that policies have become more restrictive and that they are linked with racism and the curtailment of migration.

In Chapter 4, Schönwälder introduces the German case by examining the changing position of refugees as reflected in the Basic Law (constitution). Germany, like Britain, had a history of post-war labour migration. After the oil crisis in 1973, they no longer wanted migrants and realized that their migrant workers had, in some cases, decided to have families and to settle in Germany. The mid-1970s until the early 1980s became a transitional period where Germany moved from a liberal policy to one of 'open deterrence' and laws were passed which aimed to reduce the numbers of asylum seekers entering Germany by making it more difficult to enter the country and by making it less attractive once within Germany by introducing measures such as restrictions on employment.

In the mid-1980s the attention, led by the mass media, shifted to the unwanted affects of migration on German society and warned of threats to German culture and society. Asylum seekers became linked with negative images and terminology.

By the early 1990s, there was an increase in xenophobic violence and pressure was mounted, by local authorities, on the government against the 'burden' placed on them by asylum seekers. In response to the increasing amount of social and political pressure against asylum seekers, Article 16 of the Basic Law was changed restricting asylum in Germany from 1993. This change marked the end of Germany's previously liberal policy and demonstrated the way in which asylum had become one of the most important and contested areas of social policy. Attempts were made to legitimate the restrictions by arguing that it would force a more equal share of the asylum 'burden' across Europe. The author argues, however, that in reality the policy reflects European policy towards refugees and asylum seekers more generally, that is, one of exclusion and seclusion.

In Chapter 5, Tuitt considers the legal position of refugees and explores the extent to which the legal position of refugees is compatible with their traditional 'humanitarian' status. This chapter looks as the legal concepts, especially the notion of safety, in the determination of asylum cases and maintains that the concept of safety is artificially constructed. Tuitt argues that the emphasis placed on asylum seekers to prove that their safety is at risk is a difficult and subjective one which impedes the cases brought forward by asylum seekers. The author argues that the tension lies in the fact that the judicial process relies on objective notions which may not always be open to proof and draws on cases from the United Kingdom which illustrate the difficulties inherent in the legal procedure.

In Chapter 6, Duke, Sales and Gregory examine policies of refugee reception and resettlement in different European countries and look at different systems such as reception centres and policies of dispersal. They are very critical of dispersal policies which leave potentially vulnerable people in often monoethnic localities which can result in racial harassment, especially in the current climate which is very unsympathetic towards refugees and asylum seekers. Using the policy in Britain as an example, the authors compare the reception centres which have been put in place for quota or programme refugees and compare them with the ad hoc provision for spontaneous asylum seekers.

Duke, Sales and Gregory highlight the role that voluntary sector organizations and community groups have taken in the resettlement process and assess certain areas of social policy such as education and housing. They express concern that much of the responsibility for the welfare of refugees falls on voluntary organizations and community groups who tend to fill the gaps in 'mainstream' provision. This is not without its problems and the urgency of much of their work and the precariousness of their funding means that long-term community development and empowerment has tended to suffer. Moreover, they argue that there is an urgent need for an adequately funded central programme for new arrivals because without this refugees are becoming reliant on the voluntary sector and are not developing or using their existing skills to the detriment of themselves and the society at large.

Minderhoud, in Chapter 7, looks at the social security systems in four European countries – Belgium, The Netherlands, Britain and Germany – and notes the similarities which have emerged between welfare states in terms of their treatment of asylum seekers. Minderhoud argues that the impetus for reform has been the increasing number of asylum seekers arriving in Western Europe from developing countries and social security has, according to Minderhoud, become an extension and an instrument of immigration policy.

The chapter shows the pattern of curtailing welfare for asylum seekers, of restricting access to the labour market and the role of local authorities who are increasingly forced to ensure that asylum seekers have their basic subsistence needs met, often without additional resources.

In Chapter 8, Williamson examines the situation of unaccompanied children in Britain by drawing on empirical evidence from a study of London boroughs. Unaccompanied refugee children make up a substantial proportion of asylum seekers and once in Britain, they are subsumed within the prevailing legislation and in some cases children have even been detained in detention centres alongside adults. She notes the tension between central and local government because local authorities have a statutory duty to care for children without a carer who has parental responsibilities towards them. Thus, ultimately, much of the responsibility for the care of unaccompanied refugee children falls within the remit of the local authority.

The study found that there was a worrying lack of knowledge about unaccompanied refugee children in any given locality and raises the question about how adequate services can be provided given this lack of knowledge. The study found variations between local authorities in terms of their policies towards refugee children and found that good services tended to exist in cases where there were good services for minority ethnic children and looked after children in general. Even in cases where good services existed, a problem existed with central government in terms of policy and financial constraints. The general hostility of central government towards refugees is having an adverse affect on the welfare of unaccompanied refugee children who form one of the most vulnerable groups in society.

In Chapter 9, Scott and Bolzman consider the experience of exile among older refugees. There is very little research on the situation of older refugees and the issue of ageing in exile and it is one which is very important for policy makers and service providers. Scott and Bolzman focus on the cases of Poles in the United Kingdom and

Chileans in Switzerland and raise a number of key issues and concerns which are important for service planners and providers.

After providing some context about the issues of ageing in exile, Scott and Bolzman examine four main areas which affect the lives and needs of older refugees. First, they consider the position of women ageing in exile and the ways in which experiences vary by their roles in the private and public domains. Secondly, they examine the role of the family and family life and the effects of different cultural systems and values. Thirdly, they address the health care needs of older refugees – both physical and mental health needs. Finally, Scott and Bolzman assess the role of self-help and community development and highlight its importance for older refugees.

Chapter 10 examines the situation of refugees and asylum seekers in the labour market because employment is known to be a crucial component of refugee settlement both economically and socially. Drawing on empirical evidence from a survey of refugees in Newham, East London, Bloch looks at the importance of employment and the barriers which many refugees and asylum seekers face in gaining access to the labour market. The chapter shows the high levels of work place skills and qualifications which many refugees and asylum seekers bring with them to Britain. In spite of this, refugees remain largely excluded from the labour market and the minority who are in employment find themselves working in the least desirable jobs often with poor terms and conditions of employment.

Those who were not working tended to rely much more heavily on informal contacts as a method of job seeking than they had in their country of origin. Moreover, employment aspirations were very low given the level of experience that refugees have on arrival to Britain and most felt that they had skills which had not been used in Britain. Many barriers to employment were identified of which discrimination was the most frequently cited. The chapter shows the very poor position that refugees occupy in the labour market and how they find themselves even more excluded than the most marginalized minority ethnic communities in Britain.

Chapter 11, by Levy, concludes the contributions by examining the future of asylum policy in Europe in light of the 1997 Treaty of Amsterdam. Using a case study of the former Yugoslavia, this chapter demonstrates the ad hoc approach to asylum seekers and the issues of temporary protection between and within member states.

Levy discusses the key policy issues, concerning refugees and asylum seekers, which are currently the subject of debate. These include notions of 'burden sharing', addressing the root causes of refugee producing situations and the whole notion of EU citizenship. Levy argues that a more inclusive citizenship would increase the rights of refugees and asylum seekers and would help to combat the restrictions they currently face due to national policies. Levy concludes by arguing that the EU, with the inception of the Treaty of Amsterdam, is at a cross-roads. One path is the path of increased human rights and a reduction in racism and xenophobia while the other path is that of illiberal policy and exclusion. Whichever path is taken, Levy condones the fact that the Treaty of Amsterdam allows for much greater involvement from non-governmental organizations which means that refugees and asylum seekers will at least have some representation at this level of policy making.

The contributions to this book show the way in which policies of reception, resettlement and citizenship rights towards refugees and asylum seekers vary across Europe on the one hand, while on the other hand they show the common pattern of increased restriction, suspicion and limited citizenship rights.

Given the increased prominence of refugees and asylum seekers at the level of European policy and the pattern of harmonizing policy and sharing information, this book makes a timely contribution to the debates. It provides an in-depth account of the issues which affect the daily lives of refugees and asylum seekers across Europe. It demonstrates quite clearly that refugees and asylum seekers remain among the most marginalized and excluded groups in Europe in terms of the rights and opportunities which are afforded to them. The chapters show that refugees and asylum seekers are not a threat to the cohesion of social Europe nor to the success of economic Europe. Instead, the chapters show the way in which refugees and asylum seekers could be an asset, if only they were given some basic social and economic rights.

REFERENCES

Castles, S. and Miller, M. (1993), *The Age of Migration: International Population Movements in the Modern World*, Basingstoke, Macmillan.
Collinson, S. (1993), *Europe and International Migration*, London, Pinter Publishers for the Royal Institute ofInternational Affairs.
Joly, D. (1996), *Haven or Hell? Asylum Policies and Refugees in Europe*, Basingstoke, Macmillan.

Kunz, E.F. (1973), 'The Refugee in Flight: Kinetic Models and Forms of Displacement', *International Migration Review*, Vol. 7, No. 2, pp. 125–46.

Kunz, E.F. (1981), 'Exile and Resettlement: Refugee Theory', *International Migration Review*, Vol. 15, No. 1, pp. 42–51.

Weiner, M. (1996), 'Determinants of Immigrant Integration: An International Comparative Analysis', Chapter 3 in Carmon, N. (ed.), *Immigration and Integration in Post-Industrial Societies: Theoretical Analysis and Policy-Related Research*, Basingstoke, Macmillan.

2 European asylum and refugee policy after the Treaty of Amsterdam: the birth of a new regime?

Carl Levy

Asylum seekers and refugees have been a central concern of high policy in Europe during the 1990s. The most innovative aspects in the European Union's Treaty of Amsterdam of June 1997 are a direct result of this new development. But asylum seekers and refugees have also had a major impact on the domestic politics of the member states of the European Union. Other chapters in this volume demonstrate how national welfare states in Europe have restricted access to benefits and entitlements to persons seeking asylum or those granted *de facto* refugee status (see Duke, Sales and Gregory, Chapter 6 and Minderhoud, Chapter 7 in this volume). Furthermore, the shifting boundaries between citizens, denizens and outsiders (*inter alia* labour migrants, guestworkers, Convention refugees, *de facto* refugees, protected persons, asylum seekers, detained asylum seekers and illegal migrants) has been determined not only by the economic premises of the post-Keynesian welfare state but also driven by moral panics artificially created by the manoeuvring of political parties generally of the conservative or neo-fascist right (Thränhardt, 1997; and in this volume Schuster and Solomos, Chapter 3 and Schönwälder, Chapter 4). The inflated fears of floods of Russian, Algerian, Albanian or Bosnian refugees have forced governments of the member states of the European Union to amalgamate an emergent common policy on refugees and asylum seekers with the still underweight Common Foreign and Security Policy. Nowhere is this more evident than in European reactions to the wars of succession in the former Yugoslavia or in the still shaky post-war settlements.

At the end of the twentieth century it would be tempting to picture the Treaty of Amsterdam as the legal anticipation of a fortress Europe in the twenty-first century. This judgement would probably be too hasty and extreme. As recent commentators have noted, the migration policies of the European Union and its member states are characterized by ambiguities and contradictions. Free markets, globalization and economic and refugee diasporas make it impossible to create zero immigration regimes advanced by some conservatives and all neofascists (Castles, 1993; Cohen 1997). Indeed through his recent words and deeds even Helmut Kohl has conceded that Germany is a country of immigration (Schönwälder, 1996: 173; Schönwälder, Chapter 4 in this volume). Europe too is a continent of migration and immigration. Furthermore, the integrity of the international legal regimes that have guaranteed the rights of refugees and asylum seekers since the early 1950s cannot simply be ignored by the very liberal democratic states who crafted their parameters during the Cold War, even if in the post-Cold War era some politicians and policy makers would like to forget commitments entered into in the aftermath of the Second World War or during the ideological battles with Communism before 1989.

The rights revolution in Europe and North America, deepened by the growing importance of national constitutional courts, the Strasbourg Court and the European Court of Justice also makes it difficult for European politicians and policy makers to scrap previous guarantees (Hollifield, 1992; Jacobson, 1996; Soysal, 1996). However, this culture of human rights is reinforced by economic pragmatism. The need for new forms of labour migration, suppressed by the oil shocks of the 1970s but reawakened in Europe's new post-industrial flexible labour market, may limit efforts to define away the guarantees given to asylum seekers and refugees in the international regime, since the parameters of refugee migration have been historically affected by the needs of the current labour market (Miles and Kay, 1994; Morris; 1997, Schuster and Solomos, Chapter 3 in this volume).

On the other hand, the overwhelming predominance of *de facto* refugees in Europe, who are not given the same rights guaranteed to recognized refugees under the Geneva Convention of 1951, has caused European states to address this issue at the intergovernmental, and presently, at the supranational framework of the Third and First Pillars of the (amended) Treaty on European Union (Maastricht Treaty), the Dublin Convention and the Schengen Accords. We now have the potential for the emergence of a common regime for refugees, asylum seekers and other migrants within Europe. Only a few years ago such a likelihood would have been restricted to the pipe dreams of a small group of federalists.

The emergent regime in the European Union is an excellent example of the pooling of sovereignty to address the domestic policies of the member states which has characterized the history of European integration since the 1950s. But in this case the exercise impinges on a core definition of the nation-state, namely, the determination who is and who is not allowed to cross frontiers and settle or reside within its borders. In this respect a possible future common refugee and asylum policy determined by the supranational law of the Union may be potentially more significant for endowing the Union with state-like qualities than economic and monetary union. But this possible new European regime might also contradict or undermine the international regime defended and administered by the United Nations Office of the High Commission for Refugees (UNHCR) through a process of policy-making invoking the lowest common denominator of refugee and asylum policy best practice amongst the member states of the European Union.

In order to disaggregate the complex issues raised by the Treaty of Amsterdam, this chapter will address three themes. First, it will analyse the flows of refugees and asylum seekers into Europe during the 1980s and 1990s. Secondly, it will provide an overview of European Union and intergovernmental agreements in response to these movements of migrants into Europe. Finally, it will discuss how the conflicting objectives of these agreements led to the Treaty of Amsterdam. It will assess to what extent the Treaty of Amsterdam resolved these contradictions or merely placed them within the supranational institutions and legal domain of the European Union itself.

THE FLOW OF ASYLUM SEEKERS INTO EUROPE
(1980s AND 1990s)

In the past twenty years the vast majority of refugees caused by the political and economic effects of civil wars and internal repression in the Second and Third Worlds remained outside of Europe. The largest concentration of refugees in the world in 1993 (4 million) were Afghans, Kurds and others found in Iran (Martin, 1997: 21). Within Europe the largest number of displaced persons, refugees and immigrants (1.14 million) were found in the Russian Federation in 1994 (Coleman, 1997: 121).

Richard Black has identified three categories of refugees and asylum seekers entering Europe from 1945 to 1989. The most numerous group came from Eastern Europe and the Soviet Union, followed by quota refugees mainly from South East Asia and Chile or Argentina or elsewhere, and finally asylum seekers who came spontaneously by air or sea mainly from Africa and Asia (Black, 1993: 90). The 1990s saw a large expansion of refugees and asylum seekers arriving in Europe. This expansion can be explained by the numerous ex-Yugoslavs fleeing war and ethnic cleansing in Bosnia and elsewhere in the former Yugoslavia, Roma fleeing state-inspired and vigilante violence in Romania and elsewhere in Central and Eastern Europe and finally a steady stream of spontaneous refugees from Sri Lanka, Zaire, Somalia, Liberia or elsewhere in the Third World (Thränhardt, 1997: 237–40).

Within Western Europe and the European Union, Germany received the majority of *de facto* refugees and asylum seekers (peaking in the early 1990s with 65 to 70 per cent of the grand total). Even in 1996 German received 53 per cent of all asylum applicants followed by the United Kingdom (13 per cent) and The Netherlands (10 per cent) (Eurostat, 1997b: 2). The flight of refugees affected, firstly, the poor or poorest nations of the Third World and, secondly, the battered economies of the former Second World. However, within the European Union itself the economic core and strategic centre received the most asylum applicants in the European Union. However, even within Europe, the isolated and poverty-stricken Federal Republic of Yugoslavia (Serbia and Montenegro) was affected by the largest percentage of refugees to population. The 566 000 Serbian refugees living amongst the 11 million people of the Republics of Serbia and Montenegro dwarfed the problems confronted by the German government (Elliot, 1997: 16).

Table 2.1 shows the rise and decline of asylum applications in Europe during the first half of the 1990s. In the peak year of 1992, 697 269 applications for asylum were filed in Europe. This had dropped to 281 405 by 1995. Furthermore, in the first nine months of 1996, 164 000 asylum applications were registered by the EU member states. Compared to the same period in 1995, this represented a decline of some 15 per cent (Eurostat, 1997a,b: 1).

The decline in applications in the European Union is reflected in the number of asylum applications in Germany after 1992. In 1992 Germany recorded 438 191 applications for asylum but by the end of 1996 this figure had dropped to 116 367 (*Migration News Sheet*, March 1997: 10). Table 2.2 shows how other key receiving states, such as Italy, France, Sweden and the United Kingdom, had also experienced notable decreases.

Table 2.1   Asylum applications, 1985–95 (selected years)

	1985	1990	1992	1995
EUR 15	**159 176**	**403 496**	**674 056**	**270 867**
Belgium[1]	5 387	12 945	17 675	11 409
Denmark[2]	8 698	5 292	13 884	5 112
Germany[3]	73 832	193 063	438 191	127 937
Greece[4]	1 400	10 569	3 822	–
Spain[5]	2 300	8 647	11 712	4 429
France[6]	28 925	54 813	28 872	20 170
Ireland	–	62	–	–
Italy1	5 400	3 570	2 589	1 732
Luxembourg	78	114	120	–
Netherlands	5 644	21 208	20 346	29 258
Austria[7]	6 724	22 789	16 238	5 920
Portugal	70	61	655	–
Finland	18	2 743	3 634	854
Sweden	14 500	29 420	84 018	9 046
United Kingdom	6 200	38 200	32 300	55 000
EFTA	**10 532**	**39 805**	**23 213**	**18 481**
Iceland	–	7	15	–
Norway	829	3 962	5 238	1 460
Switzerland[8]	9703	35 836	17 960	17 021
Overseas states	**28 400**	**113 775**	**135 959**	**178 736**
Australia	–	3 800	4 114	5 235
Canada	8 400	36 375	37 748	25 631
USA	20 000	73 600	94 097	147 870

These notes refer to the years 1985–93

[1] Excluding dependent children.
[2] Excluding applications outside Denmark and rejected applications at the border.
[3] Including dependent children if their parents request asylum for them.
[4] Figures for 1989–92 are the sum of the applications registered with the Greek authorities and those registered with UNHCR.
[5] Excluding dependants.
[6] Excluding children and some accompanying adults.
[7] Excluding displaced persons from the Federal Republic of Yugoslavia who benefit exceptional leave.
[8] Partly excluding rejected persons at the border (especially those lacking identity papers).

Source: Eurostat (1996) *Asylum–seekers*, Vol. 1, No. 1, pp. 4–5. I would like to thank Martin Levy-Andersson for his assistance.

Table 2.2   Asylum applications in the EU (1995–96)

	January–June 1995	January–June 1996	% Fall
Germany*	59 368	57 489	–3
UK*	19 800	14 860	–25
Netherlands	14 382	10 025	–30
France**	11 575	7 846	–32
Belgium	5 689	5 489	–3.5
Austria	–	3 509	–
Sweden	4 746	2 715	–43
Spain*	2 395	2 371	–1
Denmark	2 443	2 204	–10
Finland	420	331	–21
Italy	833	305	–63
EU	121 651	107 144	–12

Data for Greece, Ireland, Luxembourg and Portugal are not available, but numbers of asylum applicants in these countries are very small.
* Data do not include dependants.
** Data do not include minor dependants.

Source: Eurostat press release, 22 January 1997. I would like to thank Martin Levy-Andersson for his assistance.

While under 10 per cent of asylum applicants in recent years have been given refugee recognition under the 1951 Geneva Convention, many are given a variety of temporary statuses which allow them to remain in the receiving country (Coleman, 1997: 120). Thus even if asylum applications continue to fall, the numbers of *de facto* refugees or those under temporary protection are still significant.

The two reasons that best explain the decline in the flow of asylum seekers and refugees since the early 1990s are the management of the Yugoslav crisis and the general tightening of entrance into Western Europe. Of the nearly three million refugees in the former Yugoslavia created by the wars of 1991–95, only 650 000 actually left its former borders. The dubious policies of containment and 'safe havens' plus the institution of visa requirements in most of Europe by 1993–94 restricted refugee movements. Vast movements of peoples from the former Soviet Union were predicted but failed to materialize (Thränhardt, 1996). Post-Communist Poland, Hungary, the Czech Republic and Slovakia comprise a buffer zone between East and West, which has absorbed and regulated flows between the European Union and the republics of the former Soviet Union. Not only has this area served as a transit stop for the return migration of Pontic Greeks and ethnic Germans, but large numbers of refugees from the former Yugoslavia, Armenia, Georgia and elsewhere settled here in the early 1990s before these countries instituted refugee policies in line with European Union and international practice. This buffer zone between East and West has also become the destination for seasonal migrants from the East and students and venture capitalists from the West (Wallace, Chmouliar and Sidorenko, 1996).

But the buffer zone has also been a line of defence to control and limit the inflow of asylum seekers into the European Union itself. Buffer zone nations are financially assisted to process and return unfounded asylum applicants to their homelands. In this respect these candidates for membership in the EU are receiving a crash course in the ambiguities of European and global asylum policy through their signing of the Geneva Convention of 1951 and the human rights legislation of the Council of Europe while concurrently integrating the *acquis communautaire* of the European Union which may threaten their recent adherence to these solemn commitments (Ardittis, 1994; Hollifield, 1997).

This last passage has explained how Western Europe has regulated the flow of potential refugees from the source, at the same time receiving countries have tightened policies at the point of destination. The next section will examine the harmonization of European refugee and asylum policies over the past two decades.

EUROPEAN APPROACHES TO REFUGEES AND ASYLUM SEEKERS: 1985–97

Introduction

European governments responded to increased incidence of asylum seekers and *de facto* refugees in the early 1990s with a barrage of interlocking and overlapping intergovernmental and European Community/Union policies. Most observers would agree that intergovernmental and supranational policy making resulted in needless bureaucratic duplication and confusing lines of command, as well as an alarming lack of transparency and democratic accountability.

The following section will review the institutions and policies crafted by member states and non-member states of the European Union up to the Treaty of Amsterdam in 1997. All these nation-states are signatories of the Geneva Convention and have therefore recognized the rights of refugees and asylum seekers to escape danger through flight, but this has not meant that they have surrendered their sovereign right to determine who will be accepted as a Convention refugee, who will be given temporary protection, who will be recognized as a *de facto* refugee or who will be deported either to a 'safe third country' or back to their homelands. In this respect refugees cannot appeal to a regional or global legal or executive authority above the signatories of the Geneva Convention. Their only route of 'appeal' has been to apply consecutively for asylum in a series of European nation-states. One result of the recent European coordination reviewed below is the severe restriction of such a strategy in the future. In this respect and others, at least until 1997, European policy was driven by the demands and needs of nation-states who pooled sovereignty in this traditionally sensitive area in order to increase the effectiveness of their national immigration control and ease the perceived pressures placed upon their welfare systems.[1]

The Schengen Accords, the Dublin Convention and the Third Pillar of the Maastricht Treaty, the Treaty on European Union (TEU) have worked on the principle of the lowest common denominator in order to achieve harmonization of the control of migration and refugees. But as Emek Uçarer has shown, the experience of these years demonstrates the ineffectiveness of establishing 'and implementing multilaterally an exclusive regime' (Uçarer, 1997: 300). Thus the dynamics of European policy making between the middle of the 1980s to the middle of the 1990s were characterized by 'trial and error' and gradually demonstrated a move from unilateralism to multilateralism; from intergovernmentalism to 'increased supranationalism' (1997: 301). But this trend towards supranational regulation of immigration and refugee flows into Western Europe may also be used as a lever to help push through more restrictive domestic legislation.

Possible indicators for immigration and refugee policy can be adduced from the adjacent, indeed overlapping, field of social policy. In the late 1980s and early 1990s, under the leadership of Commission President Jacques Delors, European social policy seemed to herald a European Neo-Keynesianism. In fact the European Union as a regulatory rather than an activist state has implemented the TEU's social chapter using the principle of the lowest common denominator. The desire to deregulate and liberalize the European labour market to meet the challenges of globalization, and the monetarist imperatives of the Maastricht criteria, have meant that European social policy has been shaped into a series of loose frameworks. The European Court of Justice, the principle of subsidiarity and the liberalizing forces within the Commission rather than an activist and interventionist Commission have set the pace in the 1990s. But European policy can be calibrated to national objectives. Therefore, while the necessity to deregulate, liberalize and privatize the economies of member states is acted in principle by all, the effects on their welfare states has been mixed. In other words the reform of pension systems, health care or social security are set by national parliaments and treasuries even if the direction is similar throughout the European Union (Hantrais, 1995; Majone, 1996).

If we leave this adjacent field and return to refugee and asylum policy, it is interesting to note that although the Conservative government in the UK under John Major refused to sign the Social Chapter of the TEU and refused to become a member of the 'Schengenland', the 1996 Asylum and Immigration Act contained restrictive clauses 'developed co-operatively at the European level' (Harvey, 1997: 68). Recent British legislation also demonstrates a common pattern found in the laws of other member states of the EU by blending general immigration control with that of asylum and refugee policy and thereby reducing 'rhetorically the status of refugee to that of any other immigrant' (Miles and Kay, 1994: 28; Schuster and Solomos, Chapter 3). Elsewhere in this volume Patricia Tuitt (Chapter 5) emphasizes the importance of the legal identity given to refugees and asylum seekers, here it should be noted that as refugees and asylum seekers in the EU or 'Schengenland' become treated like voluntary migrants, the public may become less sensitive 'to the potential humanitarian consequences of any restrictive measures initiated' (Coleman 1997: 86).

Historical background

It is not my intention to retell in great detail the background to the Schengen Accords, the Dublin Convention and the Third Pillar of the TEU. This has been done extensively by Guild (1996), Joly (1996: 44–95), and Papademetriou (1996). Here I would like to present a summary of the state of the field on the eve of the Intergovernmental Conference (IGC) of 1996–97 (see below). But first I will provide a brief historical account of the post-war period up to the 1980s and then give the reader a synoptic overview of the patterns that have characterized policy making from 1945 to 1997.

Table 2.3   European asylum and refugee policy: TREVI to the Treaty of
Amsterdam (1976–97)

1976	Terrorism, Radicalism, Extremism and Violence International (TREVI) created under the European Political Cooperation (EPC).
1985	June: Schengen Agreement signed by France, Germany and the Benelux countries.
1986	December: Ad Hoc Group of Immigration Ministers established in London.
1987	February: Single European Act amends EC Treaty article 8A.
1990	June: Dublin Convention signed by 11 member states of EC (Denmark signs in 1991).
1990	June: Schengen Implementation Agreement signed.
1991	July: Draft of External Borders Convention presented.
1991	December: Treaty on European Union (Maastricht Treaty) is signed. Includes the three pillar structure.
1993	November: Treaty on European Union enters into force. K.4 Committee and three steering groups established. First council of Justice and Home Affairs (JHA) is held in Brussels.
1994	January: European Commission version of the External Borders Convention presented.
1995	March: Schengen Convention is applied, but France requests a six month trial period in May.
1996	March: Intergovernmental Conference starts in Turin.
1997	May: Dublin Convention ratified.
1997	June: Treaty of Amsterdam agreed.
1997	September: Dublin Convention is applied for pre-1995 member states of EU.
1997	October: Treaty of Amsterdam is signed by EU foreign ministers.

Source: Adapted from Uçarer, 1997: 302–3 and *Migration News Sheet*, various issues.

Asylum policy in Europe in the 1960s and 1970s was characterized by what Daniele Joly has called 'uncoordinated liberalism'; whereas the 1980s and early 1990s have been termed a period of 'harmonized restrictionism' (1996: 46). But this policy of 'harmonized restrictionism' was neither straightforward nor consistently successful. Harmonization was a goal more than a reality, while restriction at the national level could be calibrated to the needs of a given situation. In short, all non-members and member states of the European Union tightened their asylum and refugee policies but there were significant variations between the strictness or liberality of national regimes.

Uçarer presents a useful analytical framework (1997: 286, 288) to map the road to harmonization. The first approach involved European states acting unilaterally or bilaterally either through domestic legislation or negotiated agreements with other states in order to restrict the movement of asylum seekers. This process has not been superseded completely by successive approaches, and as we shall see shortly, implementation of intergovernmental or supranational guidelines has set the pace in this era of restrictionism. The other three approaches mentioned by Uçarer are integral to the setting of the guidelines and frameworks for national policies.

In the era of 'uncoordinated liberalism' a multilateral and global approach was advanced. European states signed the 1951 Convention Relating to the Status of Refugees and the 1967 Protocol that essentially expanded its remit to the decolonized Third World. However, there were specifically regional responses as well. The European Human Rights Convention and the Council of Europe were important parameters for European policy until the 1980s. Indeed, the Council of Europe called for the harmonization of asylum policy in Europe during the 1970s.

Two further approaches characterize policy from the mid-1980s to the mid-1990s. First, the European states could act multilaterally within the EU and via the institutions of the EU, 'where the confines of the EU, would delimit who was in and who was out of the negotiation'(Uçarer, 1997: 286). The second approach was to act multilaterally but employ the institutions of the Community (the European Commission) to coordinate the harmonization of national refugee and asylum law at the member state level. In effect this has been the method of policy making from 1993 to the IGC of 1996–97 and is also evident in the Treaty of Amsterdam. In practice, however, all these approaches mentioned still exist and still have their overlapping policies and institutions. Indeed, recently it has been argued that there might be great merit in once again relying upon the Council of Europe in post-Cold War Europe since it represents nation-states such as the Russian Federation, that do not belong to the EU, are not candidate members of the EU, nor are they members of 'Schengenland'. Such an approach would avoid the potential confusion of the European Union after the Treaty of Amsterdam where member states (Denmark, Ireland and the UK) are not associated with the Schengen *acquis* but the non-members (Iceland and Norway) are (see Levy, Chapter 11 of this volume).

From TREVI to Schengen: 1976–85

Although the first multilateral European-wide attempt to negotiate asylum policy can be found in the Schengen Accords, in reality member states had been cooperating in forms of border control through the TREVI (Terrorism, Radicalism, Extremism and Violence International) substructure of European Political Cooperation (EPC) since the middle 1970s. TREVI was aimed primarily at controlling international terrorism, but it served as a prototype for the intergovernmental organization that preceded the Third Pillar of the TEU in 1993. TREVI 'remained without a fixed secretariat and never became a genuine institution', but, 'it developed a 'wining and dining culture' from which many of the officials active in the Third Pillar's K.4 structure received their education in intergovernmental coordination (Den Boer, 1996: 395).

The Schengen Group was founded in 1985 by the core original member states of the European Community (Benelux, Germany and France), and expanded to include, by 1997, all member states except the UK and Ireland but to include the non-members, Iceland and Norway. However, the agreement to dispense with border controls within the core group was not implemented until 26 March 1995 and then delayed until 1996 (*Migration News Sheet*, August 1997: 2).

In terms of migration policy the Schengen Accords were used to fight illegal immigration by inspiring cooperation between police and customs authorities. A more distant goal was the harmonization of visa policies, and the Schengen Implementing Agreement (presented in 1990 and activated in 1995) included more detailed action on asylum and the status of refugees. It also included a common computerized system for the exchange of personal data the Schengen Information System (SIS) and EURODAC – (European Automated Fingerprinting Regulation System).

Although the Schengen Accords were delayed by German unification, Dutch concerns about the lack of judicial redress and French worries about the security of their borders after the upsurge of terrorism in France related to the civil war in Algeria, the Schengen Group was nonetheless welcomed 'as the testing ground' for the larger EU's capability to abolish internal border controls and also as a prototype for a 'EU immigration and asylum regime' (Uçarer, 1997: 293–94). Schengen provided the concepts on refugees and asylum policy later taken up by the Third Pillar of the TEU. The Schengen Implementing Agreement of 1990 anticipated its own incorporation within the European Community by creating a parallel legal instrument to that of

Title VI of the TEU. The Agreement stated that it would be compatible with Community law and Article 142 stated that once a European-wide convention for the creation of an area without internal frontiers was concluded (External Frontiers Convention), this Agreement would be incorporated into it or replaced by it. Although the method for dealing with asylum applicants was kept in the hands of sovereign nation-states, the principle of determining a sole state responsible for a specific application limited multiple applications by asylum seekers throughout 'Schengenland' (Joly, 1996: 50).

As the Schengen Agreement was expanded geographically and ratified as a Convention in the 1990s, its presence acted as a catalyst for East European states. Starting with Poland in 1990, the Schengen states signed a series of readmission agreements. By endorsing the restriction of carriage of refugees without documents, the Accords reaffirmed the domestic laws of signatories and other countries which penalized air carriers who allowed undocumented refugees on flights to 'Schengenland'. The Schengen Accords also allowed recognized refugees to be treated like third-country nationals possessing long-term residence permits. Refugees could move within the areas as long as they declared their presence to the appropriate authorities within three days of entry. On the other hand, asylum seekers were not allowed to move out of the country of application (Joly, 1996: 46–52).

The Schengen Accords have been criticized by the UNHCR, by non-governmental organizations and by individual lawyers for weakening international refugee law. The Schengen Information System was also open to abuse since there was no supranational judicial control to safeguard the rights of individuals in relation to data protection. The Convention might order signatory states to establish independent supervisory bodies to vet the SIS but there was no effective independent court of appeal (Mahmood, 1995: 183–84).

However, this anticipates my argument. For purely pragmatic reasons Schengen was flawed because it did not include a key receiving state (the UK) and it only became operational in the mid-1990s after the peak of refugee flows had passed.

Therefore, more Community-based efforts were put in place as the Schengen Convention trundled towards ratification. Following on the intergovernmental structure of the TREVI group, the Ad Hoc Group on Immigration (comprising the Ministers of Justice and Immigration of the then 12 member states of the EC) was established in London in 1986 in anticipation of the ratification of the Single European Act of 1987. From this emerged the Dublin Convention.

The Dublin Convention and the Convention on the Crossing of External Frontiers

Like the Schengen Accords of 1985–90, the Dublin Convention was also part of European intergovernmental negotiations in the early 1990s. But unlike the Schengen Accords, 'the Dublin Convention instilled an explicitly EU-wide arrangement to deal with the complexities of asylum applications lodged in member states.' (Uçarer, 1997: 249) However, it too suffered from the same laborious process of ratification experienced by the Schengen Convention. The Dublin Convention was only ratified when Ireland signed it on 15 May 1997. It came into effect for the pre-1995 members of the EU on 1 September 1997 and (at the time of writing) will come into effect on 1 September 1998 for Sweden, Finland and Austria. With the Dublin Convention in force, a committee to administer it will be formed comprising of a representative of each signatory state. The chair will come from the current holder of the Presidency of the European Council (*Migration News Sheet*, June 1997: 5–6).

The Draft Convention on the Crossing of External Frontiers was agreed by the ministers responsible for immigration in June 1991. Therefore this, like the Dublin Convention, was placed within the borders of the EC/EU. As the centrepiece of EU policy, it was later redrafted and represented by the European Commission in January 1994. Its aim is to protect the external sea and land boundaries of the EU and has been deemed vital to create a Single European Market. Disputes between the UK and Spain over Gibraltar's status and over the jurisdiction of the European Court of Justice have prevented its ratification. The Draft Convention treats asylum seekers and refugees differently than does the Dublin Convention. It is more restrictive towards refugees who are able to move and stay in another EU member state for up to three months while it allows asylum seekers the right to stay in another EU member state for up to one month if they report their presence to the proper authorities on arrival (Joly, 1996: 51–2).

Towards the Maastricht Treaty (TEU, 1985–93)

If the Conventions, as international law, have taken an inordinate amount of time to become operational (Schengen after 10 years and Dublin after 7 years), they have established the framework that carrier sanctions will be introduced in all EU states and established the principle, carried out by the Third Pillar of the TEU, of a common list of countries needing visas to enter all EU member states. In short, the Conventions have ensured, in the long run, that a tight mesh of regulations on the movement of asylum seekers are being introduced in the EU and 'Schengenland' (Joly, 1996: 65).

The Ad Hoc Committee Group of Immigration Ministers also established a sub-group to examine asylum policy. A Group of Coordinators, or the Rhodes Group, prepared the Palma Document which set the agenda for the harmonization of policies within the EC\EU itself. In many respects this was a half-way house between the purely intergovernmental TREVI group or the executive envisaged by the Schengen Convention and the role of the Community in policy making. In this case the European Commission sat in on the working group but it had little influence, and since the Ad Hoc Group remained intergovernmental, it excluded the involvement of the European Court of Justice or the European Parliament (Joly, 1996: 52–3). But to a large extent its organizational structure anticipated the structure of the Third Pillar. In effect the Ad Hoc Group established the working agenda carried forward by the Third Pillar after 1993.

Refugee and Asylum Policy under the Maastricht Treaty (1993–97)

Before I review the results of the Third Pillar (Justice and Home Affairs: JHA) of the TEU, it is best to establish an overview of its *modus operandi* and its structure. The Ad Hoc Group took steps needed to achieve 'the free movement of persons within the Union' (Joly, 1996: 52). 'In practice', Joly notes, 'it has meant that priorities were largely dictated by the measures believed necessary for the implementation of the Dublin Convention and the Convention on the Crossing of External Frontiers' (Joly, 1996: 53). However, unlike the laborious practice of ratifying a Convention, the work of Title VI of the TEU used the 'soft law' of EU Resolutions, Conclusions, Recommendations and other instruments rather than legally binding measures such as Conventions.[2] Uçarer described the process under Title VI not as the fashioning of 'legally binding instruments' but clarifying 'the rules' and decision-making procedures of the emergent regime. Procedures were 'being harmonized' and 'acceptable standard operating procedures' were 'being defined' (1997: 298). This approach was reinforced by the creation of the Clearing House (or Centre d'Information de Réflexion et d'Echange en Matière d'Asile CIREA) and the Centre for Information, – Discussion and Exchange on the Crossing of Frontiers and Immigration (CIREFI). The aim was to

align asylum practice and structures with the Third Pillar and to create
'a manual of European asylum practice' (Joly, 1996: 62). The Treaty
on European Union, Soysal notes, carefully distinguished 'between
the goals of establishing EC rules regarding the status of third country
nationals and the more limited, short-term goal of harmonized visa
and asylum policy through intergovernmental action' (Soysal, 1996:
179). Even though the TEU gave the member states the opportunity
to use new and more effective legal instruments, 'the member
states...preferred to use classic non-binding texts of intergovernmental cooperation'(Monar, 1997: 330). Therefore the usage of
Resolutions, Statements, Conclusions etc. meant that by 1997 there
had been little progress towards the creation of standardized frameworks for the admission of asylum seekers or burden-sharing of
refugees (Monar, 1997: 332). The TEU's Third Pillar had essentially
seen the continuation of the procedures of the Ad Hoc Committee of
Immigration. Harmonization, therefore, was still reliant on the intergovernmental cooperation of the slowest and least federally-minded
member state.

As has been made clear earlier, the ratification of the TEU in
November 1993 was actually not the 'zero hour' of intergovernmental
cooperation on justice and home affairs which started back with
TREVI in the mid 1970s (Monar, 1997: 327). The Third Pillar resem-
bled all the previous structures 'set on the previous ad hoc decisions'
rather than on the basis of a comprehensive strategy. The Third Pillar
therefore was, Monar argues, 'much more a codification and partial
reform of existing cooperation on justice and home affairs than a 'first
step" (1997: 327). However, if we compare the structures of pre- and
post-1993 JHA cooperation, the cumbersome series of levels had been
eliminated (see Figure 2.1).

Under Title VI of the TEU, the Third Pillar was composed of five
levels. From the bottom to summit there were: working groups, steering groups, K.4 Committee, COREPER, and the Judicial and Home
Affairs Ministers of the Council. The pre-1993 working groups at the
base of the organizational structure had been streamlined into sections administered by senior officials in Steering Groups (Steering
Group I, Immigration /Asylum, concerns us). The K.4 Committee
became the supreme coordinating body of the Third Pillar, formulating policies for the Justice and Home Affairs Council. However,
according to Article 151 of the EC Treaty, a Committee of Permanent
Representatives (COREPER) comprising of senior civil servants of
the member states tended to duplicate much of the work of the K.4

Figure 2.1 The organization of migration policy-making in the Third Pillar of the Treaty of European Union (November 1993–97)

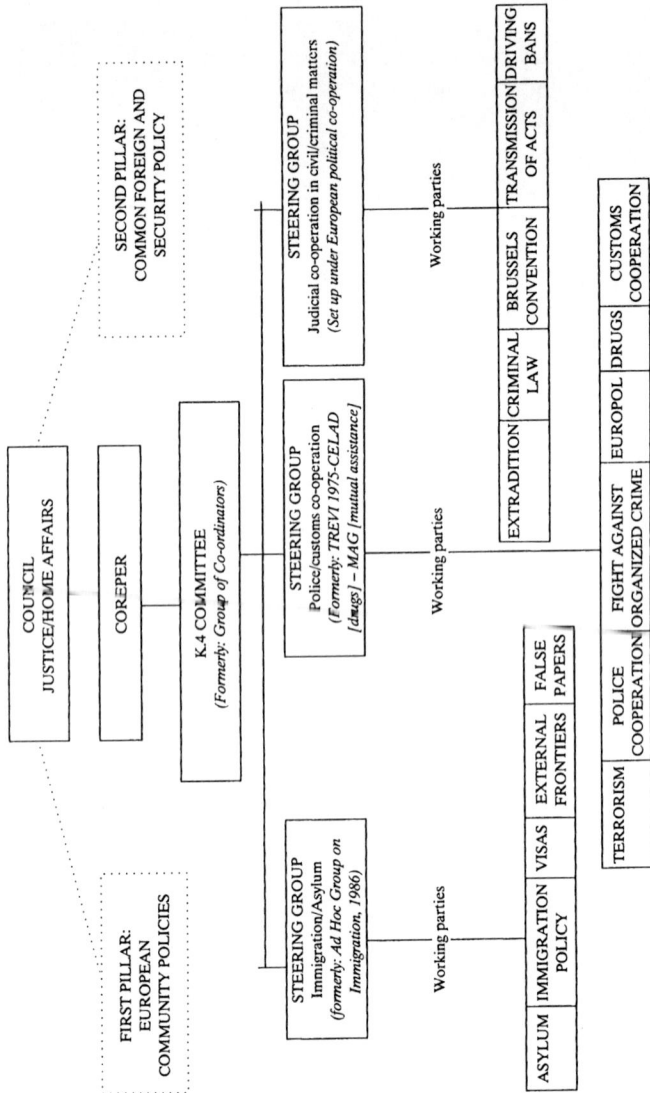

Source: Adapted from Papademetriou (1996: 78–9) and Niessen (1996: 63). (I would like to thank Martin Levy–Andersson for his assistance)

Committee. In this respect there was a tendency for K.4 and COREPER to tread on each other's toes and this led to institutional confusion at the heart of the Maastricht Treaty's Title VI. Thus during these years, tension existed between the K.4 Committee and COREPER, but also as Uçarer notes (1997: 297), the net effect of the proliferation of these bodies, 'an unwillingness to assume responsibility at any level'.[3]

But the Treaty on European Union did give some new limited competence to European initiatives if the member states had the will to exercise these options. The EC Treaty was amended by the TEU so that after 1 January 1996 Article 100C was fully communitarized. This meant that visa policy for third-country nationals could be dealt with within EC law. Secondly, although Article K was placed within the Third Pillar, the so-called *passerelle* (K.9) or bridge, made it possible to transfer asylum policy to the First Pillar. To do this the Council would have had to act in unanimity to invoke this clause. This was not done before the IGC and the signing of the Treaty of Amsterdam in the autumn of 1997.

Rhetoric and reality: member states' practice: the case of the former Yugoslavia (1991–97)

The previous passage concentrated on the reform of the formal structures and institutions concerned with European asylum policy. But the operations of the Third Pillar of the Maastricht Treaty had little direct effect on the individual regimes of the member states. The ornate discussion about structure and jurisdiction within either First or Third Pillars held little importance in the early and middle 1990s because it was the 'hard law' of the member states that determined the nature of the asylum regime in any given country. In this respect the intergovernmental initiatives may have shaped the parameters through which each member state exercised with a vengeance its own version of subsidiarity.

Nowhere is this more apparent than in the European response to the refugee crisis created by the Yugoslav wars. Without a coherent instrument to extend the 1951 Convention, European states made ad hoc decisions about reception. Austria, Germany and (non-member) Switzerland introduced visas in July 1992, Italy and The Netherlands implemented new administrative regulations, (non-member) Norway and Belgium did not process asylum applicants from the former Yugoslavia but did not stop direct applicants,

Sweden granted temporary visas, while the UK ordered that refugees get visas via consulates in Bosnia but did not have a service functioning in the country (Joly, 1996: 12–13).

At the end of November 1992, the EC states adopted a 'Conclusion on People Displaced by the Conflict in the Former Yugoslavia' (London, 30 November 1992). In the middle of 1993, EC states adopted a 'Resolution on the certain guidelines as regards the admission of particularly vulnerable groups of persons from the former Yugoslavia' (Copenhagen, 1 June 1993). But as Joly notes, despite this being a European crisis, the NGOs and the UNHCR exercised more proactive policy making on the ground than did the EC (1996: 74).

Within the European Community and the international community new concepts and practices were adopted in order to accommodate the Yugoslav refugees. First, there was the idea of internalization or the creation of 'safe havens' organized by the UN in Bosnia-Herzegovina. The massacres at Srebrenica demonstrated the grisly limitations of such a policy. Another concept was containment, namely, that refugees should either stay in the nearest safe area in the former Yugoslavia in established reception centres (Joly, 1996: 75). Thirdly, the concept of temporary protection was introduced, namely that EU states were ready 'to offer protection on a temporary basis to those nationals of the former Yugoslavia' (Joly, 1996: 76). Refugees had to arrive directly from conflict zones, be within an EU state already or could not return home due to a direct threat of human rights abuse in order to be granted temporary protection.

At Copenhagen (1 June 1993) a more liberal policy was initiated to include 'vulnerable groups', namely persons at risk of life and limb in prisoner of war camps and elsewhere, persons with serious medical conditions not treatable at home and persons who had experienced sexual assault and violence. The policy guidelines were not based on burden-sharing as Sweden, Switzerland, Austria and Germany took the vast majority of refugees. The restrictive visa policy of other member states, and the return of refugees to the first safe country, found Central Europe on the frontline.

However, large national discrepancies in the operationalization of the concept of temporary protection were noted. Indeed the differences were not only apparent in the country of reception but conditions of reception within the same country could also vary depending if the person or persons involved were admitted under the 'vulnerable group' quota or whether they had arrived spontaneously from the former Yugoslavia. 'Even', Joly notes, access to the asylum procedure was not uniform, some countries making it available immediately upon arrival, other suspending it for a few months as in Holland, or two years like Denmark, some refusing it altogether and making it incompatible with a temporary protection (1996: 77).

Patchwork policies in the 1990s

The Yugoslav emergency illustrated the contradictions of wider European responses to asylum seekers. In sum, before 1997 the European Union sought to coordinate visa policy, harmonize national entry procedures and policies towards the handling of manifestly unfounded or abusive requests for asylum and promote the concept of the 'safe third country'(while claiming to protect the concept of non-*refoulement*). However, the extremely varied responses of European nation-states towards refugees from the former Yugoslavia demonstrates that in effect 'material asylum policy' was kept firmly in the hands of the member states rather than the European Community/Union (Magleby Sørenson, 1996: 143; and Duke, Sales and Gregory, Chapter 6 of this volume). Thus the expulsion process, the issuing of work or residence permits, the rights of appeals by asylum seekers or access to welfare state were prerogatives of the member states (Magleby Sørenson 1996: 143). The policies and instruments developed by Schengen, Dublin and the Third Pillar of the TEU were based 'on reciprocal trust in the equivalence of national asylum procedures' (Hailbronner, 1995: 193). In fact, intergovernmental and supranational policy making was used as an alibi to strengthen the restrictive nature of national asylum and refugee laws that still remained widely divergent in effect.[4]

Thus the UK passed the restrictive 1993 and 1996 Acts. As Bloch notes (1997: 49), in-country asylum seekers are given precious few social rights and welfare entitlements. Those under exceptional leave to remain can claim benefits and work but unlike Sweden those under similar status are not entitled to family reunification (JUSTICE, 1997: 24). Different countries have different attitudes towards the treatment of specific groups of asylum seekers. Thus in France and Germany Algerians who are the victims of non-state violence (apparently from Islamist groups) are excluded, while in France supporters of the Islamists who are the victims of state violence have also been excluded (JUSTICE, 1997: 44). The French and the German governments have also excluded asylum seekers from Somalia, Liberia and Sierra Leone on the grounds that since the state had ceased to exist, they were under no obligation to accept the victims of non-state violence (JUSTICE, 1997: 44)!

Although the Dublin Convention was not in effect in Europe for most of the 1990s, the varying systems at work meant that its implementation from the autumn of 1997 may seriously undermine the international law of the Geneva Convention. Thus, that the Dublin Convention aims to 'ensure that an asylum applicant gets only one opportunity to have an asylum application considered' presumes 'that the same asylum application made in any member state in the same outcome'. Furthermore it 'presumes that the application of the underlining obligation not to return a refugee to a country where he or she fears persecution as defined in the UN Convention'(Guild, 1996: 117). But as Elspeth Guild has shown, 'these presumptions are not borne out in reality.' Her studies of asylum procedures in Europe show, for instance, a much greater admission of Turkish asylum seekers by Germany and France in 1991 and 1992 than by Belgium and the UK (1996: 117).

Furthermore, the Dublin Convention's definition of a 'safe third country', for those asylum seekers who are deported, may not meet the definition laid out in the Geneva Convention (Guild, 1996: 427). Thus Bosnian refugees were sent to Croatia, Iranians and Iraqis to Jordan and Ethiopians to Sudan (Wallace, 1996).

Meanwhile the constitutional courts of European states questioned the legality of the concept of 'safe third country' present in its various forms in Schengen, Dublin or the Third Pillar of the TEU. Thus the German Constitutional Court ruled in September 1993 that Greece, another member state of the European Union, could not be considered a 'safe third country', even though it was a signatory of the European Convention on Human Rights, the Dublin Convention and the Schengen Accords (Baldwin-Edwards and Schain 1994: 10). UK courts ruled that certain other EU member states might not be considered 'safe third countries' (JUSTICE, 1997: 43). While in August 1993, the French Constitutional Court ruled that domestic legislation inspired by the Schengen Accords or the Dublin Convention preventing asylum seekers from entering the territory of France might violate both the Geneva Convention and the Rights of Man of the French Constitution (Baldwin-Edwards and Schain, 1994: 10).

More generally, detention policies, adjudication and determination systems and resultant backlogs of claimants given *de facto* status also varied enormously. The UK has the highest rate of detention in

Western Europe with 700 persons detained at any time, Germany has an accelerated airport procedure with detention lasting up to 23 days but no detention thereafter, while The Netherlands only detains asylum seekers on grounds of criminal conduct or refusal to cooperate with the procedure (JUSTICE, 1997: 63). In 1997 the UK had 50 000 applicants awaiting initial decision and 22 000 appeal cases. Sweden granted permanent residence for those in Sweden before 1 January 1993 (Justice 1997: 61). As in the case of the UK, Sweden had peak arrivals in 1992/3, but unlike the UK, Sweden took swift action to ensure that the system could cope more effectively with the lower number of arrivals after that date (JUSTICE, 1997: 61). The Netherlands set up a coordinating committee to deal with the legacy of its peak years and was on its way to clearing up its backlog by late 1997 (JUSTICE, 1997: 62). In Italy the determination system was considered inadequate. Recent French and German accelerated systems lacked proper redress, while the 1996 Act in the UK removed most appeal rights for 'safe third country' cases (JUSTICE, 1997: 44–45).

Clearly the status of temporary protection has been open to different interpretations. More seriously the concept of *de facto* refugee was equally malleable. In Sweden and Denmark *de facto* refugees gives those persons status similar to Convention refugees. In Belgium, France, Germany, Switzerland and the UK there is no legal status attached to such a concept. However, unlike France and Belgium, Germany, Switzerland and the UK provide some kind of humanitarian status for *de facto* refugees, that is, authorization to stay legally in the country: the German *Duldung*, exceptional leave to remain in the UK and temporary admission in Switzerland (Lambert, 1995: 130). Meanwhile, due to the increasing importance of *de facto* refugees, The Netherlands instituted a residence permit on humanitarian grounds (VTV) while Sweden created a new permanent residence status for those affected by a situation of generalized violence which allowed beneficiaries family reunification and some social benefits (JUSTICE, 1997: 22).

Thus the net effect of the frameworks being devised by Schengen, Dublin or the Third Pillar of the TEU did not alter the patchwork nature of the asylum reception and determination throughout Europe. But these interlocking frameworks did have an indirect effect on the restrictions of Convention status. In the early 1990s liberal Sweden revised its regime so that the awarding of Convention status became rarer (Close, 1995: 134–5). Under the pressures of the growing popularity of the Haider's far right Freedom Party, the Austrian government produced stricter asylum laws as Austria was transformed from a transit to a receiving country (Wischenbart, 1992). In France pressure from the Front National resulted in a tightening of asylum laws in the early and middle 1990s. Visa requirements for Algerians were severely tightened in 1994 and in 1997 and there was a notable confrontation between police and the supporters of asylum seekers seeking sanctuary in a Parisian church (Collinson, 1996: 45; *Migration News Service*, March 1997: 3–4). Furthermore, France sought coordination with Italy and Spain against further flows of refugees from Algeria, hoping to divert any flows to neighbouring Morocco and Tunisia (Collinson 1996: 46). In traditional countries of emigration such as Greece and Italy, where large-scale immigration had been only experienced for little more than a decade, the appearance of refugees forced governments to create a policy. In both cases ethnic migrants – Italian ethnics from Slovenia and Pontic Greeks – were given special rights immediately. Italy applied a restricted Eurocentric interpretation of the Geneva Convention which may have paradoxically initially benefitted Albanians in 1991 (Vasta, 1993), but it remained the case that Italy rejected the highest proportion of asylum claimants in Europe (Papademetriou and Hamilton, 1996: 52). In fact, mini-amnesties were granted to Somalis in 1992 and both the Martelli Law of 1990 and a new proposed law in 1997 seem to point to greater cognizance of the issues. Indeed the new law proposes to establish permanent reception centres for new refugees (Vasta, 1993; Foot, 1995; Pugliese, 1996; Adler-Hellman, 1997; *Migration News Service*, March 1997: 5). The Greek government has dealt with its Albanian migration by allowing them to be incorporated in a widespread illegal second labour market (Lazaridis, 1996).

Thus if the aim of intergovernmental and supranational cooperation in the 1990s was to coordinate refugee and asylum seeker policy in Europe through reciprocal recognition of national systems, the results were extremely mixed.

The failure of Maastricht's 'Third Pillar': towards Amsterdam (1995–97)

The limitations of the Third Pillar of the TEU became quickly evident. The contesting intergovernmental and supranational elements made it difficult to operationalize. The lack of judicial review and the democratic deficit was also clear. Not only did national parliaments have little say in these aspects of asylum policy making, the European Parliament's powers were limited to mere consultation.

Article L of the TEU laid down that the Third Pillar was excluded from the judicial process of the Court of Justice. So for instance, the Florence European Council of June 1996 agreed that in principle in regard to the Europol Convention, that member states would have the liberty to accept or reject the interpretations of the European Court of Justice in terms of the Convention (Monar, 1997: 334–5).

The question of Schengen was also pressing because as Monar argues (1997: 335), it offered members the ability to arrive at 'their common aims by "eluding" the third pillar rather than by insisting on a solution within it.' But a consensus was building up to transfer Schengen to the Third Pillar. Furthermore, a general reform of the procedures of the Third Pillar gained widespread support.

Pressures for reform increased from 1995 through the start of the IGC in Turin in March 1996. The pathfinding Reflection Group declared by a majority for the communitarization of asylum and immigration policy (Monar, 1997: 336). The questions of legitimacy and transparency for the EU were very important here (Lodge, 1997: 312–13). Communitarization was later reconfirmed by the declaration of the Italian Presidency's Progress Report of 17 June 1996 (Monar, 1997: 336).

The five-level structure of the Third Pillar was also criticized, while the K.4 Committee was considered top heavy (Duff, 1997a: 128). It was also suggested that the K.4 Committee might be removed for the COREPER. Even the staunchly intergovernmental British saw merit in streamlining the decision-making structure (Monar, 1997: 336).

The financing of JHA activities was also considered limited and awkward. The Dutch government, in November 1995, said that communitarization would allow for Community funding of JHA policies instead of the limited funding received directly from member state governments (Dutch Ministry of Foreign Affairs, 1995: 181).

The major assessment of the Third Pillar was presented at the IGC Reflection Group in March 1995 (Hix and Niessen, 1996: 30). The report noted a blurring of the demarcation between the First and Third Pillars on the movement of persons and the possibility of using the *passarelle*. Not only were member states reluctant to use the bridge, they were also reluctant to employ other remedies such as Article K.3 and invoking the jurisdiction of the European Court of Justice, QMV (qualified majority voting) via Article K.3 and K.4 or the greater employment of Article K.6 to allow the European Parliament wider scrutiny. But the final report of December 1995 realized that flexibility, opt-outs and the gradual accretion of the Schengen Accords and a slower process of communitarization for several laggard states would be the future direction of policy (Hix and Niessen 1996: 42). The European Commission also issued two reports, one to the IGC Reflection Group in May 1995 and another in February 1996 to the IGC (Hix and Niessen 1996: 33). These essentially focused on the failure of the *passarelle* and therefore the Commission urged the usage of QMV in the Third Pillar while the European Parliament could expand its scrutiny of decision-making and the Commission's right of initiative could be extended to the entire JHA. The Commission argued that all elements of the Third Pillar, bar police and judicial cooperation, should be transferred to the First Pillar and that the Schengen Accords should be incorporated in the Treaty.

The European Parliament argued that asylum and immigration policies should be brought into the First Pillar but if this was not possible, the powers of the Commission, the European Parliament and the European Court of Justice should be increased in the Third Pillar (Hix and Niessen, 1996: 36). Although the European Court of Justice had no competence within the Third Pillar, it did support the incorporation of the European Convention on Human Rights within the legal system of the Community (Hix and Niessen, 1996: 37–9).

The positions of the member states were enunciated at the beginning of the IGC in March 1996. Besides Denmark and the UK, the other 13 member states were for the communitarization of immigration and asylum policy (Hix and Niessen, 1996: 59). Large majorities were in favour of increased roles for EU institutions. There was unanimous support for a reduction of the five-level JHA structure. There was near unanimity in favour of the EU's accession to the European Convention on Human Rights and Fundamental Freedoms (ECHR) and to advance common policies to fight racism and xenophobia. There was also general support for some type of flexibility clause to allow a majority of member states to establish institutions for a 'common immigration and asylum policy', which allowed Britain, Ireland, and Denmark temporary opt-outs (Hix and Niessen, 1996: 59). This last agreement was, however, not reached without controversy. The Franco-German declaration of December 1995 aroused the suspicions of Ireland and Greece, who feared that not only would this allow for opt-outs but it might also create an inner core that would place them in an excluded second tier (Hix and Niessen, 1996: 51–52).

THE TREATY OF AMSTERDAM (JUNE 1997)

The Treaty of Amsterdam moved asylum, refugee and migration policy from the intergovernmental Third Pillar to the communitarian First Pillar of the European Union. This increased the influence of the European Commission and the European Parliament. Additionally, the Court of Justice could now exercise jurisdiction in this sensitive area. The Treaty of Amsterdam also incorporated the Schengen Accords into the European Union, but mainly within the Third Pillar. The Treaty established an Area of Freedom, Security and Justice within the European Union, and for the first time, the Union acquired a direct remit in the fields of civil liberties and human rights (Duff, 1997b: 8). Institutionally, the European Parliament gained the most from Amsterdam through the expansion of the co-decision procedure, but the specific policy area concerning asylum and migration in the European Union became the centrepiece of the Treaty. 'Between the time of Maastricht and Amsterdam', Andrew Duff argues,'the question of the rights of citizens, residents and aliens of the European Union emerged as a driving force of European integration' (Duff, 1997b: 8).

It may be that the importance of immigration and asylum policy was artificially magnified by the failure of the member states to address other key issues. However, it is undoubtedly the case that the consensus to reform the Third Pillar had built up a head of steam at the 1996–97 IGC. Furthermore, the free movement of citizens and long-term residents in the European Union had become absolutely necessary in order to protect the future Economic and Monetary Union (EMU) from asymmetric shocks caused by the lack of labour mobility in the currency union. Indeed, since the early 1990s Germany has argued that a harmonized immigration and refugee policy was vital for the future progress of European integration (Hailbronner, 1990). The impending enlargement of the Union to include the former Communist countries of Central and Eastern Europe also has added pressure to expand the remit of European integration into the field of human rights.

A Critical assessment of the Treaty of Amsterdam

In order to assess the restrictive and libertarian impulses of the Treaty of Amsterdam, this section analyses its key provisions in light of the critical response of leading non-governmental organizations (NGOs).

The UNHCR and the NGOs have become increasingly important within EU policy-making circles during the 1990s. In response to criticisms about the opaque and undemocratic character of much of Union policy making, a limited audience was granted to the UNHCR and NGOs such as the European Council on Refugees and Exiles (ECRE). The UNHCR has held sessions with the Ad Hoc Group and later with the K.4 Committee (Joly, 1996: 66–7). By the time of the IGC in 1996–7, the NGOs had become accustomed to lobbying in the European Union on asylum and immigration issues. ECRE, the EU Migrants Forum and the Starting Line had pressed for the communitarization of all matters relating to the free movement of persons and for the granting of equal rights to those who had five years' residence in the European Union (Hix and Niessen, 1996: 27).

The British Joint Council on the Welfare of Immigrants (JCWI) criticized the incorporation of the Schengen *acquis* within the European Union because it would endanger the Geneva Convention (*JCWI Bulletin*, Vol. 6, No. 7, Spring, 1997: 4). Furthermore, there is much evidence that Anita Gradin, the EU Commissioner with responsibilities for migration and refugees, had close contacts with the Starting Line and other NGOs involved in European migration policy.[5] These developing contacts were recognized in the Declaration on Article 73K of the New Title IIIA of the EC Treaty, where it is stated that consultations would be established with the UNHCR and other relevant international organizations on matters relating to asylum policy.

Thus the criticisms of the NGOs help us make sense of the implications of the Treaty of Amsterdam in the light of current refugee and asylum policies in the European Union. NGO criticisms may also help us to anticipate modifications, of the more troubling and problematic aspects of the Treaty, which may be needed in the future.

At first glance the Treaty's innovations and amendments seem very impressive and wide-ranging. However, closer analysis shows that change is hedged with caution, opt-outs and possible regressive developments. Under the new Title IIIA of the amended EC Treaty, Article 73I states that within five years of the Treaty of Amsterdam coming into force member states will agree on matters assisting the free movement of people within the European Union. Articles 73J and 73K are particularly important for asylum and refugee policy. Article 73J recognized the Schengen *acquis*, and states that within five years of the Treaty implementation, the coordination of the issuing of visas between member states will be accomplished through a common list of third countries whose nationals require a visa to travel in the EU. Additionally, there will be a uniform format for this visa and member states shall coordinate measures for those third-country nationals travelling with this common visa through the EU.

Article 73K pertains more specifically to asylum policy. As a prerequisite all future EU policy on asylum seekers and refugees must be shaped within the parameters of the 1951 Convention and the 1967 Protocol. Article 73K lists the criteria and measures that member states will standardize when they handle asylum application by third-country nationals. These include minimum standards for: the qualification of a third-country national as a refugee; granting and withdrawing refugee status; granting temporary protection to displaced persons; and promoting the balance of effort (formerly burden-sharing) of refugees and displaced persons.

This apparently ambitious agenda disguises notable restrictive modifications in the original intentions of the IGC negotiations. Indeed, during the last stages of the IGC, member states became very cautious about the extent to which they desired to communitarize refugee policy. Article 73K displays a minimalist approach which shifted the intention 'from developing common rules to setting minimum standards' (Duff, 1997b: 20). Furthermore, the method of realizing these objectives were kept firmly in intergovernmental mode. This was due partially to the pressures from the *Länder* exerted upon the Federal German government, which caused Germany to switch from support of majority voting on asylum, refugees and immigration to it being subject to unanimity until it came up for review after a five (originally two or three) years transitional period. Thus the transitional five-year period was 'a compromise between the timid and the impatient' (Duff, 1997b: 20) and it is seen as a period during which a sufficient amount of trust will develop between the member states' ministers charged with immigration and asylum seekers.

After the five-year transitional period, full communitarization of asylum and migration policy under the co-decision-making procedure of the European Parliament will only happen by a unanimous vote of the Council of Ministers. Although Article 73O states that the shift to QMV will not need another IGC, 'the lifting of the tyranny of the national veto was itself made subject to the national veto'(Duff 1997b: 21). In other words, QMV can only happen through unanimity.

This compromise has drawn the criticism of the NGOs. Thus Jan Niessen (1997) of the Starting Line felt that the transferring of immigration and asylum policy from the Third to First Pillar had merely resulted in the transfer of 'some elements of decision-making procedures under the third pillar' to the First Pillar.

The ECRE was more openly critical. The transitional period was a dangerous compromise because it merely disguised a new form of intergovernmental cooperation (ECRE, 1997b: 3). While the European Parliament would now be consulted rather than merely informed about policy, it could not amend or veto relevant legislation usually granted to it in the First Pillar (ECRE, 1997b: 3). However, with the Treaty of Amsterdam the European Commission is granted the right of sole initiator for policy after the transitional period, and according to the ECRE this was 'a meaningful change' and was one the 'few unequivocal' gains of the Treaty (1997b: 1–2).

The ECRE is particularly concerned about the effect of meeting the minimum standards for asylum and refugee policy in member states as described in Article 73K. Since the definition of 'refugee' seems to be based on the Council Decision of 1996, which was severely criticized by the ECRE and the UNHCR, this was considered a potential threat to the integrity of the Geneva Convention. Furthermore, the ECRE criticized the conception of temporary protection since its institution in the EU in the early 1990s (1997a). In other words, the ECRE was concerned about how the concept of temporariness might be extended so as to threaten the separate status of *de facto* refugees. Refugees in the European Union under the functional equivalent of the British exceptional leave to remain should not be the intended beneficiaries of a harmonized regime of temporary protection because this would effectively dilute their already acquired rights and entitlements (1997b: 7).

On the other hand, Article 73L has received a far more happy reception from NGOs and the UNHCR. This Article was inspired by the experience of receiving refugees from the former Yugoslavia and allows the Council of Ministers to employ QMV on proposals from the Commission on the adequate measures required for a member state or member states to deal with displaced persons from an area of conflict. Although these beneficiaries would be under a regime of temporary protection, the Article was praised for the non-exclusivity of the definition of displaced person (ECRE, 1997b: 8).

The Area of Freedom, Security and Justice intends to be more than a venue in which the participating member states can more effectively harmonize their asylum and migration policies. For the first time the respect for human rights was made an explicit criterion for membership of the European Union. Indeed this new spirit is indicated in the amended Title I, Article F of the EC Treaty where the first sub-clause no longer refers to the 'national identities of member states', but rather, 'it now speaks of liberty, democracy, human rights and the rule of law' (Duff, 1997b: 9). Furthermore, a separate clause (Article O of the TEU), in reference to EU enlargement to the former communist countries, explicitly asks them to sign up to the principles of respect for democracy and human rights as contained in the section on the Area of Freedom, Security and Justice.

The Treaty also contains a mechanism to suspend the voting rights of a member state found guilty of the violation of human rights (Article F.1 of the TEU and a new Article 236 of the EC Treaty).[6]

But the commitment to human rights is restricted because the member states at Amsterdam did not support moves to give the Union its own international legal personality through signing up to the European Convention on Human Rights because this was considered too federalist (Duff, 1997b: 9). The fear of federalism also limited the impact of the European Court of Justice within the Area of Freedom, Security and Justice. The transfer of asylum, refugee and immigration policy to the First Pillar gave the Court the potential for jurisdiction in these areas. However, while the Court can now ensure a uniform interpretation of texts concerning asylum and immigration, its effective powers are still quite limited. In any case, the expansion of the European Court of Justice's remit to matters that pertain directly to human rights had been evident even before the Treaty of Amsterdam, and for many years the Court had regularly taken into account the actions of the European Court of Human Rights (Groenendijk, 1992: 533). The lack of judicial review at the apex of 'Schengenland' had highlighted the need for a legal remedy. Indeed the Benelux countries and Germany had plumped for a 'Schengen' Court while the French had even suggested that the European Court of Justice might be a more sensible venue (Groenendijk, 1992: 536). In the event, the Treaty of Amsterdam (Article 73P) allowed references on points of law from national courts, but ruled out citizens or asylum applicants having direct access to the Court. Nor will the Court be allowed to rule on any case in which domestic law and order or security are involved. Article 73P(3) also allows member states, the Council of Ministers, the European Commission but not the European Parliament, to seek interpretative rulings on asylum and migration law. While the extension of the Court's jurisdiction to the formerly intergovernmental province of asylum and migration law may be applauded as a step which will deepen the planned Area of Freedom,

Justice and Security, in fact, this may at first be detrimental to asylum seekers, because as the ECRE has argued, since the Court's rulings are activated through the optional decision of lower national courts seeking clarification of Community law, the very coherence of the Community's legal order might be threatened, 'as it permits lower level courts to interpret Community law in whatever way they see fit' (ECRE, 1997b: 5).

Schengen and Amsterdam: Constitutional Confusion and the Lack of Accountability

The accession of the Schengen *acquis* mainly to the Third Pillar will affect the Area of Freedom, Security and Justice. The operation of the Schengen Executive Committee under Article B of the Treaty of Amsterdam is made more complicated by the joint opt-out granted to the UK and Ireland from the other 13 member states. They can join proceedings on the unanimous decision of the 13 (Article F) but on the other hand the Danes received a separate Protocol which said that Denmark was politically but not legally attached to the Schengen within the European Union (Duff, 1997b: 31). The Danes jealously guarded their sovereignty and had previously been granted opt-outs for EMU, defence and further developments of EU citizenship. In this case the Schengen decisions take on the character of international not Community law in the same way it affected the non-member state Schengen associates, Iceland and Norway.

One of the reasons for Danish reluctance to sign the Schengen *acquis* was their distaste even for the modestly extended jurisdiction of the European Court of Justice into the new Third Pillar. Although most of the direct policy relating to asylum seekers and refugees is now in the First Pillar, the operations of Europol are within the Third. The modest extension of Court powers in the Third Pillar reflects the acknowledgement by the member states for greater transparency and accountability even here. While the new Article 191 under Chapter 10 of the TEU does not open Europol to scrutiny, the documents of CIREA and CIREFI which are of great importance to asylum policy, will now be issued by the Council of Ministers and will be open to inspection by outsiders, even if the Council itself or any member state will retain considerable power to vet sensitive material (ECRE, 1997b: 12). However, another new Article 213(b) makes EU institutions themselves responsible for European Information Service (EIS, formerly Schengen Information Service), and therefore there is still no independent supervisory body to oversee sensitive material on immigration and asylum cases, even if this will open the EIS to greater scrutiny than the very secretive SIS. Finally, the Treaty allows NGOs to gain access to final draft texts concerning migration and asylum policy at an earlier stage than was previously the case, which may facilitate greater input from them in the policy-making process (ECRE, 1997b: 13).

Although the previous aspects of the Treaty reviewed here seem to have their progressive and regressive aspects, undoubtedly the two greatest threats to the Area of Freedom, Security and Justice are: the opt-outs granted to the UK, Ireland and Denmark, and the new Protocol to the EC Treaty on Asylum for Nationals of EU member states.

Opt-Outs All Around: Denmark, Ireland, the UK and the Area of Freedom, Security and Justice

The opt-outs for the UK, Ireland and Denmark can of course mean that these three countries might retain more liberal national asylum laws than the twelve (ECRE, 1997b: 13). However, this would certainly be an optimistic reading in the case of the UK. In any case, the opt-outs will certainly lead to legal and administrative confusion. What will happen to the various Declarations, Recommendations and Decisions under the old Third Pillar? Will they be remodelled and passed through the new First Pillar? And what status will they have for the opted-out member states? Indeed a similar potential for confusion exists between the requirements of Schengen for the 13 member states and the universal application of the Dublin Convention for the 15 member states (Niessen, 1997: 3).

The Irish and British Protocol on the Area of Freedom, Security and Justice is separate from the Danish protocol. It is quite clear that the Irish were forced to sign the Protocol because of their common travel area with the UK. Indeed the Irish can leave (resile) the Protocol without a new IGC, and the Irish in a Final Declaration also announced their intention to participate in as much of the Area of Freedom, Security and Justice as the continuation of their common travel area would permit.

While the Irish and British can opt-in to the debate on measures concerning the Area of Freedom, Security and Justice the Council of Ministers will decide unanimously whether they be allowed to participate.[7] And if they do participate and disputes erupt between the rest of the member states, the other can still go ahead on a suggested proposal without the approval of the British and Irish. In this way the British and Irish cannot employ a strategy of Europe *à la carte*. However, in reality, the British are not so adamantly opposed to Schengen. In 1997 the UK had already signed 22 Schengen instruments and the British police were keen to work with their counterparts in Schengenland (Duff, 1997b: 28).

The Protocol on Asylum for EU Citizens: A Major Threat to the Geneva Convention

The Protocol to the EC Treaty on Asylum for Nationals of EU member states argues that member states be considered safe countries because of the level of protection of rights and freedoms and therefore not grant asylum to any EU national. The background to this Protocol is a diplomatic dispute between Spain and Belgium, in which the Belgian government granted asylum to an alleged member of the Basque terrorist organization, ETA. Throughout the IGC the UNHCR and the NGOs made the strongest representations against this Protocol because it was an extremely serious violation of the Geneva Convention of 1951 since it undermines the principle that each case for asylum must be judged by the receiving country on its own merits. Indeed, in a separate Declaration, Belgium stated that it would not be bound by its obligations to the Geneva Convention, while the Swedish government declared that it too would not surrender its right of decision over the granting of asylum to any applicants on their merits (*Migration News Sheet*, August 1997: 13).

CONCLUSION

The aim of the Treaty of Amsterdam is the 'progressive establishment of an area of Freedom, Security and Justice'. In this respect the dialectic behind the spread of a new rights culture, identified by Jacobson (1996) and Hollifield (1992), can be discerned in this policy objective. Jacobson writes (1996: 89)

> The state is thus in the process of being turned on its head; instead of acting as a sovereign that represents and embodies a nation, it is now accountable to international rules and institutions for the treatment of people in its jurisdiction. The concept of nationality is recast internationally as well as domestically – the two levels are obviously interlinked.

In the concluding chapter to this volume I will return to examine the possible effects upon European asylum and migration policy of European Union citizenship. Here I would like to point to specific policy areas where the quest for a common policy may undermine the first principles of an Area of Freedom, Security and Justice and be very much at variance with the new supranational culture of human rights. The following contradictions in EU member state practice need urgent rethinking.

First, the UNHCR criticizes the treatment of asylum seekers at airports: 'Member states should not resort to the creation of 'international zones' in airports to avoid obligations towards refugees' (Magleby Sørensen, 1996: 144). Certain new rapid procedures undermine member states' obligations towards refugees. Thus asylum seekers cannot be denied entry because of 'fake, non-existent or incomplete documentation.' (1996: 146). Secondly, the UNHCR has pointed out that the still unratified Borders Convention would contradict Article A of the Geneva Convention because the Borders Convention states that refugees must cross external frontiers at official crossing points and during official opening hours. But the 1951 Convention states that refugees may enter another country without restraint (1996: 146). Thirdly, carrier sanctions mean that private companies are given *de facto* competence to accept and administrate asylum seekers' claims. Fourthly, states should not detain refugees and asylum seekers while their applications are being examined. Finally (1996: 145), the UNHCR criticizes the concept of 'the safe third country'.

Amnesty International endorses the UNHCR objections and has highlighted the need for good practice in the determination of asylum claims. First, asylum seekers should be given access to a procedure that determines their status. Secondly, the asylum seeker should be given a full interview 'by a specialized authority, as well as appropriate legal assistance'. Finally, if a claim is rejected in the first instance, then the appeal should be in front of a second body of a judicial nature. The principle of non-*refoulement* should be upheld by allowing the applicant the right to remain in the country before the final judgement of the court (Wallace, 1996: Chapter 3).

If the Treaty of Amsterdam really initiates a new period of consultation with the NGOs and the UNHCR, then perhaps best practice rather than the art of the lowest common denominator will inform the search for a common European policy for asylum seekers and refugees in the twenty-first century.

NOTES

1. It was estimated that Western Europe spent $2.4 billion in 1985 on processing asylum seekers (staff, legal costs, reception centres, social aid, medical costs, etc.). By 1991 the total costs had risen to $7.5 billion (Salt, Singelton and Hogarth, 1994: 207).

2. The key Resolutions, Conclusions, Communications, Joint Positions, Recommendations and Common Positions include:

   a. The Resolution on Manifestly Unfounded Applications for Asylum adopted by the Council of the European Community (1992).

   b. The Resolution on a Harmonized Approach to Questions Concerning Host Third Countries adopted by the Council of the European Community (1992).

   c. The Conclusion on People Displaced by the Conflict in the Former Yugoslavia adopted by the Council of the European Community (1992).

   d. The Resolution on Family Reunification adopted by the Council of the European Community (1993).

   e. The Resolution on Certain Guidelines as Regards the Admission of Particularly Vulnerable Groups of Persons from the Former Yugoslavia adopted by the Council of the European Community (1993).

   f. The Communication to the Council and the European Parliament by the Commission on Immigration and Asylum Policy (Root Causes) (Com(197) 23 final, 1994).

   g. The Recommendation of the Justice and Home Affairs Council Concerning a Framework Text of a Readmission Agreement Between an EU Member State and a Third Country (1994).

   h. The Conclusion of the Justice and Home Affairs Council on the Organization and Development of the Centre for Information, Discussion and Exchange on the Crossing of Frontiers and Immigration (CIREFI) (1994).

   i. The Resolution on Minimum Guarantees for Asylum Procedures adopted by the Justice and Home Affairs Council (1995).

   j. The Resolution on Burden-Sharing with Regard to the Admission and Residence on a Temporary Basis of Displaced Persons adopted by the Council of the European Union (1995).

   k. The Common Position On Harmonized Application of the Term Refugee adopted by the Justice and Home Affairs Council (1996).

   l. Resolution of the Justice and Home Affairs Council on Non-Accompanied Children who have Applied for Asylum (1997).

3. Another informed observer also noticed the weakness of the Third Pillar of the TEU:

   > Given the fact there is no common vision, civil servants are deprived of clear direction. Consequently measures adopted tend to originate from the lowest common denominator, which is unusually restrictive. To complicate matters, the status of adopted instruments as decided by the Treaty on European Union are not frequently used. Among the devices that are not specified by the Treaty, there exists a clear

hierarchy. A Resolution is stronger than a Recommendation, which is itself stronger than a Conclusion (Niessen, 1996: 62). I would like to thank Jan Niessen for his kind responses to my e-mail enquiries.

4. Thus Helmut Kohl argued in January 1994 that Germany's new restrictive asylum laws were required so that Germany could be a good European partner and participate in further European integration. In fact, it could be argued that Germany pressed for the standardization of European practice to lessen the flow of asylum seekers to Germany. Certainly, the signing of readmission agreements by Germany and her neighbours and these newer and stricter German laws may have shifted some of the flow to other member states such as The Netherlands (Uçarer, 1997: 289).

5. From discussions with Dr Simon Hix, Department of Government, London School of Economics, September 1997. I would like to thank Dr Hix for his extremely helpful suggestions.

6. A member state can have its voting rights suspended through the request of one member state or the Commission in consultation with the European Parliament and after a decision has been made unanimously by the Council of Ministers.

7. The Danish Protocol announces that Denmark will not participate in discussion affecting the Area of Freedom, Security and Justice except those attached to old Article 100c which dealt with visas and their formats. However Article 5 of this Protocol states that Denmark can choose to implement the Directives arising. The Danes have six months to accept the Directives as law but these laws will remain as international rather than Community laws in this case. As in the case of the Schengen *acquis*, Denmark can change this relationship at any time.

REFERENCES

Adler Hellman, J. (1997), 'Immigrant "Space" in Italy: When an Emigrant Sending Becomes and Immigrant Receiving Society', *Modern Italy*, Vol. 2, Nos.1/2, pp. 34–51.

Ardittis, S. (1994), *The Politics of East-West Migration*, New York, St Martin's Press.

Baldwin-Edwards, M. and Schain, M.A. (1994),'The Politics of Immigration: Introduction', *West European Politics*, Vol. 17, No. 2, pp. 1–16.

Black, R. (1993), 'Refugees and Asylum-Seekers in Western Europe: New Challenges', in Black, R. and Robinson, V. (eds), *Geography and Refugees: Patterns and Processes of Change*, London, Belhaven Press, pp. 87–103.

Bloch, A. (1997), 'Refugee Migration and Settlement: A Case Study of the London Borough of Newham', Goldsmiths College, University of London, PhD Dissertation.

Castles, S. (1993), 'Migration and Minorities in Europe. Perspectives for the 1990s: Eleven Hypotheses', in Wrench, J. and Solomos, J. (eds), *Racism and Migration in Western Europe*, Oxford, Berg, pp. 17–34.

Close, P. (1995), *Citizenship, Europe and Change*, Basingstoke, Macmillan.

Cohen, R. (1997), *Global Diasporas: An Introduction*, London, UCL Press.

Coleman, D.A. (1997), 'Europe under Migration Pressure: Some Facts on Immigration, in Uçarer, E.M. and Puchala, D.J. (eds), *Immigration into Western Societies: Problems and Policies*, London, Pinter, pp. 121–46.

Collinson, S. (1996), *Shore to Shore: The Politics of Migration in Euro-Maghreb Relations*, London, Royal Institute of International Affairs.

Den Boer, M. (1996), 'Justice and Home Affairs: Cooperation without Integration, in Wallace, H. and Wallace ,W. (eds), *Policy-Making in the European Union*, Oxford, Oxford University Press, pp. 389–409.

Duff, A. (1997a), *Reforming the European Union*, London, Federal Trust.

Duff, A. (ed.)(1997b), *The Treaty of Amsterdam: Text and Commentary*, London, Federal Trust.

Dutch Ministry of Foreign Affairs (1995), 'Dutch Position Paper on European Cooperation in the Field of Justice and Home Affairs', The Hague, Ministry of Foreign Affairs.

ECRE (European Council on Refugees and Exiles)(1997a), 'Position Paper on Temporary Protection in the Context of the Need for a Supplementary Refugee Definition', London, ECRE, March.

ECRE (European Council on Refugees and Exiles) (1997b), 'Analysis of the Treaty of Amsterdam in so far as it Relates to Asylum Policy', London, ECRE, 16 July.

Elliot, C. (1997),'Serb Refugees Left out in the Cold', *The Guardian*, 25 October, p. 16.

Eurostat (1997a), 'Asylum-Seekers in Europe in the First Nine Months of 1995', *Asylum-Seekers*, Vol. 1, No. 1, pp. 1–5.

Eurostat (1997b), 'Asylum-Seekers in Europe in the First Nine Months of 1996', *Asylum-Seekers*, Vol. 2, No. 1, pp. 1–5.

Foot, J. (1995), 'The Logic of Contradiction: Migration Control in Italy and France, 1980–1993', in Miles, R. and Thränhardt, D. (eds), *Migration and European Integration*, London, Cassells, pp. 132–58.

Groenendijk, C.A. (1992), 'The Competence of the Court of Justice with Respect to Inter-Governmental Treaties on Immigration and Asylum', *International Journal of Refugee Law*, Vol. 4, No. 4, pp. 331–6.

Guild, E. (1996), *The Developing Immigration and Asylum Policies of the European Union*, Amsterdam, Kluwer Law International.

Hailbronner, K. (1990), 'The Right to Asylum and the Future of Asylum Procedures in the European Community', *International Journal of Refugee Law*, Vol. 2, No. 3, pp. 341–60.

Hailbronner, K. (1995),'Third-Country Nationals and EC Law', in Rosas, A. and Antola, E. (eds), *A Citizen's Europe: In Search of a New Order*, London, Sage, pp. 182–206.

Hantrais, L. (1995), *Social Policy in the European Union*, Basingstoke, Macmillan.

Harvey, C. (1997), 'Restructuring Asylum: Recent Trends in United Kingdom Asylum Law and Policy', *International Journal of Refugee Law*, Vol. 9, No. 1, pp. 60–73.

Hix, S. and Niessen, J. (1996), *Reconsidering European Migration Policy: The 1996 Intergovernmental Conference and the Reform of the Maastricht Treaty*, Brussels, Migration Policy Group, Churches' Commission on Migrants in Europe and Starting Line Group.

Hollifield, J.F. (1992), *Immigrants, Markets and States: The Political Economy of the Postwar Europe*, Cambridge, MA, Harvard University Press.

Hollifield, J.F. (1997), 'Immigration and Integration in Western Europe: A Comparative Analysis', in Uçarer, E.M. and Puchala, D.J. (eds), *Immigration and Western Societies: Problems and Policies*, London, Pinter, pp. 28–69.

Jacobson, D. (1996), *Rights Across Borders: Immigration and the Decline of Citizenship*, Baltimore, The Johns Hopkins University Press.

Joly, D. (1996), *Haven or Hell? Asylum Policies and Refugees in Europe*, Basingstoke, Macmillan.

JUSTICE/ILPA/ARC (1997), *Providing Protection: Towards Fair and Effective Asylum Procedures*, London, JUSTICE, ILPA and ARC.

Lambert, H. (1995), *Seeking Asylum: Comparative Law and Practice in Selected European Countries*, Dordrecht, Martinus Nijhoff Publications.

Lazaridis, G. (1996), 'Immigration to Greece: A Critical Evaluation of Greek Policy', *New Community*, Vol. 22, No. 2, pp. 335–48.

Lodge, J. (1997), 'The Emergent European Union: Democratic Legitimacy and the 1996 Inter-governmental Conference', in Symes, V., Levy, C. and Littlewood, J. (eds), *The Future of Europe: Problems and Issues for the Twenty-First Century*, Basingstoke, Macmillan, pp. 299–327.

Magleby Sørensen, J. (1996), *The Exclusive European Citizenship: The Case for Refugees and Immigrants in the European Union*, Aldershot, Avebury.

Mahmood, S. (1995), 'The Schengen Information System: An Inequitable Data Protection Regime', *International Journal of Refugee Law*, Vol. 7, No. 2, pp. 179–200.

Majone, G. (1996), *Regulating Europe*, London, Routledge.

Martin, P.L. (1997), 'The Impacts of Immigration on Receiving Countries', in Uçarer, E.M. and Puchala, D.J. (eds), *Immigration and Western Societies: Problems and Policies*, London, Pinter, pp. 17–27.

Miles, R. and Kay, D. (1994), 'The Politics of Immigration to Britain: East-West Migration in the Twentieth Century', *West European Politics*, Vol. 17, No. 2, pp. 17–32.

Monar, J. (1997), 'European Union – Justice and Home Affairs: A Balance Sheet on an Agenda for Reform', in Edwards, G. and Pijpers (eds), *The Politics of European Treaty Reform: The 1996 Intergovernmental Conference and Beyond*, London, Pinter, pp. 326–39.

Morris, L. (1997), 'A Cluster of Contradictions: The Politics of Migration in the European Union', *Sociology*, Vol. 31, No. 2, pp. 241–59.

Niessen, J. (1996), 'Introduction', in Guild, E., *The Developing Immigration and Asylum Policies of the European Union*, Amsterdam, Kluwer Law International, pp. 1–62.

Niessen, J. (1997), 'The Treaty of Amsterdam and the Clauses on Immigration, Asylum and Anti-Discrimination', Brussels, Migration Policy Group, 26 June.

Papademetriou, D.G. (1996), *Coming Together or Pulling Apart? The European Union's Struggle with Immigration and Asylum*, Washington DC, Carnegie Endowment for International Peace.

Papademetriou, D.G. and Hamilton, K. (1996), *Converging Paths to Restriction: French, Italian and British Responses to Immigration*, Washington DC, Carnegie Endowment for International Peace.

Pugliese, E. (1996), 'Italy between Emancipation and Immigration and the Problem of Citizenship', in Cesarani, D. and Fulbrook, M. (eds), *Citizenship, Nationality and Migration in Europe*, London, Routledge, pp. 106–24.

Salt, J., Singleton, A. and Hogarth, J. (1994), *Europe's International Migrants Data Sources, Patterns and Trends*, London, HMSO.

Schönwälder, K. (1996), 'Migrants, Refugees and Ethnic Plurality as Issues of Public and Political Debate in (West) Germany', in Cesarani, D. and Fulbrook, M. (eds), *Citizenship, Nationality and Migration in Europe*, London, Routledge, pp. 159–78.

Soysal, Y.N. (1996), 'Changing Citizenship in Europe: Remarks on Post National Membership and the National State', in Cesarani, D. and Fulbrook, M. (eds), *Citizenship, Nationality and Migration in Europe*, London, Routledge, pp. 17–29.

Thränhardt, D. (1996), 'European Migration from East to West: Present Problems and Future Direction', *New Community*, Vol. 22, No. 2, pp. 227–42.

Thränhardt, D. (1997), 'The Political Uses of Xenophobia in England, France and Germany', in Uçarer, E.M. and Puchala, D.J. (eds), *Immigration into Western Societies: Problems and Policies*, London, Pinter, pp. 175–94.

Uçarer, E.M. (1997), 'Europe's Search for Policy: The Harmonization of Asylum Policy and European Integration', in Uçarer, E.M. and Puchala, D.J. (eds), *Immigration and Western Societies: Problems and Policies*, London, Pinter, pp. 281–309.

Vasta, E. (1993), 'Rights and Racism in a New Country of Immigration: The Italian Case', in Wrench, J. and Solomos, J. (eds), *Racism and Migration in Western Europe*, Oxford, Berg, pp. 83–98.

Wallace, C., Chmouliar, O. and Sidorenko,E. (1996), 'The Eastern Frontier of Western Europe: Mobility in the Buffer Zone', *New Community*, Vol. 22, No. 2, pp. 259–86.

Wallace, R.M.M. (1996), *Refugees and Asylum: A Country Perspective*, London, Butterworth.

Wischenbart, R. (1994), 'National Identity and Immigration in Austria – Historical Framework and Political Disputes', *West European Politics*, Vol. 17, No. 2, pp. 72–90.

3 The politics of refugee and asylum policies in Britain: historical patterns and contemporary realities

Liza Schuster and John Solomos

It has been the traditional policy of successive British governments to give shelter to persons who are compelled to leave their own countries by reason of persecution for their political or religious belief or of their racial origin, but the Government are bound to have regard to their domestic situation and to the fact that for economic and demographic reasons this policy can only be applied within narrow limits (Home Office Memorandum 1938, cited in Dummett and Nicol, 1990: 158).

Asylum became a major issue in Britain from the late 1980s onwards, as the numbers applying for asylum increased suddenly and dramatically. From constituting only a small percentage of entrants they had become, within only a few years, the largest single category (excluding visitors and transit passengers). A Bill was presented to the House of Commons in 1992, with the purpose of reducing the number of applicants who could claim asylum in Britain (Shutter, 1995),[1] of reducing the time spent in Britain by applicants by categorizing some claims as inadmissible, and facilitating the speedy removal of those whose claims were rejected. The Asylum and Immigration Appeals Act finally came into force on 26 July 1993, and was followed three years later by the 1996 Asylum and Immigration Act, which denied, to certain classes of asylum applicants, access to social security and legal aid, in order to remove what was seen as an incentive to migrants to apply for asylum in Britain.[2]

This chapter will explore the changing contours of British policies relating to refugees and asylum seekers in order to contextualize contemporary trends within a broader historical framework. Given that until 1993 Britain had had no statutory law covering the granting of asylum, and that the numbers of applicants for asylum were small by comparison with other European countries, it seems surprising that the first time asylum appears in domestic law, it is in order to restrict access to it. A simple explanation would be that the most important condition necessary for granting asylum is no longer in place in Britain: asylum no longer serves any obvious purpose for the state – it has no need for refugees (as a source of labour or skills) and with the demise of the Soviet Union it is no longer needed to legitimate one ideology over another. And yet, although Britain has restricted access to asylum, it has not renounced it altogether. This raises a number of questions. What purposes has the granting of asylum served for Britain? And why does it continue to grant asylum?

The debates leading up to the introduction of the 1993 and 1996 Acts, the first to deal almost exclusively with asylum, while exposing certain party differences, also revealed areas of broad consensus, both between the main political parties and within the general population. None of the representatives of the different parties suggested that Britain cease to grant asylum. All agreed that the granting of asylum was the mark of a civilized and liberal state and that Britain had certain legal and humanitarian obligations. Occasionally reference was made to the benefits Britain derived from this practice, but essentially it was agreed that numbers were the problem – there were simply too many – they could not be controlled. Moreover, there was also an agreed concern over the types of people who were coming – 'bogus' asylum seekers, also referred to as economic migrants.

HISTORICAL BACKGROUND AND CONTEXT

Until the last decades of the nineteenth century, entry and settlement into Britain was relatively unrestricted, and for good reason. Hundreds of thousands of Britons were leaving every year, seeking opportunity and wealth in the Colonies, as well as in the United States. As a result of this large-scale emigration and the demands of the industrial revolution, there was a constant need for the population, and the labour force, to be replenished. In such circumstances, there was little resistance to the idea of granting asylum, which fitted the dominant ideology of political and economic liberalism in Victorian Britain and fulfilled practical needs. The former stressed the freedom of the individual and the latter free trade. The industrial revolution and the economic booms which followed it created an insatiable need for labour, which according to Foot, could be:

cloaked in the woolly idealism of Victorian liberalism. British politicians of both parties, particularly the Liberals, regarded themselves as champions of the right of political asylum (1965: 84).

Thus asylum fulfilled a dual function, serving both economic and political interests. Aside from political and economic considerations, it would have proved more costly to track down the fugitives than to tolerate their presence, given the absence of fingerprinting, passports with photographs and all the paraphernalia of twentieth-century surveillance. Furthermore, asylum at that time was very different than today as there was no legal definition of a 'refugee' or of asylum. Since granting asylum meant merely refusing to extradite, that is, doing nothing, it was a cheap way of asserting moral superiority. This sense of superiority received further confirmation from the new racial theories (Dummett and Nicol, 1990: 96) which became current at the time, placing North Europeans at the pinnacle of a hierarchy of 'races'.

A combination of domestic and foreign developments eventually led to a change in the *laissez-faire* entry regime from 1880 onwards. In Russia and Eastern Europe, the persecution and targeting of Jewish populations were causing increasing numbers to flee westwards, some of whom settled in Britain, but most of whom were headed onwards to America. At the same time, news of assassination attempts and bombings by anarchists and nihilists from Poland and Russia eroded liberal attitudes towards political exiles from Eastern Europe (Marrus, 1985). The contingent nature of the commitment to refugees was revealed and the way was paved for the introduction of controls. This intolerance towards aliens, expressed in the slogan 'England for the English' (Dummett and Nicol, 1990; Brown, 1995; Solomos, 1993) was heightened as British capitalism entered a period of decline, and economic crisis and high unemployment diminished the demand for labour.

STATE CONTROLS AND REGULATION

These economic, political and social factors overcame the demand for unrestricted entry, and led to the 1905 Aliens Act.[3] This was the first attempt to regulate the flow of entrants into Britain and was 'passed for the purpose of checking the immigration of undesirable aliens'.[4] The provisions of the Act only applied to steerage passengers on 'immigrant ships', that is, to those who could not support themselves, might become a charge on the rates, or were mentally ill and to those ships carrying more than twenty aliens. The Act is significant because it provided, for the first time since the reign of Elizabeth I, a mechanism for control. As a result, the Act was condemned at the time as an attack on personal liberty and because it managed to target a particular group without actually mentioning them – those coming from Russia and Poland, in particular those without means. In addition, it made a distinction between immigrants and refugees. Although there was no mention of refugees or asylum in the Act, it did specify that leave to land should not be refused to those who were seeking entry:

> to this country solely to avoid persecution or punishment on religious or political grounds or for an offence of a political character or persecution involving a danger of imprisonment or danger to life or limb, on account of religious belief (Aliens Act 1905, Section 1(2)).

Although Herbert Gladstone and his party had opposed the Act while in opposition, once in power (January 1906), they decided not to repeal it, but to soften its impact, by instructing immigration officers that in all cases where doubt about persecution existed, the benefit of such doubt should be given to the immigrant and leave to land granted.[5] Perhaps the greatest significance of Gladstone's instruction, which reinforced the discretionary power available to immigration officers, was that it confirmed the granting of asylum as an act of benevolence. Since asylum in Britain has always been an *ex gratia* act, that is, granted at the discretion of the Home Office, it is susceptible to the whims of the holder of that office and the government of the day.

The advantage of granting asylum as an *ex gratia* act is that, without surrendering control over entry, it reinforces the image of the British state as liberal – it does not have to grant asylum but it does – and implies that Britain is prepared to underwrite certain costs for the sake of certain liberal values.[6] Most importantly, however, it grants the government of the day enormous flexibility, to admit those whom it chooses and to reject those it does not want or need. While the upholding of values such as liberty, decency and fairness (terms which are conveniently vague) may be argued to form part of the national interest, historically it can be seen that it is far more likely to entail concrete advantages to Britain in terms of domestic and foreign policy.[7] The danger inherent in presenting asylum as an act of charity is that it contributes to the image of the refugee as a burden, someone to be tolerated for the sake of those liberal values rather than as someone with a positive contribution to make to the host society. Nonetheless, the Aliens Act was not a particularly effective control mechanism, and for the next few years, aliens could enter Britain almost at will.[8]

ASYLUM'S DARKEST HOURS

As a result of the anti-alien hysteria generated by the First World War, the right to appeal was suspended by the Aliens Restriction Act (1914),[9] passed in a single day, and abolished by the Aliens Restriction Act (1919)[10] along with any provision permitting refugees to land. The 1914 and 1919 Acts were again attempts to control entry, and this control was facilitated by the introduction of passports.[11] The introduction of passports also served to control exit since the warring states had no desire to lose soldiers or skills. Passports, which were introduced in spite of resistance in Britain and other European countries, as a wartime necessity, became an important part of the state's armoury in the battle to control its borders.

From 1919 to 1938 no distinction was made between aliens seeking asylum and other aliens (Dummett and Nicol, 1990: 146), although most people seeking to enter Britain at that time were victims of political and religious persecution. Kushner (1990c) and others have uncovered a lesser-known, illiberal tradition of intolerance and anti-Semitism, which did much to shape Britain's response to refugees, especially Jewish refugees from the Nazis.

The electoral failure of political anti-Semitism and fascism belies both the support such views had within the population and the impact they had on Government policy. Rather than confront the anti-Semites, the government chose instead to appease them by restricting the numbers allowed into the country. Initially, only those whom the Anglo-Jewish community promised to support were allowed to enter. This was due in part to economic considerations,[12] to prevent the refugees from becoming a financial burden on the British tax-payer, but also because it was claimed that an increase in the number of Jews coming to Britain would heighten anti-Semitism. In March 1938, concerned that this was the intention of the Germans, the Home Secretary, Sir Samuel Hoare, introduced visas which 'could be granted on the spot to "distinguished persons" assured of hospitality in Britain, [and] *non-refugee* students who are known *not* to have any Jewish or non-Aryan affiliations' (Dummett and Nicol, 1990: 157, our emphasis).

It was only as a result of public revulsion following *Kristallnacht* in November 1938, that Neville Chamberlain, in spite of his undisguised dislike of the Jews, eased admission policy, though even 'then the refugees were allowed entry only on temporary visas' (Kushner, 1990a: 199). This may have been due, in part, to a need to distance Britain from 'illiberal' Germany, but it was also seen as having practical benefits, as well as providing an opportunity to reinforce Britain's legitimacy at home and abroad. In 1938 the British Cabinet agreed that it should:

> Try to secure for this country prominent Jews who were being expelled from Germany and who had achieved distinction whether in pure science, applied science, such as medical or technical industry, music or art. This would not only obtain for this country the advantage of their knowledge and experience, but would also create a favourable impression in the world particularly if our hospitality were offered with some warmth (cited in Marrus, 1985: 153).

In spite of this cynical exploitation of the Jewish exodus for practical and propaganda purposes, the reaction to *Kristallnacht* shows that there are moments when governments could harness the concern of their populations to move policy in a more generous direction (Dummett and Nicol, 1990; Kapp and Mynatt, 1997).

After the war Britain's alleged generous treatment of the Jews, fed the myth of its 'decency' and 'liberality'. This has led to a certain complacency, a belief that there was no need to change or improve Britain's asylum policy, because Britain could be trusted to be liberal, tolerant and fair-minded. Unlike Germany, which as a defeated nation was forced to reconstruct itself as a liberal polity and to make reparations to refugees by enshrining within its constitution an obligation to grant asylum, Britain sanitized its history, forgetting its treatment of Jewish (trade unionist, socialist and communist) refugees during the second world war, and reifying the mythical 'long and honourable tradition' (Kenneth Clarke, *Hansard*, 2 November 1992, Col. 21):

THE COLD WAR AND THE END OF EMPIRE

In the aftermath of the war, representatives of the international community came together to prepare the Universal Declaration of Human Rights (UDHR) and the Convention Relating to the Status of Refugees (1951 Convention). In 1954 Britain ratified the 1951

Convention, but this had little impact on British asylum policy, since no legislation was introduced to anchor it in domestic law. Moreover, neither Article 14 (UDHR) nor the 1951 Convention impose enforceable obligations on Britain (or any other state). Instead, asylum policy in the years following the end of the Second World War was affected by four main factors: the beginning of the Cold War; the break up of the Empire; the development of the Welfare State; and a massive labour shortage, estimated at the end of 1946 at 1 346 000 (Joshi and Carter, 1984: 55).

At the end of the war, seeking a means to address this labour shortage, approximately 75 000 displaced persons (DPs) were brought to Britain,[13] but not as quota refugees to be settled. Instead they were renamed the European Volunteer Workers (EVWs) and admitted for a limited period to work in those sectors worst affected by shortages.[14] Displaced persons were not only a source of cheap labour and desirable skills, but they 'were firmly anti-Soviet, a posture that conformed to Britain's position at the opening of the Cold War' (Cohen, 1994: 75). However, the demands of the labour market and the propaganda value of the DPs did not mean that they were met with a unanimous welcome. Just as with immigration generally, the demands of the free market and capitalism met with resistance from indigenous labour, fearful of the pressure on wages. The National Union of Miners, for example, objected to Polish and Italian DPs being brought over to work in the mines (Joshi and Carter, 1984: 56; Dummett and Nicol, 1990: 176). A number of MPs argued that the government should act to remove 'this wretched prejudice' against them, since they 'would be a great benefit to our stock' (Cohen, 1994: 75–76). Other factors operating in favour of the use of DPs, was that it was possible for the government to recruit single persons without dependants, that is, only those who could make an active contribution, their entry could be controlled (in a way the entry of subjects from the Commonwealth could not) and they could be deported.

However, by the early 1950s the DP camps had been emptied of viable workers and Commonwealth migrants became the main group of new arrivals into Britain. The politics of Commonwealth immigration do not immediately concern us here (Solomos, 1993). Suffice it to say that throughout the 1950s there was increasing awareness of the question of immigration and by the late 1950s there was political pressure to control immigration. This finally led, in 1962, to the Commonwealth Immigrants Act, which was the first major piece of legislation to restrict the entry of immigrants from the Commonwealth. By this time, a clear distinction had emerged in official thinking between refugees and immigrants. Immigrants were black and came from former Colonies and the Commonwealth (regardless of their motives for leaving), while refugees were white and came from Communist regimes (regardless of their motives for leaving). In 1956, for example, several thousand Hungarian refugees were admitted into Britain with ease, as were small numbers of Czechs, Poles and Soviet citizens. Similarly, while Britain had little problem offering refuge to Czechs following Dubcek's fall in 1968, the arrival of large numbers of East African Asians from Kenya and other countries demonstrated clearly the different perceptions of the two groups and provoked a rapid and dramatic response. As a result of the arrival of East African Asians, Britain introduced the 1968 Commonwealth Immigrants Act which, having passed through Parliament in three days,[15] deprived them of the right to enter the territory of the State whose passport they held.[16]

THE RE-EMERGENCE OF ASYLUM IN LAW

When, after 56 years, reference was again made to those who sought entry for reasons of persecution, it came at the end of the Immigration Rules issued in 1970, where persecution was listed as one of the reasons for granting leave to appeal against refusal of entry clearance. This did not, however, change the discretionary nature of the granting of asylum, nor did it mark the emergence of a clear asylum policy. Asylum seekers were few in number, and came primarily from East European countries. As such, little provision had to be made for them. A brief mention in the immigration rules was deemed sufficient to regulate their entry.

Immigration Rules do not have the force of statutory law. They are regulations issued by the Home Secretary for the guidance of immigration officials and may be changed by the Home Secretary without submitting them to Parliament. The Rules stated that 'where a person is Stateless or a refugee full account is to be taken of the provisions of the relevant international agreements to which the United Kingdom is a party' and that a person should not be deported if this would mean his going to a country where he feared persecution. However, decisions on who qualified for this exemption were made at the discretion of the Immigration Officer, who had the power to decide which cases to refer to the Home Office, whose decisions are beyond the reach of the courts.[17] This has meant, therefore, that asylum has always been unapologetically subject to domestic and foreign considerations.

The Home Secretary's power to make immigration rules, and hence to stipulate the criteria for recognizing asylum seekers, was confirmed in the 1971 Immigration Act. The Act gave the Home Secretary and the immigration authorities extraordinary and largely unrestrained powers to detain asylum seekers. These may, without a court appearance, be detained indefinitely, and without proper information about the reasons for their detention.[18] Dunstan (1995: 132) has pointed out that these powers were originally intended to apply to would-be visitors to Britain who were refused entry at a port, but that, especially since the 1980s, they are being routinely used against asylum seekers.

The 1971 Act was indicative of the government's intention to assert further control over entry, especially of non-Europeans. The immigration controls were not applied indiscriminately to all Commonwealth citizens, only to those from the 'New Commonwealth', who were predominantly non-white. Differential treatment was also evident in relation to refugees. In 1973, the year that the 1971 Immigration Act became operative and the oil crisis threw economies across the globe into crisis, several thousand refugees left Chile following the overthrow of the left-wing Allende government. Three thousand Chileans were admitted into Britain as quota refugees. Their cause was assisted by a Labour government in Britain, broadly sympathetic to the Allende government. Although they were fleeing a communist regime, the reaction to Vietnamese refugees was different. Britain was perceived by the international community to have a special duty to those 'boatpeople' who found themselves in Hong Kong, a crown colony, but it took pressure from the UN to persuade Britain to take a quota of ten thousand.

THE START OF THE RETREAT

With the election of a Conservative government under Margaret Thatcher in 1979, legislation to further restrict immigration and control entry escalated. Successive Conservative governments after 1979 sought to make tougher controls on entry into Britain a point of political principle. The extent of legislation passed by the Conservatives during the 1980s and 1990s is indicated in Table 3.1.

While in opposition, Thatcher had used the immigration issue to mobilize a fear of being 'swamped by people of a different culture'. In the run-up to the 1979 election, she identified with the concerns of those who saw immigration as a threat to the cultural and social unity

Table 3.1   Legislation relating to refugees and asylum seekers

Year	Legislation
1905	Aliens Act
1914	Aliens Restriction Act
1919	Aliens Restriction Act
1948	British Nationality Act
1962	Commonwealth Immigrants Act
1968	Commonwealth Immigrants Act
1969	Immigration Appeals Act
1970	Immigration Rules
1971	Immigration Act
1980	Immigration Rules
1981	British Nationality Act
1984	Immigration Procedure Rules
1985	Change to Immigration Procedure Rules
1986	Changes to Immigration Rules
1987	Carriers' Liability Act
1988	Immigration Act
1993	Asylum and Immigration Appeals Act
1996	Asylum and Immigration Act

of Britain. Although primary immigration had virtually ceased and entry to Britain could now only be achieved via family reunion and applications for asylum, the call to restrict immigration further was perceived as a definite vote winner.[19]

As a result, the 1980s in Britain saw a number of changes in the Immigration Rules in order to increase the power of the Home Office to control entry. The three main areas of change were appeals (Immigration Rules); visas (Immigration Rules); and the introduction of the 1987 Carriers' Liability Act. The practical details of the appeals system set up by the Immigration Acts were amended by the Immigration Procedure Rules (1984), which provided for appeals to be first heard by a single adjudicator. If the appeal was lost, the applicant then had the right to appeal to the Immigration Appeal Tribunal. Those who were refused asylum did not have a separate appeal system.

A new hurdle for asylum seekers was put in place by the introduction of visa requirements. Without a visa, potential claimants are unable to embark on the journey to Britain. The Immigration Service appears unconcerned that it may be very difficult for a dissident to obtain a passport from the authorities who may be persecuting them.

Indeed in some countries visiting the British embassy to obtain a visa may in itself be seen as a subversive act. Interestingly, visas are either not required for those who are attempting to enter Britain from non-refugee-producing countries, or are much easier to acquire, but they are introduced whenever numbers of refugees from a particular country increase substantially. The Tamils in 1985 were followed in 1989 by Turkish nationals (when Kurds were fleeing Turkey) and in 1991 by Ugandan nationals.

Possibly the most significant piece of legislation to be passed in the 1980s was the 1987 Carriers' Liability Act.[20] The sole purpose of this Act was to reduce the number of immigrants reaching Britain. The effect for asylum seekers was to create another hurdle before they could leave their country of origin. The Act made carriers liable for passengers who travel without papers or with incorrect papers. Initially fines were set at £1000.[21] Ticket clerks of airline and shipping companies were turned into unofficial immigration officers with the right to refuse passage to anyone not in possession of valid passports and visas. This contravenes the spirit, if not the letter, of Article 31 of the 1951 Convention, which prohibits the imposition of penalties for unlawful entry.[22]

In spite of these new restrictions, most of the asylum seekers whose claims were rejected could not be returned to their country of origin. In these cases, exceptional leave to remain (ELR) was granted. This status is much less secure and carries far fewer rights than asylum.[23] Without granting either refugee status or asylum, it allows an asylum applicant, or those fleeing events such as civil war (who are not eligible for refugee status) to remain temporarily until conditions in their country of origin improve sufficiently to permit their return. The government originally claimed that it was granted on compassionate grounds, but then, in the debates leading up to the 1993 Act, changed tack and said it was granted to those whose length of stay in Britain made it difficult to remove them.[24] In this way, it attempted to remove the moral obligation which might be owed to such people, and to justify granting it to far fewer people. The advantage for the state of granting ELR, rather than asylum, is that it does not grant claim rights against the state, and the state retains the option to withdraw leave and deport those granted ELR. However, ELR also allows the government to point to the very low recognition rates and to use these as evidence of mass abuse of the system necessitating new and draconian measures to deal with the 'cheats', even though by the end of the 1980s the Home Office had at its disposal all the instruments required to control entry into Britain.

THE 1993 AND 1996 ACTS

The justifications offered for new legislation were the increasing number of 'would-be migrants' who were exploiting Britain's asylum provisions and the potential for 'a mass influx' from Eastern Europe. In fact, the primary factors underlying the debate at the beginning of the 1990s were not dissimilar to those at the end of the Second World War, now it was the end, rather than the beginning of the Cold War, hence the increase in the number of people coming from Eastern Europe while the numbers coming from Africa and Asia remained constant; the crisis, rather than the creation, of the welfare state; unemployment rather than a labour shortage; and whereas, after the war, Britain's identity as the centre of the Empire was crumbling, it was now Europe which seemed to pose a threat to British identity and sovereignty, especially as a result of the drive to open internal borders.

The 1993 Act was the culmination of a prolonged campaign by the Conservative government, aided and abetted by the right wing press to create an image of a besieged Britain, endangered by 'sponging', culturally alien hordes. However, the evidence adduced for this was based on data carefully selected to construct a problem which

Table 3.2   Total applications for asylum

1979	1 600*
1980	9 900*
1981	2 900*
1982	4 223
1983	4 296
1984	2 905
1985	4 389
1986	4 266
1987	4 256
1988	3 998
1989	1 640
1990	2 205
1991	44 840
1992	24 600
1993	22 370
1994	32 831

* Approximately

Sources: 1985–94 British Refugee Council and Home Office Statistical Bulletins, 1979–84; Layton-Henry, 1994: 278.

demanded a particular solution. Table 3.2 shows that the numbers applying for asylum had remained fairly constant during the ten years up to 1989, only exceeding 6000 in 1980.

The numbers applying for asylum increased in the late 1980s. In 1989, the number of people applying for asylum increase by 192 per cent, 1990 saw a 126 per cent increase and in 1991 the increase was 71 per cent. Although in absolute terms the numbers themselves were not large, especially by comparison with the number of asylum applicants reaching other European countries, the changes were used as evidence of a potentially uncontrollable influx following the collapse of the Soviet Union.[25] The figures in Table 3.3 reflect events such as the opening of East European borders in 1989 and the start of the Yugoslav conflict, while placing in context the number of asylum applications to Britain.

The figures demonstrate Britain's extraordinary ability to control entry and settlement and to respond quickly to events, and place in doubt the need for legislation. These figures were ignored in the debates. Instead, attention was focused on the recognition rates[26] in order to deconstruct the 'morally untouchable category of the deserving political refugee' and to introduce the 'disguised economic migrant' (Cohen, 1994: 82). In this way the government retained the moral high ground and demonized the majority of applicants, providing itself with a useful scapegoat for other ills. This increase in the number of refugees applying for asylum in Europe cannot be simply explained away as an increase in the number of 'economic migrants', but is due instead to the documented increase in the number of refugees generally. The Act did not address or refer to the causes of

Table 3.3 Number of asylum applications (in thousands)

	1983	1984	1985	1986	1987	1988	1989	1990	1991	1992	1993
Britain	4.3	3.9	5.5	4.8	5.2	5.3	15.6	25.3	44.8	24.5	22.4
Switzerland	7.9	7.5	9.7	8.6	10.9	16.8	24.4	35.9	41.7	18.2	24.7
Sweden	3.0	12.0	14.5	14.6	18.1	19.6	30.4	29.4	27.4	83.2	37.6
France	15.0	16.0	25.8	23.5	24.9	31.7	58.8	49.8	45.9	26.8	27.6
Germany	19.7	35.3	73.9	99.7	57.4	103.1	121.3	193.1	256.1	438.1	322.8

Source: UNHCR Report 1994 Die Lage der Flüchtlinge der Welt s.173. In the same report a list of the 50 countries with the largest number of refugees relative to population places Sweden at No. 12 (1:26.7), Denmark at No. 30 (1:88.9), Germany at No. 33 (1:97) and Switzerland at No. 49 (252.3). Neither France nor Britain appear on the list.

flight. Instead, it merely redefined those who were eligible to apply, reducing numbers who were granted asylum or permitted to remain legally by introducing criteria that were almost impossible to fulfill.[27]

Having first argued that the purpose of the bill was to prevent only 'bogus' asylum applicants from gaining access to Britain and the benefits it provided, the government went on to assert that Britain could not afford to take all of the 'genuine refugees' who might wish to come, no matter how pressing their claim, since there were simply too many of them. It was therefore claimed that Britain could not be expected to grant asylum to every 'genuine' refugee. The State's first duty must be to its citizens, and with that in mind the State had a right to select from among even the 'genuine' refugees those who had ties to Britain (Anne Widdecombe, *Hansard*, 15 July 1996, Col. 823) or who would prove an asset to Britain. This argument was used to justify those provisions which would affect 'genuine' asylum seekers, such as the 'safe third country rule'.

It is worth recalling that the claims that 'many people are now using asylum claims as a means of evading immigration control'[28] were being made just as the war in Yugoslavia was forcing millions to flee ethnic cleansing. Rather than suggest that, as Britain has the power to control entry to a greater degree than other European states, and receives far fewer refugees than France or Germany, it could take in quota refugees,[29] the British government failed initially to take advantage of this propaganda opportunity, and in 1992 introduced visas for those fleeing the Yugoslav conflict. In November 1992 the government announced that it would be willing to receive 1000 ex-detainees and their dependants (estimated at a further 3000) from Bosnia and other parts of the former Yugoslavia on an exceptional basis, for an initial period of six months. However, 18 months later, less than 1600 had been admitted.

At the same time as the numbers of people seeking refuge in Britain increased, it was facing economic difficulties, which helped to shape the debate. In 1990–91, rising inflation, a worsening balance of payments and a fall in industrial production saw Britain enter a period of deep and prolonged recession. In the drive to cut public spending, benefit fraud and cheats were targeted. By focusing on the tiny percentage of applicants who were actually granted asylum, asylum seekers were targeted as cheats – a drain on the public purse (the tabloid press focused on the numbers of applicants granted Convention status *at the first hearing*, ignoring the numbers actually permitted to remain legally:

By claiming asylum, those who have no basis to remain here cannot only substantially prolong their stay, but gain access to benefit and housing at public expense... Of the 40 000 asylum applicants currently being supported on benefit, very few will be found to merit asylum or exceptional leave to remain... My right honourable friend the Secretary of State for the Environment has concluded that the same arguments apply in relation to social housing (Michael Howard, *Hansard*, 20 November 1992, Col. 336).

These 'bogus' refugees were depicted as 'illegal' immigrants exploiting Britain's 'lax' asylum laws to take advantage of Britain's welfare benefits:

The easiest way to clamber on board the Great British Gravy Train is to enter the country on a visitor's visa or slip in illegally. Then if you're caught, just claim political asylum (*Daily Mail*, 13 March 1995).

In response to the alleged burden on the welfare state, local authorities were relieved of the duty to accommodate asylum seekers awaiting a decision, once they have temporary accommodation, even if this is only a floor in a church or a volunteer's home. The Member for Harborough summed up the argument thus:

Our duties to our citizens include the duty to protect our welfare and benefit budgets and our housing system at a time of economic stringency... Those who should not be here but who have got round the system by false applications are of no benefit to our own people (Edward Garnier, *Hansard*, 2 November 1992, Col. 61).

Nonetheless, even after the 1993 Act curtailed access to housing, it was still felt that Britain offered too many incentives by way of benefits. The end result of this pressure was the Asylum and Immigration Act 1996 (see Minderhoud, Chapter 7 in this volume). The 1996 Act restricted access to child benefit, housing and other social security benefits, as well as extending the scope of the 'fast track' asylum appeals procedure with the introduction of 'White Lists' (Gillespie, 1996: 86). The new housing provision provides that only those who apply for asylum within three days of entry, and are without temporary accommodation, will be entitled to housing. This time restriction also applies to child and social security benefit claimants. Lest the impression be given that the concerns of the proponents of the new Act were driven solely by self-interest, these 'bogus' claimants were further accused of behaving immorally by making it difficult for genuine asylum seekers, by 'clogging up the system', and prolonging the processing period.

It was suggested during the debates in the House, that the liberal polity itself was endangered by refugees. The only time that the proponents of the Bill alluded to the fact that most asylum seekers arriving in Europe went to Germany was when warning of the consequences large numbers of asylum seekers would have for social harmony, that is racial violence, hostel burning and the rise of the far right. Douglas Hurd, the then foreign secretary, chairing an informal meeting of EC foreign ministers in 1992, said that Britain could not increase its refugee intake. The government would not risk a resurgence of the racial tension and 'considerable political and economic dislocation' seen in the 1960s and 1970s (*The Times*, 14 September 1992). Again, during the second reading of the 1992 Bill, members held up the spectacle of the violent attacks on hostels for asylum seekers in Germany as a warning of what might happen in Britain if the influx of asylum seekers was not checked:

> A vast horde of aspirant economic migrants is creating pressures in Europe, leading to political responses that are extremely distasteful to democrats ... We should face up to the fact that the United Kingdom is not immune to such pressures ... We have good race relations, and, by and large, the days of National Front marches are gone; but that improvement is based on public trust in our tight immigration controls. If those controls are doubted, we shall risk a resurgence of the National Front and other such nasty activists (Jacques Arnold, *Hansard*, 2 November 1992, Col. 71).

Opponents of the bill, mostly though not exclusively on the Labour benches, were accused of offering an 'open door' policy which would fatally damage the race relations in Britain:

> Kenneth Baker, the Home Secretary, formally announced the Bill to cheers at last year's Tory party conference, where he accused his Labour opposite number of 'attempting to pander to ethnic minorities' (*The Times*, 15 February 1992).

However, *The Times*, although normally a supporter of the government, went on to warn of the consequences of such attacks:

> His supposed crackdown on 'bogus' refugees inspired a stream of vitriol in the popular press against a 'flood' of illegal immigrants. Mr Major should tell his ministers to button their lips in the run-up to the election, even if a bill would still be introduced should he win.

Another dimension in recent debates appears to be the perception that those coming are 'more' different than previous entrants, that they will change British identity. In spite of the increase in numbers coming from Europe, refugees, especially since the collapse of the Soviet Union, are assumed to come from Africa and Asia, and therefore from very different cultures. These fears were particularly evident during the Salman Rushdie affair (Solomos, 1993; Cohen, 1994: 191). Given the small number of refugees entering Britain, relative to other European states, it is difficult to understand this perception of a threat to British identity. If however, one takes seriously the claims that liberal, humanitarian and 'civilized' values and tolerance are an integral part of what it means to be British, then it is this restrictive legislation which constitutes a threat to British identity. Britain has always seen itself as a beacon of liberal progressiveness, drawing those from less enlightened regimes 'because of the standards and values that they believe we encapsulate and personify' (Patrick Cormack in *Hansard*, 15 July 1996, Col. 862). It seemed logical that those denied free speech, free association, religious and political freedom would want to come to a country where such freedoms were fundamental rights. That Britain was attractive for these reasons confirmed its superiority over other countries and the granting of asylum confirmed Britain's image of itself as free and fair and of its political system as a proper model for the rest of the world. To abandon this mythical tradition would call into question those 'liberal' values which underpin the nation's self-image.

Even supporters of legislation designed to restrict entry for asylum seekers to Britain ritually reaffirmed their state's commitment to continue this liberal tradition of providing sanctuary 'to those who genuinely fear persecution'. On the one hand, it was reasserted time and again that of course there was an obligation to 'genuine' refugees, and that the legislation was only designed to keep at bay 'bogus' refugees, who it was asserted, make up the majority of claimants. The nature of this obligation was left suitably vague, to be decided by the government of the day as need and interest dictated.

OPPOSITION TO RESTRICTIVE LEGISLATION

Opposition to the new legislation came from many different sources: lawyers; groups such as refugee organizations; the Joint Council for the Welfare of Immigrants; Human Rights organizations; Amnesty International; Church organizations and political parties. However, some on the opposition benches accepted the government's premises that the majority of asylum seekers were bogus, and that stricter controls would be necessary.

Let us make clear – beyond doubt I hope – that bogus asylum seekers must be prevented from entering the country. This is an honourable and sensible objective and our amendment reflects our determination to ensure that bogus asylum seekers are identified and denied entry (Roy Hattersley, cited in Greater Manchester Immigration Aid Unit, 1993: 7).

As a result, during the course of the parliamentary debates, senior members of the opposition concentrated on the details of the legislation. Tony Blair, for example, stressed the impact that measures, such as the curtailment of leave for those making an in-country application, the accelerated appeals procedures which would affect many more asylum seekers than those whose claims were 'manifestly unfounded', and the removal of certain rights to appeal would have on 'genuine' asylum seekers. Given the difficulty of obtaining a visa to enter Britain, some of those intent on seeking asylum would purchase a ticket for a destination (often in Eastern Europe) which entailed a stop en route in Britain, intending to disembark and claim asylum when the aircraft touched down in Britain. The 1993 Act extended the provisions of the Carriers' Liability Act so that airlines must now demand transit visas for Britain from intending passengers. Lawyers and refugees campaigns have pointed out the implication of this provision for 'genuine' asylum seekers.

Church groups have been particularly concerned about the hardships which are to be imposed on asylum seekers, such as the measures supposedly targeting 'bogus' refugees included fingerprinting to prevent multiple social security claims and the curtailment of leave for those who have entered on a student or visitors visa (the only possible way of entering for an asylum applicant since visas are not granted abroad to those seeking asylum), but who subsequently applies for and fails to receive asylum. It further enables the Home Office to detain such rejected applicants pending deportation. It was left to opposition backbenchers such as Max Madden, Jeremy Corbyn and Robert Maclennan to point out the racist nature of the legislation (*Hansard*, 2 November 1992, Col. 65).

PROSPECTS FOR THE FUTURE

The election of a Labour government on 1 May 1997 led to expectations of an asylum policy more concerned with social justice than narrow national interest. Part of the reason for these expectations lies in the way in which sections of the Labour Party opposed key elements of the legislation introduced by the Conservatives during the 1990s. Early indications about the extent of any reforms that will be introduced by the new administration are not all that positive. According to a spokesperson at the Immigration Department at Lunar House there has been little change in the aftermath of the 1997 General Election.[30] Reviews have been instituted into legal aid for asylum seekers, the asylum appeals process, spending and the regulation of immigration advisors, in order to weed out those who are incompetent or unscrupulous. It seems likely, however, that any adjustments will be minimal. Early indications are that they will include tinkering with the White List, proposing a code of conduct for immigration advisors and computerizing records at the Asylum Directorate in the hope of reducing the backlog of outstanding cases. While this might have positive implications for a small number of asylum seekers and/or refugees, it is unlikely that the Carriers' Liability Act 1987, the Asylum and Immigration Appeals Act 1993, or the Asylum and Immigration Act 1996 will be repealed or significantly changed.

In this environment the politics of asylum and refuge are likely to remain deeply contested in British political culture. It is for this reason that those interested in the question of the rights of refugees and asylum seekers in the coming century need to learn some of the lessons of the past and explore avenues for new policy agendas and initiatives that offer the chance for a radical rethinking of both the past and the present.

NOTES

1. It also removed the right of appeal against refusal to enter from visitors, prospective students and students coming for less six months.
2. Michael Howard, *Hansard*, 11 December 1995, Col. 702.
3. See Foot, 1965: 84–100 for an analysis of the campaign which led to the passing of the Act.

4. From a letter from the Secretary of State for the Home Department to members of immigration boards, 9 March 1906, cited in Landa, 1911: 315.
5. Gladstone's liberal concern sparked furious attacks from the right, who argued that the 'benefit of the doubt' rule fatally undermined the Act. However, those who successfully appealed against refusal to land were very few: 505 (1906); 43 (1907); 20 (1908);10 (1909); and 5 (1910) (Landa, 1911: 225).
6. 'Britons must bear in mind that the national attributes of which we are justly proud – liberty, decency and fairness – are not free goods. One of the costs they impose is that we may not return people – even inconvenient people – to dangerous places for subjection to unspeakable acts' (Ann Winterton, *Hansard*, 15 July 1996, Col. 816).
7. See quotation at the start of the chapter.
8. Nonetheless, according to a report in *The Times*, a ship was fined shortly after the Act came into force, when two of its passengers, political refugees fleeing death or imprisonment, escaped (Dummett and Nicol, 1990: 161).
9. The 1914 Act was repealed by the 1971 Immigration Act.
10. Parts of which were repealed by the 1971 Immigration Act. The 1919 Act was passed as a temporary measure, but was renewed every year until 1971.
11. Passports were used before the war in South America and in Southern Africa for the purposes of transnational travel, and internally they were in use in Russia. In Britain and France the legislation which governed the issuance of passports, had passed into desuetude (Plender, 1988: 77).
12. Between 1933 and the outbreak of war, 20 000 Jewish women had come to Britain as domestic servants, but this was because of a shortage of labour in nursing and domestic service, and not the result of a generous asylum policy. See Kushner, 1990b.
13. See Cohen, 1994 for a discussion of the ethnic discrimination at work in the selection of workers from the DP camps.
14. Kay and Miles suggest that these refugees may also be referred to as 'unfree labour', since they did not have the right to 'return to the labour market to find an alternative buyer' (Kay and Miles, 1992: 10), they could not return to their home countries, and were without the protection of a State. They did not even have the protection of the International Refugee Organization, since it was not party to the EVW scheme
15. A cabinet minister at the time reflected later that the introduction of this legislation 'would have been declared unconstitutional in any country with a written constitution and a Supreme Court' (Richard Crossman, cited in Robertson, 1989: 317).
16. This right is reaffirmed in the Preamble to the Declaration on Territorial Asylum, and Art. 3(1) of the Fourth Protocol to the European Convention on Human Rights reads 'No one shall be deprived of the right to enter the territory of the state of which he is a national', but the United Kingdom has consistently refused to ratify this Protocol.

17. 'The 1971 [Immigration] Act does not allow the courts of this country to participate in the decision making or appellate process which control and regulate the right to enter and remain in the United Kingdom. This is not surprising. Decisions under the Act are administrative and discretionary rather than judicial and imperative' (*Bugdaycay* v *Secretary of State for the Home Department* [1987] 1 All ER 940).

18. According to the 1971 Immigration Act an asylum seeker has the right to appeal against refusal of entry clearance. If an asylum seeker applied for leave to enter as a visitor or a student (a common occurrence, given the difficulties a dissident would have going to the British Embassy and requesting permission to enter as an asylum seeker) and was refused, s/he had a right of appeal. However, s/he could not win such an appeal, as 'there are no provisions in any Act or rules for entry clearance for asylum' (Shutter, 1995: 96). This anomaly was corrected by the 1993 Asylum and Immigration Appeals Act by abolishing this right of appeal.

19. This remained a Conservative strategy throughout their 18 years in government.

20. This followed an incident at Heathrow airport involving 58 Tamil asylum seekers, who arrived without valid documents. The Home Office decided to detain the Tamils pending deportation. However, after a widely reported protest by men during an attempt to deport them, and representations by lawyers, the Tamils were allowed to put their case, and most were allowed to remain.

21. Since increased to £2000.

22. As S. Cohen points out, the Carriers' Liability Act was not without precedence. The 1905 Aliens Act was interpreted in such a way that those awaiting a decision on entering the country and those refused entry had to be kept on board the same boat on which they arrived – and the general assumption was that the Master of the ship was liable to a fine if the detainee escaped (Cohen, 1988: 15).

23. Although it is not a legal status under the 1951 Convention, Britain is not the only state to grant it.

24. While ELR is still granted to more applicants than asylum, prior to 1993 the percentage of ELR granted was considerably higher.

25. In 1992, Kenneth Baker, the then Home Secretary warned: 'There could be 7 million people seeking exit visas from Russia'. According to the UNHCR report cited above, Russian citizens have not come in large numbers. The same report compiled a 'Top 10' list of countries of origin for the years 1988–92. While Turkey and the former Yugoslavia have been in the top three in each of those years, Russian was not anywhere to be seen.

26. Grants of asylum had sunk from a high point of 31% (2210) in 1989, to 23% (920) in 1990, 8% (505) in 1991 and 3% (1115) in 1992 (Home Office Statistical Bulletin, 17/94). On the basis of two years, 1991 and 1992, reports in the press referred to the tiny percentage of 'genuine' refugees, ignoring those granted ELR (55% (3860) in 1989; 60% (2400) in 1990; 36% (2190) in 1991; and 44% (15 325) in 1992) or those who were granted asylum on appeal.

27. Britain is not alone in this. Redefining refugees out of existence is the preferred solution of the Northern/Western states.
28. Kenneth Baker, Home Secretary, Second Reading of the Asylum Bill, November 1991.
29. According to Home Office Statistics, the total number of refugees resettled – quota refugees plus individual asylum grants – in the UK during the 1980s was 14 897. This is a tiny fraction of those resettled in Austria, France, Germany or Sweden.
30. He could not confirm that deportations to Algeria and Zaire had been suspended, though solicitors representing asylum seekers have informed us this is the case.

REFERENCES

Addo, M. (1994), 'The Legal Condition of Refugees in the United Kingdom' *Journal of Refugee Studies*, Vol. 7, Special issue 'Symposium on the human rights of refugees', pp. 96–110.

Amnesty International (1993), *Passing the Buck: Deficient Home Office Practice in 'Safe Third Country' Asylum Cases,* Amnesty International British Section, London, AIBS/RO/1/93.

Brown, R. (1995), 'Racism and Immigration in Britain', *International Socialism*, No. 68, pp. 3–35.

Burgess, D. (1991), 'Asylum by Ordeal', *New Law Journal*, Vol. 141, No. 6487, pp. 50–2.

Carter, B., Green, M. and Halpern, R. (1996), 'Immigration Policy and the Racialization of Migrant Labour: The Construction of National Identities in the USA and Britain', *Ethnic and Racial Studies,* Vol. 19, No. 1, pp. 135–57.

Cohen, R. (1987), *The New Helots: Migrants in the International Division of Labour*, Aldershot, Gower.

Cohen, R. (1991), 'Asylum Policies and Public Attitudes: The British, German and French experience', Paper for a Conference on *World-Wide Refugee Movements, Development Politics and Human Rights* organized by the Berlin Institute of Social Research in collaboration with the New School of Social Research (New York) and the Friedrich-Naumann-Stiftung, New York City, 8–9 November 1991.

Cohen, R. (1994), *Frontiers of Identity*, London, Longman.

Cohen, R. (1996), 'International Migration and the Future of the Nation-State', *New Community*, Vol. 22, No. 1, pp. 159–63.

Cohen, S. (1988), *From the Jews to the Tamils: Britain's Mistreatment of Refugees*, Manchester, Manchester Law Centre.

Cohen, S. (1989), *Imagine There's no Countries: 1992 and International Immigration Controls against Migrants, Immigrants and Refugees*, Manchester, Greater Manchester Immigration Aid Unit.

Cornelius, W.A., Martin, P. and Hollifield, J.F. (1994), *Controlling Immigration: A Global Perspective*, Stanford, Stanford University Press.

Dummett, A. (ed.) (1986), *Towards a Just Immigration Policy*, London, Cobden Trust.

Dummett, M. and Nicol, A. (1982), 'The Role of Government in Britain's Racial Crisis', in Husband, C. (ed.) *Race in Britain: Continuity and Change*, London, Hutchinson, Chapter 5.

Dummett, A. and Nicol, A. (1990), *Subjects, Citizens, Aliens and Others: Nationality and Immigration Law*, London, Weidenfeld and Nicolson.

Dunstan, R. (1995), 'Home Office Asylum Policy: Unfair and Inefficient?', *Immigration and Nationality Law and Practice*, Vol. 9, No. 4, pp. 132–5.

Faist, T. (1995), 'Ethnicization and Racialization of Welfare-State Politics in Germany and the USA', *Ethnic and Racial Studies*, Vol. 18, No. 2, pp. 219–50.

Foot, P. (1965), *Immigration and Race in British Politics*, Harmondsworth, Penguin.

Freeman, G. (1986), 'Migration and the Political Economy of the Welfare State', *ANNALS, AAPSS*, Vol. 485, pp. 57–63.

Freeman, G. (1995), 'Modes of Immigration Politics in Liberal Democratic States', *International Migration Review*, Vol. 29, No. 4, pp. 881–902.

Gillespie, J. (1996), 'Asylum and Immigration Act 1996: An Outline of the New Law', *Immigration and Nationality Law and Practice*, Vol. 10, No. 3, pp. 86–90.

Goodwin-Gill, G. (1983), *The Refugee in International Law*, Oxford, Clarendon Press.

Goodwin-Gill, G. (1995), 'Asylum: The Law and Politics of Change', *International Journal of Refugee Law*, Vol. 7, No. 1, pp. 1–18.

Harvey, C. (1995), 'Excluding Refugees?' *New Law Journal*, Vol. 145, No. 6718, p. 1630.

Harvey, C. (1996), 'The United Kingdom's New Asylum and Immigration Bill', *International Journal of Refugee Law*, Vol. 8, No. 1/2, pp. 184–7.

Holmes, C. (1988), *John Bull's Island: Immigration and British society, 1871–1971*, London, Macmillan.

Holmes, C. (1991), *A Tolerant Country?: Immigrants, Refugees and Minorities in Britain*, London, Faber.

Joly, D. (1988), *Refugees in Britain: An Annotated Bibliography*, Centre for Research in Ethnic Relations, Bibliographies in Ethnic Relations, No. 9.

Joly D. (1989), *Reluctant Hosts: Europe and its Refugees*, Aldershot: Avebury.

Joly, D. (1996), *Haven or Hell: Asylum Policies and Refugees in Europe*, London, Macmillan.

Joshi, S. and Carter, B. (1984), 'The Role of Labour in the Creation of a Racist Britain', *Race and Class*, Vol. 25, No. 3, pp. 53–70.

Kapp, Y. and Mynatt, M. (1997), *British Policy and the Refugees: 1933–1941*, London, Frank Cass.

Kay, D. and Miles, R. (1988), 'Refugees or Migrant Workers? The Case of the European Volunteer Workers', *Journal of Refugee Studies*, Vol. 1, No. 3/4, pp. 214–36.

Kushner, T. (1990a), 'Beyond the Pale? British Reactions to Nazi Anti-Semitism, 1933–1939', in Kushner, T. and Lunn, K. (eds) *The Politics of Marginality*, London, Frank Cass pp. 143–160.

Kushner, T. (1990b), 'Politics and Race, Gender and Class: Refugees, Fascists and Domestic Service in Britain, 1933–1940', in Kushner, T. and Lunn, K. (eds) *The Politics of Marginality*, London, Frank Cass pp. 49–58.

Kushner, T. (1990c), 'The Impact of British Anti-Semitism, 1918–1945', in Cesarani, D. (ed.) *The Making of Modern Anglo-Jewry*, Oxford, Basil Blackwell, Chapter 10.

Lambert, H. (1995), *Seeking Asylum: Comparative Law and Practice in Selected European Countries*, London, Martinus Nijhoff.

Landa, M.J. (1911), *The Alien Problem and its Remedy*, London, P. S. King and Son.

Layton-Henry, Z. (1994), 'Britain: The Would-be Zero-Immigration Country', in Cornelius, W., Martin, P. and Hollifield, J. (eds) *Controlling Immigration: A Global Perspective*, Stanford, Stanford University Press, Chapter 8.

London, L. (1989), 'British Government Policy and Jewish Refugees 1933–45', *Patterns of Prejudice*, Vol. 23, No. 4, pp. 26–43.

London, L. (1990), 'Jewish Refugees, Anglo-Jewry and British Government Policy, 1930–1940', in Cesarani, D. (ed.) *The Making of Modern Anglo-Jewry*, Oxford, Basil Blackwell, Chapter 9.

Macdonald, I. (1994), *Immigration Law and Practice in the United Kingdom*, London, Butterworths.

Marrus, M. (1985), *The Unwanted: European Refugees in the Twentieth Century*, Oxford, Oxford University Press.

McKee, R. (1996), 'The Asylum Appeals (Procedure) Rules 1996 – A Survey of the Main Changes and their Likely Effects', *Immigration and Nationality Law and Practice*, Vol. 10, No. 4, pp. 136–38.

Miles, R. (1993), *Racism after 'Race Relations'*, London, Routledge.

Parekh, B. (1986) '"The New Right" and the Politics of Nationhood', in Cohen, G., Bosanquet, N., Ryan, A. and Parekh B., *The New Right, Image and Reality*, London, The Runnymede Trust, pp. 33–45.

Parekh, B. (1994), 'Three Theories of Immigration', in Spencer, S. (ed.) *Strangers and Citizens: A Positive Approach to Migrants and Refugees*, London, Rivers Oram/Institute Public Policy Research, Chapter 3.

Pellew, J. (1989), 'Communication: The Home Office and the Aliens Act, 1905', *The Historical Journal*, Vol. 32, No. 2, pp. 369–85.

Plender, R. (1988), *International Migration Law*, London, Martinus Nijhoff.

Randall, C. (1993), 'An Asylum Policy for the UK', in Spencer, S. (ed.) *Strangers and Citizens: A Positive Approach to Migrants and Refugees*, London, Rivers Oram/IPPR, Chapter 7.

Robertson, G. (1989), *Freedom, The Individual and the Law*, Harmondsworth, Penguin.

Shutter, S. (1995), *Immigration and Nationality Law Handbook*, London, Joint Council for the Welfare of Immigrants.

Solomos, J. (1992), 'The Politics of Immigration since 1945', in Braham, P., Rattansi, A. and Skellington, R. (eds) *Race and Anti-Racism: Inequalities, Opportunities and Policies*, London, Sage, Chapter 1.

Solomos, J. (1993), *Race and Racism in Britain*, 2nd Edition, London, Macmillan.

Spencer, S. (ed.) (1993), *Strangers and Citizens: A Positive Approach to Migrants and Refugees*, London, Rivers Oram/Institute Public Policy Research.

Stevens, D. (1993), 'Re-introduction of the United Kingdom Asylum Bill', *International Journal of Refugee Law*, Vol. 5, No. 1, pp. 91–100.

Supperstone, M. and O'Dempsey, D. (1994), *Immigration: The Law and Practice*, London, Longman.

Vicenzi, C. (1993), *Current Law Statues Annotated: Asylum and Immigration Appeals Act*, Vol. 1, Chap. 23, pp. 1–35.

Wasserstein, B. (1979), *Britain and the Jews of Europe 1939–1945*, Oxford, Clarendon Press.

Williams, B. (1985), 'The Anti-Semitism of Tolerance: Middle-Class Manchester and the Jews 1870–1900', in Kidd, A.J. and Roberts, K.W. (eds) *City, Class and Culture: Studies of Cultural Production and Social Policy in Victorian Manchester*, Manchester, Manchester University Press, pp. 74–102.

Wrench, J. and Solomos, J. (eds) (1993), *Racism and Migration in Western Europe*, Oxford, Berg.

4 'Persons persecuted on political grounds shall enjoy the right of asylum – but not in our country': asylum policy and debates about refugees in the Federal Republic of Germany

Karen Schönwälder

'There is the so-called "right of asylum" but it is much more a right on the part of the Government to grant asylum than a right on the part of the alien to have it.' This is how David Renton explained the position of the British government to the House of Commons in 1961 (15 November 1961, *Hansard*, col. 431). Until 1993 the situation in the Federal Republic of Germany was different. In West Germany's *de facto* constitution of 1949, the Basic Law, Article 16 states that 'Persons persecuted on political grounds shall enjoy the right of asylum.' (*Politisch Verfolgte genießen Asylrecht*). This generous and internationally exceptional provision gave refugees the right to enter West Germany and to have their applications for asylum considered. If they were found to be victims of political persecution, they had the right to stay. If their application was rejected, they had the right to challenge this decision before a board and then the courts. Clearly the politicians who drafted this clause were motivated by the experiences of persecution and exile after 1933. Article 16 also states that no German may be deprived of his or her citizenship – as practised by the Nazi regime with many of its opponents. The democratic successor state to the Nazi regime, which had turned so many Germans and Europeans into refugees, wanted to grant generous conditions to people fleeing from persecution, and it was felt that Germans, at least in so far as they themselves had found refuge abroad, owed future refugees hospitality in return (Münch, 1993: 17–21; also Roos, 1991: 87). Roughly forty years later the situation was seen differently. In May 1993 the newly unified Federal Republic of Germany amended Article 16 of the Basic Law, thus restricting severely the right to political asylum. Cynics have suggested that Article 16 now reads: 'Persons persecuted on political grounds shall enjoy the right of asylum – but not in our country'. A liberal tradition shaped by the moral commitments owed to the Nazi past was discarded. This decision was accompanied by one of the fiercest political controversies in German post-war history.

Before the mid-1970s, neither the academic nor the general public showed much interest in the situation of refugees and the right to asylum. Numbers were relatively low and the reception of those seeking asylum in West Germany confirmed Cold War images of unbearable conditions in the Socialist countries, since most of the asylum seekers of the immediate post-war years came from Eastern Europe. Until 1966 official West German statistics did not even distinguish between regions of origin. In 1966, 4108 asylum applicants in a total of 4370 came from Eastern Europe (Marx, 1985: 381). Until 1973 their share exceeded 50 per cent of the applications. But the years 1973–74 constitute a turning point in the history of political asylum in the Federal Republic of Germany. Not only did the structure of the asylum seekers change as more and more refugees came from non-European countries, but policies were also transformed as regional and federal governments increasingly tried to invent mechanisms to deny refugees a right to asylum. Asylum became the subject of public debate and would, in particular in the later 1980s and early 1990s, turn into one of the most important and most controversial themes of domestic politics.

The number of individuals applying for asylum in West Germany in the 1970s remained low by present standards, but it continued to rise. While in the mid-1970s fewer than 10 000 persons applied per year, in 1978 the authorities received 33 136 applications; in 1979 the figure was 51 493, and in 1980 more than 100 000 people sought asylum in the Federal Republic. Their countries of origin reflected the political conflicts and crises of the time: among them were opponents of the military dictatorship in Chile, Palestinians, Pakistanis, refugees from the 1978–79 Iranian revolution and victims of the 1980 putsch in Turkey.

However, already in 1973, when only 5595 people applied for asylum, the liberal Free Democrat Minister of the Interior, Genscher, pointed at what he perceived as a problem of abuse (quoted in Wolken, 1988: 64). The alleged 'abuse' of the right to political asylum (*Asylmißbrauch*) would become one of the key terms of the political debate. It helped to portray refugees as people who, with a few exceptions, simply sought to gain access to the superior living standards in Germany without being genuine victims of persecution. When most of the refugees had come from socialist countries this accusation had rarely been levelled in spite of the fact that far from every East European was found to fit the criteria which defined a victim of political persecution.[1] The negative label of the 'economic refugee' was applied already in the early 1960s (Münch, 1993: 54–5). Nevertheless, the Ministers of the Interior of the regional states (*Länder*) in 1966 decided not to expel East European refugees whose applications for asylum had been rejected. Only the Yugoslavs were exempted. Unquestionably, political sympathies and antipathies influenced the attitudes towards refugees. But the increasingly negative stance towards refugees was also linked to migration policy in general. In 1973 the Federal Employment Agency ordered a stop to the recruitment of the so-called 'guestworkers'. Suddenly those who had been urged to come and help build West Germany's prosperous society were called a 'social problem'. Only reluctantly the German public began to realize that the famous saying, 'we needed workers, and people came', meant people not only performed their duties but had families, needed decent accommodation and occasionally the services of a doctor, had children and in many cases decided to settle in Germany. In 1973 official statistics recorded about 4 million foreign residents in the Federal Republic. Refugees formed only one part of this group.[2] However, as unemployment rose, public debates often focused on them as symbolizing an illegitimate and threatening 'stream' of paupers flowing into West German society just as West Germans were beginning to lose their confidence in the permanence of the economic miracle. To the present day, West German governments have refused to accept that Germany is a country of immigration and an increasingly multicultural society. At the same time, politicians have been unable to revise or stop immigration. The asylum article in the Basic Law came to represent the 'open door' through which foreigners circumvented the political intentions of the government.

Since 1978 there has been a succession of laws on asylum procedure which had initially been regulated in the Aliens Act of 1965.[3]

Reinhard Marx has described the years from 1974 to 1982 as a transitional period in which an initially liberal attitude and the predominance of the rule of law were transformed into a policy of open deterrence (1985: 386). Instead of protecting the victims of political persecution – the prior aim – policy began to be defined as the prevention of the abuse of the right to asylum. Among the main measures introduced were attempts to accelerate the asylum procedures by reducing the possibilities to appeal against decisions concerning status. Other measures aimed at making a stay in Germany more unpleasant. Before they could obtain a work permit, asylum seekers now had to wait for one and later two years.[4] The welfare benefits they were thus forced to rely on were cut back and mostly paid in kind. Since 1982, asylum seekers have been housed in mass accommodation where they have also been fed, and their residence permits have not allowed them to move beyond the district in which they reside (also see in this volume Duke, Sales and Gregory, Chapter 6 and Minderhoud, Chapter 7).

While these measures aimed at making West Germany less attractive as a country of refuge, other measures were aimed at preventing potential asylum seekers from reaching the borders of the Federal Republic. Thus in 1980 visa requirements were extended to a range of countries (India, Bangladesh, Sri Lanka, Ethiopia, Afghanistan and Turkey), including some in which political persecution was common and from which an above average number of applicants for political asylum were usually recognized. Airlines were required to transport only those passengers with the necessary documents. Critics have attacked these latter measures as violating the constitutional right to political asylum (Münch, 1993: 83–4).

In 1983 a report by the United Nations High Commissioner for Refugees (UNHCR) stated that Germany had introduced measures of deterrence which were unique in Europe. The UN officials were particularly worried about the internment of the refugees in camps and the psychological effects these conditions might have on them. Not only were the refugees forced to be idle and a burden on the taxpayers' pocket, mass accommodation bred tensions and created additional pressures on people who had often suffered from torture or war. As Manfred Zuleeg has argued, the treatment of the asylum seekers demonstrated how the state used a policy that fostered poverty in order to achieve political aims (1985: 302). The resultant low recognition rates have been cited by its supporters to demonstrate the correctness of this policy. Indeed, in recent years the proportion of applicants whose right to political asylum was recognized by the authorities was usually below 10 per cent. However, this figure would be misinterpreted were it taken to indicate that 90 per cent of the asylum seekers are 'abusers'. Roughly the same number as those recognized by the authorities are usually successful in court. Additionally, in 1989, for example, 34 per cent of those whose claims were rejected were granted a right to stay in Germany according to the Geneva Refugee Convention; a further 17 per cent could not be expelled because they came from civil war regions (*Die Zeit*, 11 October 1991). Nevertheless, the definition of political persecution applied by the German authorities and courts is fairly restrictive. Thus courts have ruled that torture does not justify a claim to political asylum if it forms part of the common procedures of penal law in a country (Münch, 1993: 34, 221). Furthermore, many experts have argued that the accepted definition of the political refugee is too restrictive and no longer captures the complex reasons for involuntary migration.

At the same time, it is generally accepted that some applicants for asylum are most probably seeking work rather than refuge. But by refusing to offer legal access to the German labour market, the government encourages migrants to attempt the only route open and thus contributes to the swelling of the number of asylum seekers. Supporters of an immigration law for Germany argue that the introduction of quotas for labour immigrants would encourage potential migrants to apply for a place on such a scheme instead of putting pressure on the complex and overburdened asylum process.

Since the 1980s, a 'refugees lobby' has developed in Germany which publicly attacks maltreatment of refugees. The Churches, welfare organizations, human rights organizations such as Amnesty International and, in the *Bundestag*, the Green Party (represented since 1983) as well as occasionally SPD and FDP deputies, have demanded a more liberal and humane policy. The previously cited critical UNHCR report and the tragic case of Cemal Altun encouraged more sympathetic reporting of the fate of refugees.

In 1983 Altun committed suicide by jumping out of the window of a court room. In spite of having obtained initial recognition as a political refugee, he was threatened with extradition to Turkey and held in custody for several months. His case highlighted the inhumane aspects of West German policy towards asylum seekers and the problematic influence of foreign policy considerations on government policy because the German government wanted to extradite him in the interest of German – Turkish relations (Wolken,

1988: 75; *Gemeinschaftskommentar*, 1993: II, 15). And yet, public debates and the reporting of mass circulation papers have largely been dominated by attacks on the alleged 'asylum-swindlers' and by dramatic visions of human 'floods' threatening Germany.

Political interest in refugee issues and related public debates was influenced by the balance of political parties. West German policy towards refugees had already become more restrictive when government and parliamentary majority were Social Democratic-Liberal. Encouraged by the need to come to an agreement between the federal and the regional governments, asylum policy has not generally been marked by deep divisions between the two major political parties, the SPD (Social Democratic Party) and the CDU/CSU (Christian Democratic Union/Christian Social Union). Nevertheless, pressure for further restrictions usually came from those *Länder* governed by the conservative parties CDU and CSU, and the CDU constantly attacked Helmut Schmidt's SPD-FDP government (1974–82) for its supposed failure to stem the 'flood' of refugees. Indeed, the West German political establishment, particularly Conservatives, have displayed little reluctance to use the issues of refugee flight and asylum for political advantage. But when the Christian Democrat, Helmut Kohl, became Chancellor in 1982, the new governing coalition initially downplayed the asylum issue. Without an amendment to the Basic Law, which requires a two-thirds majority in Parliament, there was little they could do. A political campaign would have raised expectations on the right of the political spectrum which the government would have been unable to fulfil.

In 1985, however, the CDU-right winger and regional Minister of the Interior, Lummer, fought the Berlin elections on the issue of the *'Asylantenproblem'* (the asylum seekers problem).[5] In the run-up to the 1987 federal election, the situation in Berlin brought the asylum issue back on the national agenda over the issue of the so-called 'hole in the Wall', through which, it was claimed, East Germany channelled refugees into the Federal Republic.[6] In 1986 Chancellor Kohl expressed his support for a change to Article 16 of the Basic Law. Thus after a few years in office, Kohl's Chancellorship witnessed an end to the all-party consensus on the inviolability of the constitutional right to political asylum (Wolken, 1988: 82–3).

During the 1980s the terms of the debate over political asylum were different from those of the previous decade. While in the 1970s 'abuse', the 'fake asylum seekers' (*Asylmißbrauch*, *Scheinasylanten*) and Germany's 'limited capacities' had been the key terms, now attention shifted towards an unwanted permanent immigration of minority groups with different cultures and traditions and the accompanying changes to the population structure of the Federal Republic (see, for instance, the bill quoted in Marx, 1985: 392; Schönwälder, 1996). While previously claims to political asylum had been denounced as illegitimate, attention now focused on the unwanted effects of refugee immigration on German society. Articles began to appear in the quality press which questioned the possibility of the peaceful coexistence of culturally distant ethnic groups in the Federal Republic. The Germans, it was claimed, were entitled to assert their right to what was left of their territory – against Turks, Africans and Asians. 'It cannot go on like this', the respectable *Frankfurter Allgemeine Zeitung* exclaimed in 1986 in a leader. 'Refugee-spring tides from all over the world', millions of potential asylum seekers, were not only threatening to create 'unbearable, explosive conditions' in Germany. Within a few decades Germany would become a country with an Asian-African majority, shaken by social, national and religious conflicts; the state would be forced to abandon the German nation in the western part of Germany (Reißmüller, 1986).

Not only did this article conjure up the already familiar image of the poor and discontented of the world descending upon Germany, it also drew upon racist attitudes by portraying the refugees, who by this time often came from Poland, as Africans and Asians, and, in a way more common to extreme right propaganda, it told the Germans that they were fighting for their national survival. Closing the door to the refugees became a matter of life or death for the nation.

Of course this article represented only one example. But a number of studies have demonstrated how, from about 1980, refugees or so-called '*Asylanten*', were increasingly linked with negative associations. Images of 'floods', even 'spring tides' or 'avalanches' helped to dehumanize the individual refugees who were likened to the elements of a natural catastrophe. The Ministers of Interior of regional states spoke of an 'avalanche-like inflow of economic refugees' or a 'deluge-like swelling of the asylum-flood' (quoted in *Gemeinschaftskommentar*, 1993: II, 6). Ute Gerhardt has noted that military metaphors such as 'invasion' or 'assault' began to be used to describe the refugee problem (1993: 245). Wildly overstated predictions of ten, twenty or even one hundred million potential asylum seekers encouraged fears in the population (see the quotes in Münch, 1993: 106, 182). In Germany asylum became the focus of debates but was also linked to broader issues of immigration and ethnic plurality. In this controversy, the call for a positive commitment to a multicultural and open society clashed with the reaffirmation of a 'national identity' and an appeal to defend the 'German' character of the Federal Republic's territory and society. The threat of Germany's culture being inundated (*Überfremdung*), a key spectre of traditional German nationalism, was conjured up again.

From about 1980, hostility against 'foreigners' grew in the West German population. Already in 1980 and 1981 arson attacks on refugee hostels were committed. The extreme right began to campaign on the immigration issue and formed groups which demanded an '*Ausländerstop*' (a stop to [the immigration of] foreigners). Hostile and racist attitudes towards immigrants and refugees played a part in the electoral successes of the right-wing *Republikaner* and the NPD in 1989 (and the following years), when extreme right-wing deputies were elected to the Berlin Parliament and the Frankfurt city council. However, hostility against those declared '*Ausländer*' (aliens) did not increase consistently. Some authors even claimed that hostility towards foreigners actually declined during the 1980s (Reuband, 1989). While this assumption is questionable, it is likely that there were peaks and slumps in popular attitudes and that these were related not only to economic and political crises but also to public debates (Schönwälder, 1991).

Politicians and the media can influence the way in which refugees are perceived, they play a part in whether they are summarily denounced as welfare 'scroungers' or met with sympathy. Although one should not unduly generalize, the debate about refugees and asylum has often been conducted in a rather irresponsible way which helped to strengthen negative perceptions and contributed to hostility towards foreigners. In 1982, an opinion poll still recorded 51 per cent of those interviewed in support of the generous constitutional right to political asylum. Only 28 per cent wanted its abolition (IfD, 1982:7). Since 1989, however, various opinion polls have demonstrated majority support for restrictions, although even at the height of the debate, in late 1992, an *Emnid* poll for *Der Spiegel* (7 December 1992, no. 50: 65) found that 39 per cent wanted the Basic Law article on asylum to be retained in its present form (Köcher, 1991).

It is difficult to tell how far attitudes were related to the current numbers of asylum seekers. In 1981 and the following years the number of applicants for political asylum had declined steeply to less than 50 000 per year. From 1985 onwards, numbers rose again to exceed 100 000 in 1988 and reach 121 000 in 1989 and almost 200 000 in 1990. In 1991 256 000 and in 1992 438 000 people applied for asylum in Germany. Although these figures seem huge, it has to be remembered that they reflected the changes in Eastern Europe and the war in the former Yugoslavia.[7] Due to political inflexibility and also, perhaps, to an interest by the government in dramatizing the 'asylum problem', the war refugees from the former Yugoslavia were forced into the asylum procedure. Rarely was it mentioned that in spite of their huge numbers the asylum seekers, for instance in 1990, represented a smaller group of immigrants than the ethnic Germans (*Aussiedler*) from Eastern Europe and those migrating from East to West Germany. Images of threatening 'floods' usually contained African, Asian and Turkish faces and misrepresented the real process of migration to Germany. While politicians appealed for the solidarity of fellow Germans in the Federal Republic with immigrants of alleged German descent, asylum seekers from Africa and Asia were usually identified as the main abusers of Germany's asylum laws.

In 1991 the debate about asylum reached a new stage. In September 1991 a hostel in Hoyerswerda (Saxony), inhabited mainly by Sinti and Romanies, was attacked and set on fire. Shortly afterwards two Lebanese girls suffered life-threatening injuries when a fire bomb was thrown into the window of a refugee hostel in Hünxe (North-Rhine-Westphalia). In 1991, the authorities recorded 2368 illegal acts, including 338 arson attacks, associated with xenophobia or racism. In 1992, the situation became even worse when 701 arson attacks were recorded and 17 people died. Rostock, Mölln and, in 1993, Solingen – the locations of violence and murder – came to symbolize disturbing new features of the newly unified Germany and to reveal a previously unknown aggressive and murderous potential in contemporary German society.

Politicians immediately distanced themselves from such acts of violence. But there was also much understanding, for instance on the part of the author Martin Walser, for the grievances which motivated the violence (1993), and the political response seemed to suggest, as Jürgen Habermas bitterly remarked, that the real problem behind the hatred of foreigners were the foreigners themselves. Habermas (1992) referred to the political shift which had taken place in favour of substantial changes to the constitutional provision of political asylum. Legal changes were immediately announced following the attack at Hoyerswerda and the siege of Rostock, where in August 1992 a huge crowd – cheered on by the locals – launched an assault on the accommodation of refugees and Vietnamese workers.

Between the summer of 1991 and May 1993 the theme of asylum dominated the newspaper headlines in Germany. For weeks it was the major political topic. Increasingly the demand was put forward that, in order to stop the violence, its supposed cause had to be eliminated and, therefore, Germany's borders had to be closed to refugees. The conservative parties and parts of the media stepped up their campaign for a change to Article 16 of the Basic Law. The Bavarian CSU wanted to abolish an individual right to asylum altogether and replace it with an 'act of grace' on the part of the state. Attacks on the SPD, whose votes were necessary for a change to the constitution, increased. The CDU party secretary Volker Rühe suggested that the local organizations of the party should campaign with the slogan that 'every additional asylum seeker is an SPD asylum seeker'. In fact, in 1990, it had been an SPD politician, its subsequent chairman Oskar Lafontaine, who gave the campaign for constitutional reform new impetus. The SPD- governed state of Bremen in 1991 – shortly before the regional elections – (illegally) refused to accept new applications for asylum by Poles and Romanians (Münch, 1993: 116; *Frankfurter Allgemeine Zeitung*, 8 August 1991). Many local authorities, including several dominated by the Social Democrats, revolted against the burden placed upon them to house refugees and pay benefits (although they were compensated for this).

In August 1992 the SPD began to give way to the pressures. While just a little over a year previously, the liberal FDP, represented by the Minister of Justice, Klaus Kinkel, declared that his party would not agree to changes to Article 16, now also their position had changed. At the end of 1992 the three governing parties and the Social Democrats agreed on the legal changes which were subsequently passed by the federal parliament by a vote of 521 to 132. Critics, among them Jürgen Habermas, have seen this as a major turning point in post-war German history, as a departure from moral commitments arising from the Nazi past. The Berlin political scientist Alfons Söllner saw a 'morass of political non-culture' emerging in the course of the attacks on the right to asylum. A 'key component' of Germany's political culture had been called into question (1993: 127–8).

The dimensions of the debate about asylum in Germany can only be properly understood if it is placed in the context of, on the one hand, Germany's relationship with its past and, on the other hand, the immediate effects of unification. 'Never again' was one slogan of the many thousands of people who in 1992–93 demonstrated against racist violence and for peaceful coexistence of natives and newcomers in

Germany. The fires of Rostock and Solingen raised the memory of the 'Kristallnacht' ('the night of broken glass'), the anti-Jewish Nazi pogrom of 1938, and the events which followed and led to the Holocaust. The rejection of a nationalist and Nazi past is still a powerful force among Germans and it encourages distrust of any renewal of nationalism. Two years after unification the question was posed as to where this new powerful Germany was heading. Were the restrictions of the constitutional right to political asylum a major step towards the formation of an ethnically defined, more nationalist identity? Or had Germany, as some supporters of this move might phrase it, finally stepped 'out of Hitler's shadow' and become a 'normal' state which could act free of any annoying limitations arising from past crimes?

While the worst fears of a surge of nationalist and violently racist politics have not come true, Germany has certainly managed to build a more effective 'wall' around its territory and the European Union (see in this volume, Levy, Chapter 2). Rather than prioritizing both the protection of refugees against racist persecution in Germany and tackling the causes of refugee movements abroad, the 'defence' of the state against the flow of refugees has gained the upper hand. In the amended Basic Law the original Article 16, as quoted above, was retained. Its substance, however, was significantly altered. Key changes are, firstly, the introduction of a safe third country rule. Therefore, anyone who enters the Federal Republic via a member state of the European Union or another state which has been qualified as safe is denied access to the asylum procedure. In fact, Germany has created a *cordon sanitaire* around its own territory which makes it impossible to reach the country (and gain access to the asylum procedure) other than by air. Secondly, the claims of those asylum seekers are generally regarded as unfounded who come from countries which are on a list of states where persecution is assumed to be non-existent. (In 1993 this included Gambia, Ghana and Romania.) Thirdly, expulsions were made easier and the possibility to appeal against a negative decision of the authorities was reduced. The SPD achieved a few concessions: a separate status for war and civil war refugees was introduced to avoid forcing people into the asylum process who were obviously not asylum seekers in the official sense. A slight relaxation of the naturalization procedures for immigrants was also agreed. No agreement was achieved on the demand for an immigration law.

Supporters of the 1993 reform claim that the individual right to asylum has been retained while restricting the rights of particular groups, namely those coming from or via 'safe countries'. The numbers of asylum seekers, it is claimed, had become intolerable and Germany had to adjust its practice to that of other European states in order to achieve a more equal distribution of the burden. But the rights of genuine victims of political persecution would still be protected (Hailbronner, 1993). Critics, among them *Terre des Hommes*, Amnesty International and the German pressure group *Pro Asyl*, have challenged the latter claim. Refugees, it is pointed out, can no longer reach Germany without major difficulty. Indeed, compared to the 1992 record figure of over 400 000 applicants, numbers declined significantly to 323 000 in 1993 (the new legal provisions came into force on 1 July) and about 127 000 in 1994 and 1995 respectively (Pollern, 1996: 87; also see in this volume, Levy, Chapter 2).

While the supporters of the constitutional change may claim this as a success, critics argue that in all probability many victims of political persecution were excluded from Germany. The invention of 'safe countries', it is further argued, obscures the reality of individual cases of persecution even in states where persecution is not the norm. Under current rules, many individuals are denied a proper investigation of their claims because their application for asylum is automatically assumed to be unfounded. Furthermore, allegedly safe countries to which refugees are expelled may not be safe. Thus Greece has been accused of expelling refugees to Turkey, Poland and Lithuania.

In a much publicized case, Germany expelled seven Sudanese men who showed signs of torture after the Sudanese government promised not to persecute them for fleeing to Germany. Can regimes such as the Sudanese be trusted? Additional criticism has been directed against the increased use of the detention of rejected asylum seekers and against the accelerated procedures for the determination of status carried out at Frankfurt's airport, where applications for asylum are decided while the refugee remains officially outside German territory (also see in this volume, Levy, Chapter 2). Increasingly, the authorities have turned to expulsions and since 1993 more than 30 000 persons per year have been forcibly removed from the country (Pollern, 1996: 91; the organization *Pro Asyl* gives higher figures).

The alternative to the policy of deterrence has been the call for a more liberal attitude to immigration in general and a humane treatment of all refugees in particular. During the controversy of 1992–93, parliamentary deputies of the *Bündnis 90*/Green Party suggested a radical law on the legal position of refugees. It stated that anyone fleeing from persecution for political reasons, but also because of their sexual preferences or gender and from war or military service, should be granted asylum. In Germany the applicants would enjoy a right to a labour permit and to participation in an education or training course. This suggested that the law had the clear and positive acknowledgement of the fact that Germany is a multi-ethnic country and might have formed the basis for a more relaxed attitude of Germans towards this reality. Furthermore, since the German population is ageing it needs immigration to make up a future demographic deficit. A positive and rational immigration policy is required. Greens and Social Democrats have called for an immigration law with an immigration quota, but which would not limit the rights of victims of persecution. The introduction of such a law is, however, controversial even among the supporters of a more open attitude to immigration. Additionally, there have been demands that countries which cause refugee movements, such as Germany's NATO partner, Turkey, should be placed under more pressure.

The legitimacy of the recent restrictions to the right to political asylum in Germany has been linked by its supporters to the demand for a European solution in which the burden of refugees and asylum seekers would be shared equally. The general tendency of German legal measures is indeed in line with the practice of the European Union. But this trend, one of exclusion and seclusion, of desperate attempts to shut the European Union off from the crises and conflicts within Europe itself also entails protecting the European Union from the increased global mobility of migrants, even if only a small proportion of the world's refugees ever reach this continent (see also Chapters 2 and 11 in this volume by Levy). But all this is far from the guiding principles of West Germany's Basic Law of 1949, which while not practised consistently, did promise to offer a more generous welcome to the victims of political persecution.

NOTES

1. Reinhard Marx has pointed out that the courts were more generous towards refugees from Hungary after the 1956 Revolution than towards Algerian refugees from their war of independence. However, not every East European was automatically recognized as a refugee. The figure was around 50 per cent in the early 1950s, but only 13.6 per cent in 1965 (Marx, 1985: 380–1).
2. No-one knows how many refugees actually live in Germany. In 1985 the government estimated their number at about half a million, while the

UNHCR gave a figure of 115 000 (Marx, 1985: 393). Numbers are highly controversial, and the Minister of the Interior has been accused of overestimating refugee numbers in order to strengthen the case for restrictions. Critics point to the vague estimates of family members and the lack of information on people leaving Germany (see for instance Roos, 1991b: 91).

3. In 1978 and in 1980 laws on the acceleration of the asylum procedures were passed. In 1982 the *Asylverfahrensgesetz* (law on the asylum procedure) was passed and in 1987 and 1988 further legal changes came into force.

4. In 1980 a waiting period of one year was introduced. It was extended to two years in 1981 and to five years in 1986; the *Länder* partly applied their own more restrictive rules. For East European refugees the waiting period was shorter. In 1991 the restrictions were lifted and asylum seekers now have access to jobs for which there is no German or other privileged foreign applicant. In fact this usually means employment in catering and agriculture. All the measures referred to above apply to refugees waiting for a decision on their application for asylum. In connection with the changes to the Basic Law, the *Asylbewerberleistungsgesetz* (law on benefits for asylum seekers) was passed which excluded asylum seekers from the normal welfare benefits and further emphasized the payment of benefits in kind.

5. Lummer has published a sensationalist book entitled *Asyl: ein mißbrauchtes Recht* (Asylum: an Abused Right). Subheadings on the cover are: 'Timebomb of our Society', 'Politicians' Cowardice' and 'The Tricks and the Costs'.

6. In 1985 almost 30 000 persons who had entered West Berlin coming from the East Berlin airport applied for asylum. From October 1986 the GDR no longer admitted transit passengers who did not possess a visa for their further journey.

7. Of the 193 000 applicants in 1990, 35 000 were Romanians, 22 000 Yugoslavs, 16 000 Lebanese. In 1991 there were 75 000 Yugoslavs among 256 000 applicants.

REFERENCES

Frankfurter Allgemeine Zeitung (FAZ), various articles.
Gemeinschaftskommentar zum Asylverfahrensgesetz 1992 (1993), Neuwied, Luchterhand.
Gerhardt, U. (1993), '"Fluten", "Ströme", "Invasionen" – Mediendiskurs und Rassismus', in Hessler, M. (ed.), *Zwischen Nationalstaat und multikultureller Gesellschaft: Einwanderung und Fremdenfeindlichkeit in der Bundesrepublik Deutschland*, Freiburg, Hitit, pp. 239–53.
Habermas, J. (1992), 'Die zweite Lebenslüge der Bundesrepublik', *Die Zeit*, 11 December.

Hailbronner, K. (1993), 'Die Asylrechtsreform im Grundgesetz', *Zeitschrift für Ausländerrecht und Ausländerpolitik*, Vol. XIII, pp. 107–17.

House of Commons (1961), 'Parliamementary Debates', *Hansard*, Vol. 538.

Institut für Demoskopie Allensbach (1982), *Allensbacher Berichte*, No. 18, p. 7.

Köcher, R. (1991), 'Besorgnis, nicht Radikalisierung', *Frankfurter Allgemeine Zeitung*, 9 October, p. 5.

Marx, R. (1985), 'Vom Schutz vor Verfolgung zur Politik der Abschreckung. Zur Geschichte des Asylverfahrensrechts in der Bundesrepublik Deutschland', *Kritische Justiz*, Vol. XVIII, pp. 379–95.

Münch, U. (1993), *Asylpolitik in der Bundesrepublik Deutschland: Entwicklung und Alternativen*, 2nd updated edn, Opladen, Leske and Budrich.

Pollern, H.-I. von (1996), 'Die Entwicklung der Asylbewerberzahlen im Jahre 1995', *Zeitschrift für Ausländerrecht und Ausländerpolitik*, Vol. XVI, pp. 86–92.

Reißmüller, J.G. (1986), 'So geht es nicht weiter', *Frankfurter Allgemeine Zeitung*, 15 July.

Reuband, K.-H. (1989), 'Wächst in der Bundesrepublik die Ausländer-feindlichkeit?', *Neue Praxis*, Vol. XIX, pp. 270–74.

Roos, A. (1991), 'Für das Grundrecht auf Asyl. Anmerkungen zur Debatte um eine "realistische" Flüchtlingspolitik', *Vorgänge*, Vol. XXX, No. 3, pp. 84–100.

Schönwälder, K. (1991), 'Zu viele Ausländer in Deutschland? Zur Entwicklung ausländerfeindlicher Einstellungen in der Bundesrepublik', *Vorgänge*, Vol. XXX, No. 4, pp. 1–11.

Schönwälder, K. (1996), 'Migration, Refugees and Ethnic Plurality as Issues of Public and Political Debates in (West) Germany', in Fulbrook, M. and Cesarani, D. (eds), *Citizenship, Nationality and Migration in Europe*, London, Routledge, pp. 159–78.

Söllner, A. (1993), 'Asylpolitik im "deutschen Frühling". Eine zeit-geschichtliche Momentaufnahme', in Butterwegge, C. and Jäger, S. (eds), *Europa gegen den Rest der Welt? Flüchtlingsbewegungen, Einwanderung, Asylpolitik*, Köln, Bund, pp. 127–144.

Walser, M. (1993), 'Deutsche Sorgen', *Der Spiegel*, No. 26, pp. 40–7.

Wolken, S. (1988), 'Asylpolitik in der Bundesrepublik Deutschland: Politik gegen politische Flüchtlinge?' in Thränhardt, D. and Wolken, S. (eds), *Flucht und Asyl. Informationen, Analysen, Erfahrungen aus der Schweiz und der Bundesrepublik Deutschland*, Freiburg Lambertus, pp. 62–97.

Zuleeg, M. (1985), 'Politik der Armut und Ausländer', in Leibfried, S. and Tennstedt, T. (eds), *Politik der Armut und die Spaltung des Sozialstaats*, Frankfurt, Suhrkamp, pp. 295–308.

5 The precarious safety of the refugee

Patricia Tuitt

INTRODUCTION

That states can reliably determine whether another state is likely or not to produce refugees is a view which has underpinned refugee policy in the United Kingdom and other Western European countries in recent years. In many countries this policy has been enshrined in the law. The United Kingdom Asylum and Immigration Act 1996 by Section 1 amends Schedule 2 of the 1993 Asylum and Immigration Appeals Act to apply an accelerated determination process to claims by refugees subject to certification on the basis that their claim relates to countries in which there is 'in general no serious risk of persecution'.[1] This chapter argues that whilst safe country concepts are implicit in the idea of 'refugee', the refugee's security has become less assured since 'safety' and its companion notion 'fear' have been conceived of as justiciable. I attempt to demonstrate this by exploring the origin and contemporary relevance of the 'safe country' concept.

ORIGINS OF THE SAFE COUNTRY CONCEPT

I will begin by stating the primary sense in which the 'safe country' concept is employed in refugee discourse. It is fundamental to an understanding of what it is to be a refugee that those we designate 'refugees' are seeking asylum from a place which is unsafe. The lack of safety as perceived by the refugee and the receiving state may extend to the whole of the refugee's country of nationality or domicile or may be confined to specific regions. A country which can be proved to be safe in its geographical entirety cannot, by definition, produce refugees since the refugees' disenfranchisement attaches to the state or nation. The history of refugee movements thus reads, at the very least, as an implicit finding that certain states are unsafe in respect of certain groups of nationals or residents at certain times.

In the early period of significant refugee movement, the so-called 'classic' refugees' concern for their safety stemmed from their opposition to the established religious order (see Zolberg *et al.*, 1991: Chapter 1). The seventeenth century witnessed the flight of several thousand Protestants from France and Salzburg to countries all over Europe between 1685 and 1732 (Zolberg *et al.*, 1991: 8–9). Earlier, in the reign of Mary Tudor, 30 000 Englishmen fled to Holland as a result of the re-establishment of Roman Catholicism (Plaut, 1992: 38). In the eighteenth century, democratic revolutions spawned thousands of victims whose beliefs conflicted with dominant political ideologies. Asylum was sought from Austria, Prussia, Russia and of course France, indeed most countries in Europe were forced to house fleeing political refugees. In recent years minority ethnic and cultural groups have comprised a significant number of the displaced populations of the world, a manifestation of challenges to the very centre of nationhood rooted in the early twentieth century and the mass population displacements of that time. In the inter-war years Jews and Armenians represented the largest refugee populations in Europe (Zolberg *et al.*, 1991: Chapter 1). Eastern Europe now provides contemporary examples of this phenomenon. This brief history demonstrates that the safe country concept existed in some guise or other since the related concepts of refuge, and asylum – a concept which can be located in the writings of Euripides, Sophocles and Virgil (Arboleda and Hoy, 1993: 68).

However, as central to the refugee experience as was the factual existence of states which were unable to secure the physical safety and integrity of certain groups, 'safety' had not emerged as an independent, forensic and ultimately justiciable category. Undoubtedly the unsafe state provided the background against which the need for refugee protection arose; however, it appears that at least before this century, the mere existence of fleeing migrants meant that the state from which they fled was deemed, without more proof, to be unsafe. This presumption, which effectively worked to the benefit of the refugee, arose largely because of the complex mix of social and political factors which determined the movement of people between states before mass regulation of immigration in the twentieth century.

The need to define refugees was not perceived as necessary since most who were compelled to flee were 'readily received by rulers in Europe and elsewhere' (Hathaway, 1991: 1). Indeed, Hathaway speaks almost glibly of the 'freedom of international movement' (1991: 1) enjoyed by refugees at this time. A freedom, which as Marrus (1985) observed, aided governments as much as migrants since such governments were able to utilize the talents and industry of its immigrants in the promotion of its economy. It follows logically from the position stated by these writers that the 'unwritten laws' applying to refugees – a law which was nothing more nor less than the exercise of the sovereign power to grant admission to a state to foreign migrants (Grahl-Madsen, 1966–72: 9) – did not depend for its operation upon precise proof of fear or absence of safe conditions in the country from which asylum was sought.

SAFETY IN THE LEGAL DOMAIN

The preoccupation with the notion of 'safety' as an objective concept capable of precise definition and articulation is traceable to the drive in the early twentieth century to define the refugee in terms of the law. This process was, as Hathaway claimed, a particular feature of the adoption of 'instrumentalist immigration policies in Western states' (1991: 1). Abstracting the notion of safety from the primary, essentially 'climatic' sphere within which it had previously operated aided the controlling function of the law. Under the law the presence or absence of a 'safe' state or safe conditions of existence would only be acknowledged once determined through a carefully structured forensic process.

A WELL-FOUNDED FEAR OF PERSECUTION

The particular forensic process which has emerged is structured around the legal concept of a 'well founded fear of persecution' – a principal element of the definition of refugee under Article 1.A (2) of the Geneva Convention Relating to the Status of Refugees 1951. Although the Geneva Convention was not the first formal legal definition of refugee, it was the first to foreground the argument that the refugee's 'fear' for his or her safety and, relatedly, the safety of a state could be subjected to reasoned processes (for an analysis of earlier definitions see Goodwin-Gill, 1996: Chapter 1). Unlike earlier refugee definitions, the Geneva Convention declined to accord refugee status according to 'political or social categories' and promoted instead a determination process geared principally to an examination of the 'merits of each applicant's case'.[2] Whilst the well-founded fear concept has not been imported into other major regional refugee conventions such as the Organization of African Unity Convention Governing the Specific Aspects of Refugee Problems in Africa 1969 and the Cartegena Declaration 1984 which binds African and Latin American states respectively, the concept remains an overwhelmingly strong benchmark of refugeehood, not least because of the dominant position the Geneva Convention has acquired in international refugee law.[3]

CONSTRUCTING SAFETY

Once appropriated by the law, safety acquired a carefully qualified status. What it was to be safe or unsafe in the refugee domain became not a question or issue of fact encompassing, potentially at least, all forms of injurious action, howsoever occasioned, but a 'fiction' or 'term of art' in relation to which the causal link between the injury or threatened injury and the putative refugee's civil or political status became dominant. Thus at the outset a refugee's reasonable apprehension of fear was co-extensive with a fear of persecution upon one or other of the grounds of 'race, religion, nationality membership of a social group, or political opinion ...' (Convention, Article 1.A(2)).

The requirement that the fear of injurious harm must relate to a negation of the state of origin of one or other of its primary responsibilities toward its citizens placed causation rather than need as a curious but central concern within this particular field of human rights, and held many refugees hostage against the law's limited imagining of fear and safety in this domain. In particular, victims of natural disaster cannot unequivocally claim their state of existence unsafe under Geneva Convention criteria.[4] As the literature devoted to examining the persecution standard of the Convention suggests, women refugees' claims which are based upon gender violence especially, often fail to overcome the causation hurdle.[5] Safety and freedom, then, were carefully measured against the possibilities of safety and freedom in a world in which much was, and still is, capable of compromise. In setting the Convention standards of safety, what was compromised were those injuries which did not serve the 'strategic goals' of western states (Hathaway, 1991: 6), and which tended against the 'orderly departure' of refugees from one state to another. Individually targeted persecution for which the state – through its organs were directly or vicariously held responsible – emerged as a privileged form of injury within the field of refugee law.

The disjuncture between safety operating within the legal domain and the broader ethical human rights sphere, has been noted by many writers. Criticism extends beyond the failure to include any but the most basic human rights standards within the definition of refugee within the Geneva Convention (see for example, Coles, 1988 and Gibney and Stohl, 1988), but surrounds, in addition, the treatment of refugees in host states. Detention measures have been a particular target for criticism – many practices seemingly are used to deter refugees from seeking asylum rather than being last resort measures to ensure that an asylum claim is properly scrutinized (see Helton, 1990). Whilst refugees may be secure against the most extreme breaches of human rights under the Convention and through the limited operation of Article 3 of the European Convention on Human Rights which prohibits 'torture, inhuman or degrading treatment or punishment' (for the effect of this article on refugee claims, see *Amerkrane* v. *UK* 1973; *Vilverajah* v. *UK* 1991), they are routinely denied rights at the level of discrimination, social rights and primary access to justice (see in particular: Joint Council for the Welfare of Immigrants (JCWI) and Liberty, 1995; Dunstan, 1994).

PROOF OF A WELL-FOUNDED FEAR

Against the background of this artificially constructed notion of safety the demands of the forensic process required the refugee not merely to assert 'fear' and to seek asylum from a state, the conditions of which may raise a *prima facie* case that he or she may be in fear or unsafe, but to prove 'fear' of persecution as a past, present or prospective reality – the dominant emphasis resting on the latter temporal experience of 'fear' (see Hathaway, 1991: Chapter 3; *R.* v. *Secretary of State* for *the Home Department ex parte Sivakumaran*, 1988). As Douzinas and Warrington justly observe, this presents 'fear' as 'interpretable realities' (1995: 222–3). The wealth of scholarly writing, judicial decisions and policy initiatives at government and non-governmental level related to the 'well-founded fear' concept also attests to the officially held view that these concepts are accessible at the level of the community. Most notably, however, refugees are increasingly estranged from the creative processes involved in constructing the notion of 'safety'. The forensic process denies refugees the choice to articulate their fears or to articulate, at a more abstract level, what 'fear' might mean. Thus the finely drawn debate over whether the 'well founded fear' is a subjective or objective concept is a prime example of this process of disenfranchisement.

OBJECT AND SUBJECT IN LAW

A substantive part of the discourse on refugee law is focused on the question of to what extent the refugee can convey his or her own fears consistently with a reliable process of adjudication. In legal terms this fundamental question centres around the apparent distinction between an adjudication process which focuses upon objective factors when determining the well-foundedness of a fear of persecution as opposed, or in preference, to one in which subjective factors are privileged.

Perhaps as a legacy of the uncodified law relating to refugees, described earlier in this chapter, interpretation of the well-founded fear criterion, until the late 1970s, tended towards the view that the refugees' so-called 'subjective' feelings of 'terror' could undermine, or at least challenge, any official designation relating to the 'objective' circumstances surrounding a claim. It was thought through an application of one literal meaning of the term 'fear' that the well-founded fear concept, as enshrined within the Geneva Convention, was constructed of mainly 'subjective elements' (Fragaman, 1970: 53; Posner and Kaplan, 1981: 18; Sexton, 1985: 733).

Upon this view, 'fear' itself was definable only by the refugee and thus, except where extraneous evidence clearly contradicted a refugee's story, the focus of judicial inquiry was almost entirely upon the credibility of the refugee applicant. Fear as 'terror' is a personal perception which cannot be shared, or as Douzinas and Warrington claim, it is a violent emotion which 'brings interpretation to an end' (1995: 223). What was seen to be interpretable and could, therefore, be shared, however, was the refugee's expression of his/her fears. At this level, then, the well-founded fear inquiry centred on matters relating to the timing of the application, the manner of entry into the host state, the consistency of the story related by the refugee during the various stages of the inquiry and the extent of cooperation generally demonstrated by the refugee applicant. Whilst this was, and still is, labelled a 'subjective' inquiry, it is clear from the judicial authorities emerging through this particular process, that forensic examination itself confounds the objective/subjective distinction – for the process requires an external examination of the subjective which cannot itself be objective. The object/subject division is at the heart of law, and the claim to objectivity endemic in the law inevitably involves the claim that what is pronounced by the law in its objective determination is inherently more reliable. Behind the subject/object distinction lies the real question which is one fundamentally organized around power: the extent to which, within the forensic process, the refugee's conveyance of his/her personal fears is given authority. Since the late seventies, the share in interpreting fear and safety has rested disproportionately, it is argued, on matters extraneous to the refugee applicant.[6]

THE EMERGENCE OF SAFETY AS AN ABSTRACT CONCEPT

The prime example of evidence of this type is comprised of documentary sources – emerging through the courts and tribunals, government organs or within the academy. These sources have worked together to construct a notion of safety which although derived from lived experiences, nevertheless operates at a more general, abstract level, sometimes seemingly far removed from what is happening in the refugee's state of origin (see generally, Tuitt, 1996: Chapters 5 and 6). Lord Keith was anxious to privilege evidence of this type in the *Sivakumaran* case (mentioned above), for evidence relating primarily to the conditions in the state from which asylum is sought was, in his view (a view supported by the rest of the House of Lords) more likely to produce a result in the adjudication process closely consistent with the aims of the Convention, that is to say to:

afford protection and fair treatment for those to whom neither is available in their own country and does not extend to allaying of fear not objectively justified, however reasonable those fears may appear to be from the point of view of the individual in question. (*R.* v. *Secretary of State*, 1988: 196).

The subject/object division was clearly maintained in *Sivakumaran*, the House of Lords stridently rejecting what was seen to be the pro-refugee 'subjective' pronouncement of Lord Donaldson when the case was heard in the Court of Appeal. Lord Donaldson sought to argue that the refugee's subjective assessment of the risk of persecution will only be impeached if there is no good reason for that fear 'looking at the situation from the point of view of one of reasonable courage circumstanced as was the applicant for refugee status' (1988: 1052–3).

Lord Donaldson's conclusions were drawn from the principled stance that when interpreting fear, 'the adjectival phrase "well-founded" qualifies, but cannot entirely transform, "the subjective nature of the emotion"'. In rejecting Lord Donaldson's test, the House of Lords decision ensured that the 'well-founded' fear test was no longer one substantially (in some cases exclusively) a test of the refugee applicant's credibility, but rather the elusive 'condition of the state of origin or domicile' from which, according to Lord Keith, the refugee's exposure to persecution prospectively 'can only be determined'.

CONTESTING DOCUMENTARY SOURCES

The move from a scrutiny of the refugee applicant toward a scrutiny of the country of origin, is in one view, a fairly logical progression in the development of international refugee law since such developments are marked by an expansion of relevant literature, thus creating more evidence from which reasoned conclusions about the safety of refugees can be drawn. The forensic process thus is uniquely one in which documentary sources – in particular governmental sources – have great authority, so much so, that the written word assuring the safety of a state is seldom open to serious challenge. Such was the position of the Appeal Court in the case of *Dursan* v. *Secretary of State for the Home Department*, 1993, when it dismissed the argument that the Minister of State for the Home Office was required to prove by direct evidence brought before the court that a state deemed safe, in this case France, was indeed safe for the particular refugee applicant:

> The Secretary of State in Immigration matters, and in particular, refugee matters, is in constant contact with all sorts of other countries through British missions abroad and foreign missions in this country, and it has been stated over and over again in the context of refugee cases, that the Secretary of State is entitled to rely upon the information which comes to him through diplomatic and other channels (*Dursan* v. *Secretary of State for the Home Department*, 1993: 170).

The potential range of documentary sources embodied in the voice of the state is vast, and this is virtually matched by that collated by non-governmental organizations like Amnesty International and the International Red Cross Organization, not to mention the host of refugee organizations which have sprung up to cope with the growing demands of displaced populations. The curious result of this prolifera-tion of information is that the scrutiny of the credibility of refugees has shifted, crucially, to the credibility of documentary sources, and relatedly, the imbalance between refugee groups and other organiza-tions in terms of the availability of these sources. This has led to some significant legal battles over which sources of evidence are more com-pelling and the extent of the duty to disclose sources and their content – both questions being resolved strongly in favour of official sources and representatives (Shah, 1995).

As I observed in an earlier work, apart from creating an evidential fortress around some countries, thereby ensuring that their safety can seldom be impeached (Tuitt, 1996: 103), this shift to generalizing or abstracting the concept of safety has led governments confidently to assume that they can, consistently with their obligations towards refugees under international law:

> single out, at an early stage, those applicants who have nothing to fear in their home country, and who can therefore be presumed to have abused the asylum procedures to circumvent immigration law (Hailbronner, 1993: 32).

This sums up the aim behind the safe country concept in its modern guise. Its place within administrative and judicial inquiries into asylum cases has two dimensions. The first, of less general relevance to this chapter, is trained on the question of asylum, rather than refugee status. That is, irrespective of the merits of the inquiry on the well-founded fear of persecution, does the refugee demonstrate a need to be granted temporary refuge in the place where the asylum applica-tion is lodged? A deceptively simple question which is answered in the negative whenever the refugee in question is travelling or transiting through countries deemed safe. In this context, the safe country concept has a largely administrative connotation meaning that the state will not itself persecute the refugee nor return (*refouler*) the refugee to a state in which he/she may suffer persecution.

The other dimension to modern-day notions of safety in the refugee field is to raise a rebuttal by using the presumption in law that refugees emerging from countries deemed from time to time by the Secretary of State to be 'safe' have no 'well-founded' fear of persecution on grounds of the Geneva Convention – thus going to the heart of the refugee inquiry. The refugee applicant may produce evidence to rebut the pre-sumption, but as indicated earlier, the finding that a refugee emerges from a 'safe' state allows the determining authorities to dispose fully of his/her claim within a very short time from the commencement of the application. n. 7 Rebutting such a strong presumption is thus a formidable task for a refugee applicant who, for the most part, does not receive legal aid. Evidence suggesting a 'reasonable likelihood' that the refugee applicant has been tortured in the country from which he/she seeks asylum must be adduced (Section 1(5). Immigration and Asylum Act, 1996).

CONCLUSION

From being an exceptionally fluid notion, 'safety' in refugee inquiries has acquired an almost academic quality. The security of refugee claimants in western states rests upon the interpretation of factors which, precisely because of the violent contexts wherein they reside, defy precise analysis and interpretation. Safety can never be scientifically determined and thus the greatest practicable discretion should be encouraged. Whilst some undeserving cases may succeed, the safety of the majority of refugees will be assuredly less precarious.

NOTES

1.   Where such certification is made, the refugee applicant has no right of appeal to the Immigration Appeal Tribunal and can only challenge a negative finding before a Special Adjudicator (thus preserving the appeal rights established under Section 8 of the Asylum and Immigration Appeals Act 1993). However, the time limit for lodging an appeal is two days following certification. Within ten days after the appeal papers have been lodged, the case must be fully disposed of (for a comprehensive analysis of the effect of these procedures see, Winterbourne, Shah and Doebbler, 1996).

2.   Hathaway (1991: 2–6) charts three phases in the development of refugee protection in this century. The 'juridical perspective' ensured that status was granted to refugees from whom 'de jure' protection of the state had been withdrawn, e.g., through withholding passports. The aim was 'to facilitate the international movement' of persons so placed (Hathaway, 1991: 3). The 'social perspective' aimed largely to protect those displaced as a result of the National Socialist regime in Germany: 'the helpless casualties of broadly based social or political occurrences which separate them from their home society' (Hathaway, 1991: 5). The 'individualist

perspective' encompassed the Geneva Convention regime, the main tenets of which are explained in the body of this chapter.

3. There is no single definition of refugee, but most works on refugee law speak of international refugee law as being co-extensive with the regime of legal protection established under the Geneva Convention and the New York Protocol to the Convention Relating to the Status of Refugees, 1967. The Convention and Protocol are, on present authority, the only conventions binding on all states in the international community. Whilst the Convention is the most widely ratified treaty governing refugee protection, it is binding not merely because of its status as a signed treaty but because it is generally thought that the main obligation imposed on states under Article 33, which prohibits states from returning refugees to the frontiers of states where they may face persecution on Convention grounds, has evolved into a rule of customary law (see for discussion, Goodwin-Gill, 1982: 302; Hyndman, 1992: 49–52, 59–71; Noble, 1982: 252).

4. It is widely accepted that the Geneva Convention does not cover modern refugee producing phenomena, especially those which beset the developing world, e.g. famine, drought, civil war. The response to this lacuna in the law in the late 1970s/ early 1980s until, in fact, the huge expansion of inter-continental refugee movement later in the 1980s, was to grant so-called 'B' status (exceptional leave in the UK) to those refugees falling outside the Convention definition, but who were nonetheless felt to be deserving of temporary protection. Such status provided them with some of the benefits of full refugee status, with some significant omissions, e.g. an automatic right to a passport and family reunion (see Goodwin-Gill, 1986; Perluss and Hartman, 1986; Hailbronner, 1986 and Tuitt, 1996: Chapter 3). States have retrenched significantly from this position in recent years. In the UK, both the 1993 and 1996 Asylum Acts have reaffirmed the position that the proof of persecution as defined under Article 1.A(2) is a necessary condition to gaining temporary or permanent asylum (see Section 1(4)(a) of the Asylum and Immigration Act 1996).

5. In the recent past, women were denied adequate recourse under international refugee law because of the view that gender violence (in particular rape or other forms of sexual assault) were perpetrated because of a 'personal motive', thus failing to establish a nexus between the harm and responsibility of the state (see Bhabba and Shutter, 1994: 248–51). More recently, cases have been allowed providing that a link to the five grounds of persecution can be established, leading to rather strained interpretations of cases (see for example, *Olympia Lazo-Majono* v. *Immigration and Naturalization Service*, 1987). Most claims are brought under the social group or political opinion grounds of persecution (see Castel, 1992). Women rape victims have gained some ground, particularly where the rape is part of a policy of ethnic cleansing, as occurred in the former Yugoslavia (see generally for recent developments, Spijkerboer, 1995). This, however, has done little in recognition of gender oppression and violence in its broader form, and many commentators feel that without the addition of 'gender' as a separate ground of

persecution under the Convention, the problems faced by women refugees will not be remedied (Kobayshi, 1995).

6. Both the 1993 and 1996 Asylum Acts allow credibility factors to influence heavily the process of an asylum claim. For example, paragraphs 5(3) and 5(4) of the 1996 Act state that claims made by refugees without passports or in possession of invalid passports, will be subject to certification. Certification also occurs, where the claim is manifestly fraudulent. The latter allowing the determining authorities to consider a whole host of factors which rely on the credibility of the refugee applicant, it has been argued that often what is deemed fraudulent by the authorities is a perfectly sound psychological reaction to a refugee's fear of authority. This is seldom given much weight by determing authorities (see Anker, 1987: Tuitt, 1996: 86–91).

7. The issue turns on the scope of Article 33. The Convention clearly only operates at the level of absolute necessity, thus the principle that refugees should not search widely for a 'desirable' place of refuge is sound. However, which countries are deemed 'safe' is not always satisfactory, particularly where the claim of lack of safety is related to the incompatibility of asylum procedures between states (see, for particular criticism, Amnesty International, 1993). Refugees in the past have claimed that certain countries, in particular Germany, are not safe for refugees because of the existence of organized racist groups. But such claims have been universally unsuccessful (for a comprehensive discussion, see Tuitt, 1996: Chapter 6).

REFERENCES

Amekrane v. *United Kingdom* (1973), 16 YB 356.

Amnesty International (1993), *Passing the Buck: Deficient Home Office Practice in 'Safe Third Country' Asylum Cases*, London, Amnesty International.

Anker, D. (1987), 'Discretionary Asylum: A Protection Remedy for Refugees Under the Act of 1980', *Virginia Journal of International Law*, Vol. 28, No. 1, pp. 1–72.

Arboleda, E. and Hoy, I. (1993), 'The Convention Refugee Definition in the West: Disharmony of Interpretation and Application', *International Journal of Refugee Law*, Vol. 5, No. 1, pp. 66–90.

Asylum and Immigration Act (1996), London, HMSO.

Bhabba, J. and Shutter, S. (1994), *Women's Movements: Women Under Immigration, Nationality and Refugee Law*, Stoke On Trent, Trentham Books.

Castel, J. (1992), 'Rape, Sexual Assault and the Meaning of Protection', *International Journal of Refugee Law*, Vol. 4, No. 1, pp. 39–56.

Coles, G. (1988), 'The Human Rights Approach to the Solution of the Refugee Problem: A Theoretical and Practical Enquiry' in Nash, A. (ed.),

Human Rights and the Protection of Refugees Under International Law, Montreal, Human Rights Foundation.

Douzinas, C. and Warrington, R. (1995), *Justice (Mis) carried: The Ethics and Aesthetics of the Law*, London, Harvester and Wheatsheaf.

Dunstan, R. (1994), *Prisoners without a Voice: Asylum Seekers Detained in the UK*, London, Amnesty International.

Dursan v. *Secretary of State for the Home Department* (1993), IMM AR, 169.

Fragaman, A. (1970), 'The Refugee: A Problem of Definition', *Case Western Reserve Journal of International* Law, Vol. 3, No. 1, pp. 45–69.

Gibney, M. and Stohl, M. (1988), 'Human Rights and US Refugee Policy', in Gibney, M. (ed.), *Open Borders? Closed Societies? The Ethical and Political Issues*, Westport Conneticut, Greenwood Press.

Goodwin-Gill, G. (1982), 'Entry and Exclusion of Refugees: The Obligations and Protective Functions of the United Nations High Commissioner for Refugees', *Michigan Yearbook of International Legal Studies*, New York, C. Boardman Co., pp. 291–337.

Goodwin-Gill, G. (1986), 'Non-Refoulment and the New Asylum-Seekers', *Virginia Journal of International Law*, Vol. 26, No.4, pp. 897–918.

Goodwin-Gill, G. (1996), *The Refugee in International Law*, Oxford, Clarendon Press.

Grahl-Madsen, A. (1966–72), *The Status of Refugee in International Law*, Leyden, A.W. Sijthoff.

Hailbronner, K. (1986), 'Non-refoulement and Humanitarian Refugees: Customary International Law or Wishful Legal Thinking?', *Virginia Journal of International Law*, Vol. 26, No. 4, pp. 857–96.

Hailbronner, K. (1993), 'The Concept of "Safe Country" and Expeditious Procedures: A Western European Perspective', *International Journal of Refugee Law*, Vol. 5, No. 1, pp. 31–65.

Hathaway, J. (1991), *The Law of Refugee Status*, Toronto, Butterworths.

Helton, A. (1990), 'The Detention of Refugees and Asylum-Seekers: A Misguided Threat to Refugee Protection', in Loescher, G. and Monahan, L. (eds), *Refugees and International Relations*, Oxford, Clarendon Press.

Hyndman, P. (1992), 'Asylum and Non-Refoulement: Are There Obligations Owed to Refugees under International Law?', *Philippine Law Journal*, Vol. 57, pp. 43–65.

Joint Council for the Welfare of Immigrants and Liberty (1995), *The Last Resort: Violations of the Human Rights of Migrants, Refugees and Asylum Seekers*, London, JCWI.

Kobayashi, A. (1995), 'Challenging the National Dream: Canada's Immigration Laws' in Fitzpatrick, P. (ed.), *Nationalism, Racism and the Rule of Law*, Dartmouth, Aldershot.

Marrus, M. (1985), *The Unwanted: European Refugees in the 20th Century*, Oxford, Oxford University Press.

Noble, P (1982), 'Refugees, Law and Developments in Africa: Transnational Legal Problems of Refugees', *Michigan Yearbook of International Legal Studies*, New York, Clark Boardman and Co., pp. 255–87.

Olympia Lazo-Majano v. *Immigration and Naturalization Service* (1987), 813 F2d 1432 (9th Cir 1987).

104   *Refugees, Citizenship and Social Policy in Europe*

Perluss, P. and Hartman, J. (1986), 'Temporary Refuge: Emergence of a Customary Norm', *Virginia Journal of International Law*, Vol. 26, No. 4, pp. 551–625.

Plaut, W. (1992), *Asylum: A Moral Dilemma*, Conneticut and London, Praeger.

Posner, M. and Kaplan, S. (1981), 'Who Should We Let In', Human Rights Vol. 9, No. 3, pp. 16–21.

R. v. Secretary of State for the Home Department ex parte Sivakumaran (1988), AC 958.

Sexton, R. (1985), 'Political Refugees: Non-Refoulement and State Practice: A Comparative Study', *Vanderbilt Journal of Transnational Law*, Vol. 18, No. 4, pp. 731–806.

Shah, P. (1995), 'Refugees and "Safe Third Countries"' *Immigration and Nationality Law and Practice*, Vol. 9, No. 1, pp. 3–13.

Spijkerboer, T. (1995), *Women Refugees: Beyond the Public/Private Divide*, Amsterdam, Dutch Emancipation Council.

Tuitt, P. (1996), *False Images: Law's Construction of the Refugee*, London, Pluto.

Vilvarajah v. United Kingdom (1991), Series A No. 215.

Winterbourne, D., Shah, P. and Doebbler, C. (1996), 'Refugees and Safe Countries of Origin: Appeals, Judicial Review and Human Rights', *Immigration and Nationality Law and Practice*, Vol. 10, No. 4, pp. 123–35.

Zolberg, A., Suhrike, A. and Aguayo, S. (1991), *Escape from Violence: Conflict and the Refugee Crisis in the Developing World*, Oxford, Oxford University Press.

6 Refugee resettlement in Europe
Karen Duke, Rosemary Sales and Jeanne Gregory

INTRODUCTION

As refugees have become a focus of increasing political concern in the 1990s, it is the conditions of entry to European states which has dominated debate and policy making in Europe. The 1951 Geneva Convention, which forms the basis for current international law governing refugee status, gives equal importance to the social rights of refugees within the country of asylum. These include residence rights, employment, social welfare, education and housing (European Consultation on Refugees and Exiles, 1983). Most European states provide at least the minimum levels set out in the Convention to those to whom they grant full refugee status (Convention status), but there has been only limited development towards harmonization of policy in this area. As European integration has brought common policies of closure, resettlement policy remains largely under the control of individual states and reflects individual notions of nationhood and citizenship.

Refugees have distinctive needs which necessitate specific policies if resettlement is to be successful. They have been forced to flee, usually at short notice, often leaving behind family as well as jobs, homes and possessions: in fact everything that made up their identity. Although some refugee flows involve movement towards countries with colonial ties (for example Algerians to France) in many cases refugees seek asylum in countries with which they have no former connection, and they may have little knowledge of the language, culture or job market. Labour migrants, however reluctantly they may leave their homeland, and whatever the mixture of motives involved in their decision to migrate,[1] are generally able to prepare themselves in some way for employment in the country of exile, and have some positive expectations of the move. For refugees, preparation is impossible and the

105

experience of exile, particularly in the early days, is dominated by a sense of loss. Their needs cannot be met merely by the provision of services on the same basis as nationals. Successful resettlement depends on programmes which allow them to find a place in the new society, for example by converting their skills and qualifications so that they can be used in the new situation.

Most research on refugee settlement has been conducted in a single country (for example Carey-Wood *et al.*, 1995; Gold, 1992a) and often focuses on specific issues, such as mental health, employment or housing. Joly and Cohen (1989) brought together experience from a number of different European states, while Joly (1996) compared French and British policies in relation to Chilean and Vietnamese refugees. These contributions are useful in illuminating the different assumptions underlying policy in the different states, and providing axes of comparison. They are, however, concerned mainly with the situation in the 1980s when the majority of refugees in Europe were 'programme refugees' who had secure legal status, generally from the moment of entry.

The experience of asylum seekers in the 1990s has been very different. The majority reaching Europe are 'spontaneous refugees' (Koser, 1996) who have to fight their case for refugee status within Europe and may endure months or years of uncertainty. They face increasingly restrictive legislation, initiated both at a European level, the so-called 'Fortress Europe' (Kofman and Sales, 1992), and by individual states. These policies have been aimed at deterring asylum seekers both by making it more difficult to enter or remain within Europe, and by denying them access to social rights in the country of exile. As external policing has increased, the abolition of internal borders within Europe has produced more rigorous internal policing of immigrants. Welfare services are being used for surveillance, with access conditional on proof of immigration status (Owers, 1994).

The dramatic rise in the number of asylum seekers across Europe from the late 1980s has been accompanied by a fall in the proportion granted Convention status. In the United Kingdom, for example, it has declined from 59 per cent in 1982 to less than 10 per cent after 1991 (Home Office, various dates). Full refugee status is now given to only a small proportion of asylum seekers across Western Europe (see Table 6.1). Some countries continue to accept applicants on humanitarian grounds (Salt *et al.*, 1994) although this category too is being tightened, and there are major differences between states in the rights accorded to this status.

Table 6.1 Number of applications for asylum and grants of Convention
status in Europe, 1991–95

	Applications	Convention grants
Austria	53 960	7 624
Belgium	45 989	5 186
Denmark	65 504	11 595
Finland	9 479	56
France	149 150	29% in 1992; 16.3% in 1995
Germany	1 272 063	8.5% in 1995
Greece	3 113[a]	231
Ireland	940	22
Italy	30 765	2 034
Luxembourg	905	13
Netherlands	159 186	30 292
Norway	27 522	369
Portugal	4 255	147[b]
Spain	34 131	3 047
Sweden	177 000	2 573[c]
United Kingdom	148 610	5 330

[a] Figures for August 1993–95.
[b] Includes humanitarian status.
[c] Figures from 1992. Total residence permits – 99 800.

Note: Unless percentages are given, decisions are not linked to applicants in
the same period.

Source: Liebaut and Hughes, 1997.

Current policies are producing a growing number of asylum
seekers in Europe whose legal and social status is insecure. Attacks
on the rights of asylum seekers, both in material terms and at an ideological level – through, for example, the denigration of 'bogus
asylum seekers' by politicians and sections of the media – affect all
refugees, including those with Convention status. The Geneva
Convention includes the obligation to grant at least temporary
asylum (European Consultation on Refugees and Exiles, 1983: 13).
Measures to deter asylum seekers, such as the removal by the United
Kingdom government of benefits from in-country applicants, contradict the spirit of the Convention. They have diverted the efforts of
those concerned with refugee rights towards dealing with immediate
needs for shelter rather than long-term strategies, undermining the

process of long-term settlement, which Joly argues, should properly begin on entry (Joly, 1996: 95). In the words of an asylum seeker in Ireland:

> I spent six years studying at university. I worked for a petroleum company and I speak several languages but here I can't do anything for this society or myself ... I can't plan my life. (*The Guardian*, 29 July 1997: 7)

Hostility towards asylum seekers threatens the security of refugees, whatever their legal status. Racist attacks have been common in Europe, particularly in France, Germany and Italy, while our studies revealed high levels of racial harassment in Britain (Carey-Wood *et al.*, 1995; Gregory and Sales, 1997). The far right has had some electoral success, particularly in France, with appeals to anti-foreigner feeling. Immigration and asylum became electoral issues for the first time in the 1997 Irish election as an independent candidate stood on an anti-immigration platform.

In spite of the increasingly inhospitable climate for refugees in Europe, many are proving extraordinarily resilient and have been able to make a new life in exile. Much research on refugees suggests that women find it easier than men to adapt to changed status (Kay, 1989; Buijs, 1993; Refugee Council, 1996; Gregory and Sales, 1997). Men have generally lost status in both public and private spheres through the loss of employment and their 'breadwinner' role, and often a political position. Women have generally been able to preserve more continuity, maintaining primary responsibility for the family. This has often meant taking on new roles, from choice, because of the absence of husbands or from financial necessity. They have tended to be more flexible in the type of jobs they are prepared to take on, both paid and unpaid. Women, however, have found it difficult to be accepted as refugees in their own right (Crawley, 1997) and their residence status is often dependent on men, making them vulnerable to abuse.

This chapter focuses particularly on British resettlement policy. The first section, however, places this in the context of European policy towards refugees and asylum seekers. The second section compares British resettlement policy in the 1970s and 1980s with current policy, illustrating current refugee experience by looking at a number of specific issues in the resettlement process (health, housing and education: for employment see Bloch, Chapter 10 in this volume). The final section draws some policy conclusions.

REFUGEE RESETTLEMENT POLICIES

Most European states carry out at least their minimum obligations to those to whom they grant Convention status. The content and structures of their policies towards refugees, however, differ considerably. The Danish Refugee Council conducted a comparative study of the legal and social rights of refugees, asylum seekers and those with humanitarian status in 16 Western European countries (Liebaut and Hughes, 1997). This shows that most Convention refugees have the same formal rights as nationals. Their precarious economic status, however, means that their ability to gain access to these rights is often restricted.

Unemployment among refugees remains extremely high even after several years of settlement (Liebaut and Hughes, 1997). A major obstacle to employment is lack of appropriate qualifications and experience and adequate facility in the local language; while refugees face discrimination in racially segregated labour markets. They tend to be concentrated in inner city areas with high unemployment rates. While most states allow access to the labour market unconditionally, some, for example Belgium and Greece, continue to require work permits. Even when legally entitled to work, many employers are reluctant to take on refugees, whom they may regard as temporary residents.

Welfare benefits in most European states (particularly France, Germany and Italy) are largely based on contributions through employment (Esping Anderson, 1990). This has been an increasing trend in other European states, particularly Britain, and is likely to be hastened by European integration (Kofman and Sales, 1996). These conditions mean that the level of benefits obtained by refugees are unlikely to exceed the bare minimum. This may also affect access to health care, where provision is partially tied to contributions, as for example in Germany. Refugees are, however, generally unable to draw on extended family networks to supplement state provision. Low incomes also affect access to housing. Portugal actively discriminates against refugees and other migrants by limiting municipal housing to households containing at least one Portuguese citizen (Liebaut and Hughes, 1997: 194). The shortage of housing in other European states means that refugees are often housed in inadequate and overcrowded conditions.

A major issue affecting the resettlement process is family reunion. Separation from family is a major source of stress during exile, making it extremely difficult to put down roots. The right to family life is enshrined in various international instruments, including the Universal Declaration of Human Rights (European Consultation, 1983: 15). While most European states grant family reunion unconditionally to immediate family, Austria, Belgium, Italy and Portugal place the same conditions as imposed on other migrants, i.e. that the applicant can support them without 'recourse to public funds' and has secure accommodation. In view of the precarious nature of refugees' lives, this is likely to be an insuperable obstacle for many refugees. These restrictions mark a significant break with the spirit of the international convention. No agreement exists in relation to the definition of family, and most confine it to spouse and dependent minor children, although some (for example Denmark, The Netherlands and Sweden) widen this to include parents if the applicant is able to support them.

European states differ markedly in the way they organize the reception of refugees. Some, such as France, and the Scandinavian countries have permanent centralized settlement programmes, while others such as Portugal, Greece and Ireland provide more ad hoc support. This partly reflects the recent arrival of asylum seekers in the latter countries. Ireland, for example, incorporated the Geneva Convention into national law only in 1996 and measures to support refugee resettlement included in the new Refugee Act have not yet come into effect. Ireland has experienced a substantial rise in asylum seekers since 1995 and the Irish Refugee Council (IRC) is calling for the urgent establishment of an integrated reception policy (IRC, 1997). While Portugal and Greece offer minimal support to asylum seekers, they are able to claim relatively generous benefits in Ireland. Britain has a long tradition of receiving asylum seekers, but has always refused to set up a permanent programme, preferring to see refugee flows as temporary (see Schuster and Solomos, Chapter 3, in this volume). Joly, comparing British and French programmes for receiving Chilean and Vietnamese refugees, argues that the differences reflect fundamental philosophical differences about the nature of citizenship in the two states. Refugees in France

> were not to be made to feel that they were the beneficiaries of charitable individual or local initiatives: they were to be taken on by the national collectivity, that is, fully funded by central government departments (Joly, 1996: 95).

France offered a more generous programme during this period, with funding extended to cover needs, rather than limited to a predetermined budget as in Britain (Joly, 1996: 95). While these programmes have been curtailed in the 1990s, with restrictions on asylum rights, they continue to be underpinned by the civic republican concept (Kofman, 1995) in which full citizenship is seen as resting on participation in civic life. Refugees are encouraged to acquire French values and language: the state offers 520 hours of tuition in French language and culture, which is compulsory to those housed in reception centres.

Germany has received by far the largest number of refugees in Europe, the majority from Eastern Europe. Germany has had an ambivalent relationship to refugees. On the one hand, the state has, since the Second World War, proclaimed its commitment to providing asylum. On the other hand, Germany has never seen itself as a country of immigration (Rathzel, 1991). The concept of citizenship is exclusionary, with German nationality acquired primarily by *jus sanguinis* (through blood ties) rather than *jus soli* (by birth in the country) as is the tradition in France and Britain (Anthias and Yuval-Davis, 1992). There has been some convergence as rights to citizenship have been restricted in Britain and France while it has become somewhat easier for foreigners to acquire German citizenship. Many second and third generation migrants, nevertheless, still do not have German citizenship. These contradictions came to a head in the 1990s, when a wave of anti-foreigner feeling, targeted mainly at refugees, precipitated a major constitutional amendment in 1993 which limited the right to asylum (see Schönwälder, Chapter 4 in this volume).

German policy toward resettlement is characterized by authoritarian treatment of asylum seekers – for whom living in reception centres is compulsory even if they have relatives in Germany – relatively ungenerous conditions, and limited support for integration. There is, for example, no national system of support for children with limited German language within the school system (Liebaut and Hughes, 1997: 97). As in France, there is no provision for mother tongue classes. This is provided in state schools in the Scandinavian countries, which have traditionally emphasized a more multi-cultural model of incorporation than either Germany or France (Soysal, 1994). In Britain, where multi-cultural policies have been initiated at local rather than national level, individual education authorities support such classes.

Differences between state programmes are reflected in whether primary responsibility for refugee resettlement rests with national or local state agencies, and the degree to which responsibility is devolved to voluntary agencies, such as the Red Cross, the churches and community groups. France has a highly centralized system, run by the

Ministry for Social Affairs and Integration, and there is a branch of the National Office for Employment specifically for refugees. In The Netherlands, Denmark, Sweden and Norway, local authorities take a major role, but they are funded by the state. Others, such as the United Kingdom, Spain, Italy and Greece are more dependent on voluntary organizations, although they may be partially subsidized by the state.

There are major differences in states' attitudes to the dispersal of refugees, which are related to their policies on receiving asylum seekers. Most have reception centres which can accommodate at least some asylum seekers on arrival. Several states, including Belgium, Norway and Denmark, allocate asylum seekers particular localities. In Germany, dispersion to the *Länder* (regions) is based purely on the numbers already there. Similarly in The Netherlands refugees have little choice about where to move. In Britain, dispersal was attempted with programme refugees in the 1970s, but there is no centralized policy for spontaneous refugees, most of whom move to London or other major cities (Carey-Wood *et al.*, 1995). British local authorities receive little direct state support for refugee settlement and some have tried to disperse asylum seekers to areas with few refugees, a move precipitated by shortage of housing. This policy is strongly resisted by refugee organizations, since they deprive refugees of supportive networks and access to special services.[2]

Dispersal may allow refugees greater possibilities of finding employment, a view strongly supported by Robles (1989) writing of Spanish resettlement programmes for Vietnamese refugees. It also spreads the cost of accommodation and other services more evenly. Compulsory dispersion, however, has serious implications for civil liberties. As we argue below, community groups play a major role in the resettlement process, and these tend to be most securely established in large centres of population. For refugees, torn from home and family, the isolation of life in a small foreign town, with few fellow nationals, may be extremely isolating. They are also more likely to suffer racial harassment in more monocultural areas. The notion of 'burden sharing' can imply a negative view of asylum seekers, which does not recognize the contribution they can make to the life of their new country.

CONDITIONS FOR ASYLUM SEEKERS

A greater disparity exists between states in provisions for asylum seekers, who are an increasing proportion, as refusals of refugee status increase. The range of difference is illustrated by the amount of financial support available (Table 6.2). Fairly generous benefits are available in some states, while in others which rely heavily on reception centres, help is largely confined to pocket money and benefits in kind. Conditions in German reception centres have been a cause for concern to non-governmental organizations (NGOs) (Liebaut and Hughes, 1997: 93). In Greece and Portugal asylum seekers receive minimal state help, and rely on charity for basic needs. In Britain, benefits were removed in 1997 from in-country applicants and those appealing against refusal. A court decision based on the National

Table 6.2   Income of asylum seekers

	Adult monthly allowance, $	
Austria	36.5	(pocket money – payable to those under 'federal care': approximately 30% of asylum seekers)
Belgium	639	
Denmark	174	(plus board and lodging)
Finland	384	(excludes accommodation)
France	247	(plus one off payment of 380 – no allowance for children)
Germany	26	(pocket money)
Greece	none	
Ireland	617	
Italy	480	(payable for 45 days)
Luxembourg	343	
Netherlands	76	(pocket money plus clothing)
Norway	139	(pocket money)
Portugal	none	(for 96% under accelerated procedure)
	178	(for those in normal determination procedure)
Spain	271	(6 months; or $50 pocket money if in reception centre)
Sweden	315	(105 if meals provided)
United Kingdom	173	(plus housing benefit to port applicants)
	zero	(in-country applicants and refusals – food vouchers provided by local authorities)

Source: Liebaut and Hughes, 1997.

Assistance Act of 1948 stated that local authorities were responsible for the provision of basic needs, but they are not allowed to supply cash.

There is increasing differentiation between groups of asylum seekers in relation to income and access to accommodation. In most states asylum seekers are not allowed to work, although in some they may apply for a work permit after a certain length of time (three months in Finland and Germany, six in the United Kingdom). Belgium, Spain and Sweden have some flexibility. Many asylum seekers work illegally, particularly in Greece, Italy and Portugal where limited funds are available, and in Britain where welfare payments have been withdrawn.

HUMANITARIAN STATUS

As Convention status is given more rarely, the importance of other forms of residence status has increased. Some states grant temporary protection to asylum seekers who they have determined do not meet the criteria for Convention status, but for whom it would be unsafe to return. The major group in Europe are from former Yugoslavia, for whom many European countries have provided collective temporary protection. In some cases, (for example in Norway) these programmes have been extended so that they now have an indefinite right to remain. Others have acquired individual rights which provide a variety of social rights and possibilities of permanent residence (see Table 6.3). A crucial difference between humanitarian and convention status is that the former does not grant unconditional and immediate family reunion, which is generally offered only in limited cases. Finland, which grants a tiny number of Convention statuses, and Sweden are the only countries which allow it unconditionally. Elsewhere, refugees must wait for a period of stipulated residence, for example four years in Britain, after which they may apply on the same basis as legal migrant workers for whom it is conditional on income and accommodation. These conditions often pose insuperable barriers to refugees, few of whom are able to find secure employment in their country of exile. Women, particularly those with children, are least likely to be in work, and are unlikely to be able to call on extended family networks in order to support them in meeting the criteria.

Table 6.3 Humanitarian status available to asylum seekers in European states (excluding provisions for asylum seekers from former Yugoslavia)

Austria	Temporary residence permit for limited time, extendable for maximum of one year (this is rarely granted)
Belgium	No *de facto* humanitarian status
Denmark	Humanitarian status rarely granted Exceptional residence permits – mainly granted to lone children
Finland	Convention status rarely granted; residence permits on need for protection or humanitarian grounds provide same benefits as Convention
France	Convention status is the only formal status, but humanitarian status may be granted to those who have lived a long time in France – provides same status as migrant workers 'Territorial asylum' available for Algerians
Germany	Duldung – tolerated residence – equivalent to waiver of deportation order because of risk of return. Does not imply right of residence
Greece	Temporary residence on humanitarian grounds granted for six months and renewable; no social rights attached
Ireland	Humanitarian permission to remain (HPR) – residence permit renewable annually. After five years may apply for permanent residence
Italy	Temporary protection for Somalis – renewable annually
Luxembourg	Residence on humanitarian grounds – no legal basis, and does not imply right to work; tolerated residence for those whose residence permits are not renewed – renewable monthly
Netherlands	Residence status for humanitarian reasons – no legal status, and no social rights attached Provisional residence permits for humanitarian reasons for those who withdraw asylum applications – one year renewable annually – may apply for it to be made permanent after three years
Portugal	Residence permit for humanitarian reasons and exceptional reasons (mostly former colonies)
Spain	Residence on humanitarian grounds available to groups of displaced persons renewable annually for three years. Rights as for migrant workers
Sweden	Protection for those other than Convention refugees imply same rights as Convention status. Temporary protection – usually maximum of two years
United Kingdom	Exceptional leave to remain (ELR) renewable up to seven years, then indefinite leave to remain. Generally same social rights as Convention status apart from family reunion.

Source: Liebaut and Hughes, 1997.

RECEPTION AND RESETTLEMENT POLICY IN THE UK

Resettlement programmes in the 1970s and 1980s

Britain's reluctance to establish a permanent, central programme for the resettlement of refugees in Britain has meant that special temporary programmes have been developed for refugees on an ad hoc basis: for example for Chileans and Ugandan Asians in the early 1970s, Vietnamese in the late 1970s and early 1980s, and more recently, Bosnian evacuees in the 1990s. Before the recent increases in asylum seeking, the largest groups were dealt with through these specific resettlement programmes. Small numbers of 'trickle' refugees who were not part of these programmes were granted refugee status or asylum in their own right (Field, 1985).

During this early period, the British government provided funding for reception and resettlement and established policy objectives, but did not become directly involved in policy implementation, which was delegated to quasi-governmental organizations (Hale, 1993). For example, funding for the Chilean programme was provided by the Home Office through a Joint Working Group consisting of voluntary agencies,[3] as well as the Chile Committee for Human Rights and the Chile Solidarity Campaign (Field, 1985; Kaye, 1987; Joly, 1996). The Uganda Resettlement Board was set up in 1972 to deal with reception and resettlement arrangements for Ugandan Asians. The Board was controlled and funded by the Home Office, although it involved voluntary sector representatives (Bristow, 1979; Levin, 1981; Field, 1985; Marret, 1989). Similarly, when the Vietnamese began to arrive in 1979, another new structure was established, the Joint Committee for Refugees from Vietnam, consisting of representatives from voluntary agencies and the Home Office. Its tasks included co-ordinating the resettlement programme, calling forward refugees from Hong Kong and providing a forum for discussion of policy. In addition, an Advisory Council on the Reception and Resettlement of Refugees from Vietnam was established with a wider membership (Jones, 1982; Field, 1985).

A central feature of policy towards these groups was 'front end loading'. This involves providing resources and support during the initial stages of resettlement in the expectation that less support, particularly financial, would be needed in later stages as economic self-sufficiency was attained (Stein, 1979; Field, 1985; Joly, 1996). Refugees were usually housed at first in reception centres funded by central government and managed by voluntary agencies and moved to permanent homes as soon as these could be located. These centres offered services such as English language courses, medical help, an opportunity to learn systematically about life in the UK, arrangements of subsequent accommodation, enrolment of children in local schools and childcare.

After refugees left the reception centres, no specialist assistance was available, leaving them reliant on mainstream services. Local authorities were expected to take over responsibility, although in contrast to other European countries such as The Netherlands, Denmark and Sweden, no extra funds were made available. Joly (1996) found that local authorities lacked knowledge about refugee groups living within their areas, and this inhibited the development of appropriate services and specific local policies. She commented that their responses were ad hoc rather than based on a concerted policy (Joly, 1996: 126).

A conscious policy of 'dispersal' was adopted for both Ugandan Asian and Vietnamese refugees. This policy was undermined by the isolation it created for many refugees, high unemployment in many areas of initial settlement and lack of resources available to local authorities to provide for special needs such as education and training. As a result, Ugandan Asians began to move away from their initial places of resettlement to areas with existing East African communities (Community Relations Commission, 1974). Similarly, secondary migration occurred amongst the dispersed Vietnamese community (Robinson and Hale, 1989; Robinson, 1993). It was evident that these 'accommodation-led' strategies had not been successful and a much more comprehensive approach was needed (Joly, 1996).

The policy of 'front end loading' also failed, with many refugees experiencing continuing unemployment and other problems, necessitating further support or 'post-settlement work'. Refugees were, however, officially considered 'resettled' once accommodation had been found for them and policy began to focus on 'community development' with refugees receiving support and advice from members of their own communities (Joly, 1996). 'Community self help' has remained the cornerstone of British resettlement policy. Commenting on reception and resettlement policies during this early period, Jones (1982), who conducted research on the Vietnamese population, argues:

All too often it is thought that new refugee situations are isolated, deviant and non-recurring. A direct consequence of such beliefs has been the common failure in refugee programmes to learn from the lessons of the past, a failure to develop an institutional memory, and a constant need, in connection with each new situation, to re-invent the wheel. (Jones, 1982: 49)

Current resettlement policy

The majority of asylum seekers coming to Britain in the 1990s are non-quota refugees, for whom there is no co-ordinated programme. They may be given assistance with immediate needs such as housing, translation and interpretation and transport by specialist organiza-tions like the Refugee Arrivals Project (RAP) at Heathrow and Gatwick airports, the Refugee Councils and refugee community groups. Referral to these agencies may be made by the Immigration Service or friends and relatives already in the UK. Access to more permanent support is, however, limited and uneven.

Current resettlement policy is based on two key approaches: equal access to general state provision and support for community self-help (Carey-Wood, 1994). The principle of equal access to state services has been increasingly eroded during the 1990s, with restrictions on the rights of asylum seekers to benefits and other services. Those with full refugee status or exceptional leave to remain (ELR) have a formal right to equality, but in practice access is limited by discrimination – both individual and structural – by service providers, as well as the difficulties posed by language and poverty.[4]

Most refugees, especially spontaneous refugees, have moved to large cities, primarily London. The boroughs which attract the largest numbers tend to be the poorest. Although attracting no state funding for this purpose, some local councils and health authorities provide special programmes to assist in resettlement such as language courses, translation and advocacy services. These projects are, however, threat-ened by increasingly stringent budgetary restriction. The restructuring of welfare services, the introduction of market conditions, and the requirement to meet externally imposed targets have made it difficult to sustain programmes aimed at meeting specific needs.

The Voluntary Services Unit (VSU) of the Home Office has central government responsibility for the reception and resettlement of refugees. Their policy is to provide assistance through voluntary organ-izations, community groups, local authorities or through special pro-grammes within statutory agencies. The VSU provides grant aid to refugee agencies to work with statutory bodies to help refugees gain access to services and fosters the development of self-help through refugee community groups (Carey-Wood *et al.*, 1995).

The major recipients of VSU grant-aid are the Refugee Council, the national refugee umbrella organization in the UK, and Refugee Action,[5] the main agency providing help with reception and resettlement for Vietnamese refugees. Some of these funds are used to support other agencies working with refugees. Grant-aid is also provided to the Scottish and Welsh Refugee Councils, and the three English regional councils, the Midlands, North and North-east. The councils are involved in a wide range of activities and services for refugees, including facilitating access to employment, training, and housing; and advice, translation and interpretation, education and lobbying.

Refugee community groups

National and local refugee community groups are voluntary organizations managed by refugees themselves. They are generally specific to particular national, ethnic, cultural, political, or religious groups. Some have established national networks to respond to needs in different parts of Britain, but most concentrate their activities in London although they have contacts around the country. Some organizations have developed in response to particular needs, for example, women's groups and services to the elderly.

Several studies have pointed to the important role refugee community groups play in the resettlement process (Rogg, 1974; Jones, 1982; Field, 1985; Dalglish, 1989; Eisenbruch, 1991; Gold, 1992a; Beiser, 1993; Carey-Wood, 1994; Schwarzer *et al.*, 1994; Carey-Wood *et al.*, 1995; Duke and Marshall, 1995). They provide a 'voice for refugees', contact points for isolated individuals, expertise in dealing with refugee issues and flexible and sensitive responses to the needs of their target populations. They also provide cultural and social activities which offer refugees the chance to maintain their own customs and religion, talk in their own language, celebrate their traditions and exchange news from their home country.

The difficulties refugees experience in accessing mainstream services have resulted in the development of 'refugee specific initiatives' (RSIs) (Carey-Wood, 1994). Such initiatives can include refugee community groups, adapted services in the statutory and voluntary sectors or the appointment of a refugee worker in a mainstream service. These initiatives '... can act as intermediary, interpreter, innovator, campaigner, negotiator, representative and advocate for refugee individuals or whole communities in a much more targeted way than larger, bureaucratic organizations' (Carey-Wood, 1994: 32). Community groups therefore provide a major link between individuals and the formal agencies concerned with employment, training, housing and welfare. Reliance on these groups as the major focus of resettlement policy is, however, problematic.

The refugee population in the UK is diverse in terms of class, region, ideology, ethnic and national identity, religion, age and gender, and community groups may exclude isolated subgroups within their populations. Surveys commissioned by the Home Office found that women, single parents, the elderly, and those living outside London were particularly likely to be isolated (Carey-Wood *et al.,* 1995; Duke and Marshall, 1995). Refugee women experience difficulties in finding suitable childcare to enable them to seek assistance or participate in community events. Groups are generally controlled and run by men, often to the exclusion of women, a problem which emerged in our local study of the Somali community (Sales and Gregory, 1996). Summerfield (1993) found that women often initiate community organizations, but when they achieve formal status and funding, men tend to take them over, assigning women to subordinate roles.

Refugee communities may include people from opposite sides in a civil war and some may be suspicious of fellow nationals, fearing they will report on their activities to the authorities in the home country. One Spanish speaking voluntary advice worker reported that he was frequently asked to interpret for Latin American refugees, in preference to someone from their own country (Calvar, 1996: 9).

Funding for community groups is obtained primarily through charitable funds and 'special' statutory sources.[6] These tend to be short term, insecure and often subject to annual renewal, taking time and resources away from actual work with refugees and making it difficult for groups to make long-term plans. They depend on high rates of voluntary work by members. Over a third of respondents in both Home Office surveys had done such work, often full-time, including organizing cultural events, interpreting and translating, providing welfare and advice services, teaching religion and culture, fund-raising campaigns, administrative and secretarial tasks, helping those still living in their home countries and providing childcare (Carey-Wood *et al.,* 1995; Duke and Marshall, 1995). In addition, because the work is unpaid, there is high staff turnover resulting in loss of skills and expertise.

Evidence from the two surveys suggested that some individuals become overly dependent on their community group. This results in less pressure to adjust personally, to learn the language, and handle their own affairs within British institutions. There was a danger of the groups becoming inward-looking, monopolizing the relationships of their members, instead of empowering them to become independent.

Carey-Wood (1994) found that individual casework has been the main priority of refugee community groups due to the urgent needs of new arrivals for legal work and assistance with basic needs such as benefits, housing, food and clothing. Groups are often overwhelmed by the volume of casework so that longer term community development and resettlement work is neglected. Official strategy has been to place more and more work in the hands of voluntary agencies, extending the use of unpaid labour. The 1996 Asylum Act marks a dramatic acceleration in this trend, as thousands of asylum seekers were deprived of an income, diverting the energies of refugee community groups and other voluntary groups towards ensuring the basic survival of people denied assistance from the state.

These issues are reflected in an analysis we carried out of community groups. Vietnamese and non-Vietnamese were examined separately,

Table 6.4   Issues dealt with by Vietnamese community groups (% of groups involved in each activity)

	%
Welfare rights	86
Cultural and social activities	71
Housing	70
Interpreting and translation	69
Education	67
Employment, training and business	65
Health	64
Mother tongue classes	57
Services to the elderly	57
Liaising with central and local government	55
Family reunion	43
Skills support and training	41
Services to women	39
Young people	39
Race equality	20

Source: Refugee Action, 1996, mailing lists.

using records from Refugee Action and the Refugee Council respectively. A total of 54 Vietnamese groups and 179 non-Vietnamese refugee community groups were identified.[7] Over half (59 per cent) of the Vietnamese groups are based in the London area. Thirteen per cent have a national remit, whilst 87 per cent deal with specific geographical areas. The majority (98 per cent) have management committees and almost three quarters (73 per cent) have workers attached to them. The groups deal with a multitude of issues and activities (see Table 6.4).

The structures and activities of Vietnamese community groups reflect their more secure legal status and longer establishment within British society. Family reunion, however, remains a major issue. In contrast non-Vietnamese groups appeared to have less formal structures and to be more dependent on voluntary labour for their core work. The main activities focused on securing legal rights for their members, and advice on welfare. Cultural and social activities were a lower priority (Table 6.5).

These groups are much more concentrated in London (96 per cent) and the majority deal with a specific nationality (87 per cent), having developed around the main refugee populations in the UK (see Table 6.6). This creates potential problems of duplication of activities and resources, competition for scarce funding, and the possibility of newer groups being excluded. Some local authorities and refugee

Table 6.5   Issues dealt with by non-Vietnamese community groups (% of groups involved in each activity)

	%
Asylum issues (policy, campaigning, casework)	74
Education	73
Welfare rights	67
Health	56
Housing advice	48
Services to women	45
Cultural and social activities	40
Interpreting and translating	35
Employment and training	32
Publications	10
Race equality	10

Source: Refugee Council, 1996, mailing lists.

Table 6.6   Non-Vietnamese refugee community groups by nationality

	%
Somali	25
Kurdish	10
Latin American	9
Tamil	6
Eritrean	6
Ugandan	4
East European	3
Iranian	3
Iraqi	3
Zairian	3
Ethiopian	3
Afghan	2
Other African	7
Other	16

Source: Refugee Council, 1996, mailing lists.

groups have attempted to develop structures to bring together refugees (e.g. consultative forums) with varying success. The need to co-ordinate activity and resources was recognized at a recent conference organized by the London Borough of Waltham Forest, when one of the main proposals to emerge was for a dedicated centre serving all refugees, with secure and long-term funding.

ISSUES IN THE RESETTLEMENT PROCESS

Health

Refugees have specific health needs, which are addressed through existing services, and through a limited number of special programmes. As well as the health problems some arrive with, social deprivation, including unemployment and sub-standard housing impacts on refugee health. The increased role of the internal market in health care has made it easier to exclude refugees and other groups with specific, and possibly expensive needs. Some authorities have established programmes to promote access to health care, for example Health Advocacy and Counselling Services for Turkish and Kurdish speaking communities based in Hackney. These programmes are, however, vulnerable to budgetary pressures.

Research on health needs has demonstrated problems for refugees in accessing mainstream health care (Buduk, 1993; City and Hackney Health Authority, 1992). Everybody, regardless of immigration status, is entitled to medical care if they present themselves to a doctor or hospital in need of treatment, but cuts in benefits for asylum seekers have made many unsure of their rights. A significant proportion of refugees are not registered with a general practitioner: one estimate suggested that registrations among new arrivals in London was as low as 74 per cent (Newham Refugee Centre, 1996: 5).

Several studies have shown a relationship between pre-migration trauma such as torture, refugee camp experiences and dangerous journeys to the country of asylum and psychological stress during resettlement (Chung and Kagawasinger, 1993; Carey-Wood *et al.*, 1995; Duke and Marshall, 1995; Hauff and Vaglum, 1995; Mghir *et al.*, 1995). Two thirds of Carey-Wood *et al.*'s (1995) sample experienced stress, anxiety and depression while physical health problems affected 16 per cent. Many also suffered physical disabilities as a result of their experiences (Refugee Council, undated). The effects of war and persecution are compounded by adverse experiences in exile, such as social and cultural isolation, unemployment, accommodation problems, language difficulties and concern about friends and relatives who remain in their home countries. Stress is aggravated by anxiety about legal status and delays in processing applications. Separation from their families, who have no right to join asylum seekers or people with ELR, increases stress.

Several studies have revealed a lack of understanding among health care professionals of issues affecting refugees' health and difficulties in the interpretation of their symptoms (Silove *et al.*, 1991; Gold, 1992b; Forbes Martin, 1992; Fuller, 1993; Carey-Wood *et al.*, 1995; Stephenson, 1995). A survey of general practitioners working in the London Borough of Newham, which has an estimated 18 000 refugees (Newham Refugee Centre, 1996: 5), found that most had no expertise in dealing with victims of torture, or knowledge of the resources available. Informal sources of practical and psychological support through community groups and family members are extremely important in reducing the severity and likelihood of mental illness (Field, 1985, Eisenbruch, 1991; Gold, 1992b; Noh *et al.*, 1992; Beiser, 1993; Schwarzer *et al.*, 1994; Carey-Wood *et al.*, 1995; Duke and Marshall, 1995).

Housing

Carey-Wood *et al.* (1995) found that housing was the most urgent issue facing refugees, with over a quarter having experienced homelessness in the UK. Difficulties in securing suitable accommodation hamper the resettlement process. Asylum seekers are overwhelmingly dependent on rented accommodation, particularly in the public sector. Their rights have been reduced by the 1993 Asylum Act, with the duty of local authorities to provide housing increasingly limited, and discretionary (Refugee Council 1995a). Only temporary accommodation may be offered, and this is only where no alternative, however inadequate, exists.

A number of other problems arise for refuges in relation to housing, which affect their access to other social rights. Language barriers make it difficult to negotiate with housing authorities; refugees fleeing from state repression often find state officials, including housing officers, intimidating, a perception given added weight since current legislation requires housing officers to report to the Home Office on the immigration status of housing applicants. Delays in processing benefit applications can lead to rent arrears and conflict with housing authorities; and the restriction of asylum seekers to temporary accommodation makes it more difficult for families to settle. Families may move frequently, disrupting children's schooling. Temporary accommodation may be dispersed, making it difficult to establish community networks and increasing isolation. Isolation is also increased as a result of racial harassment (London Borough of Waltham Forest, 1994; Gregory and Sales, 1997).

Education

Education, particularly for young people, has a central role in resettlement. Schools are one area of authority which is widely recognized, and to which most refugees will come with positive feelings. Many refugee children arrive with high hopes and expectations, and their initial experiences at school are crucial in determining whether they are able to settle and succeed, or, as often happens, feel rejected and alienated and drop out. This is particularly likely if there is no one able to speak their language among the teaching staff. Most refugee families have high ambitions for their children, but shortage of family income may create overriding pressures on young people to seek work, and thus to abandon their studies.

A number of refugee pupils and former pupils were interviewed in a secondary school in North London. All reported that they had felt excluded when they first started school, and most had been bullied. Those who did not speak English well were unable to join in lessons at levels appropriate to their ability. While some had made remarkable progress, others had become discouraged, and teachers reported a high rate of absenteeism.

Many teachers and other professionals are reluctant to talk to the pupils about their experiences, through indifference, or fear that speaking about traumatic experiences may upset the children. Denial of their experiences can, however, leave children isolated. This particular school had developed some model practices in relation to supporting refugee children and allowing them to recount their experience. But even here, support was patchy and uneven, and very much depended on the chance of which class children were assigned to. Extra help given to refugee children is heavily dependent on the goodwill and commitment of individual teachers. Recent changes in education policy make this commitment difficult to sustain. Teachers are increasingly exhorted to meet targets, to aim for high examination results. In a situation of increasingly straightened resources, schools and other education institutions are being forced to compete against each other in financial and academic terms. Some children will become too 'costly' to teach.

CONCLUSION

The current climate of hostility towards asylum seekers, together with restraints on welfare spending make it an inauspicious time to be developing positive policies towards refugee resettlement. With refugee organizations increasingly devoting their energies towards maintaining the basic needs of asylum seekers, welfare services across Europe are being restructured, in order to meet the Maastricht criteria for monetary union. Significant refugee flows to Europe are, however, likely to continue for the foreseeable future, and there is an urgent need to develop appropriate policies which draw on the best practice in planning resettlement. Some form of harmonization – based on standards of living which preserve human rights and dignity – is also necessary to prevent competitive downgrading of conditions between European states (see Levy, Chapter 11 in this volume). While restrictive policies have been pursued by inter governmental bodies and national states, the European Commission and Parliament have attempted to pursue a more positive role in this area (Hoskyns, 1996). Recent political changes in European states, the increasing powers of the European Parliament, and the growing political presence of refugee and migrant groups in Europe open up the possibility of developing more constructive policies at national and European level.

In Britain an adequately funded central and continuing programme is urgently needed to support refugees through the initial phases of resettlement and to ensure that refugees are enabled to make as full a use as possible of their skills and experience. Reliance on voluntary labour, whatever its positive elements, cannot be a substitute for a permanent funded programme. Many local authorities have developed excellent local initiatives, often in conjunction with refugee community groups. This expertise needs to be generalized through the development of more productive relations between national and local authorities, including appropriate financing.

Constructive policies to support refugees and asylum seekers would be in the spirit of the international and European conventions to which European states are signatory. They would also benefit the countries of asylum directly through allowing refugees to contribute to the social and economic life of the country of exile.

NOTES

1. The distinction between refugees and 'economic migrants' is not always clear cut. For example, many Turks left in the 1970s largely for political reasons, but did not claim refugee status. Many women leave home as a result of sexually repressive laws and practices but are not able to claim refugee status (see Tuitt, Chapter 5 in this volume).

2. Information from Hackney Refugee and Migrant Support Group, July 1997.

3. These included Christian Aid, British Council for Aid to Refugees (BCAR), Ockenden Venture and the World University Service.

4. For further discussion of racism in the provision of welfare services see, for example, Williams, 1989; Braham, Rattansi and Skellington, 1992; Solomos, 1993; Miles, 1993.

5. From April 1994, as a result of the termination of the Vietnamese programme, Refugee Action merged with the Refugee Council's Development Unit to provide services to all refugee groups in the UK.

6.   These special statutory sources include the Community programme, the
     Urban Programme, Section 11 Ethnic Minority Grant, European
     Funding and inner city funding initiatives.
7.   These were not comprehensive lists. They contained only the community
     groups of which the Refugee Council and Refugee Action had knowledge.

REFERENCES

Anthias, F. and Yuval-Davis, N. (1992), *Racialized Boundaries*, London,
     Routledge.
Beiser, M. (1993), 'Mental Health of Immigrants in Canada', in Robinson, V.
     (ed.), *The International Refugee Crisis: British and Canadian Responses*,
     Basingstoke, Macmillan.
Braham, P. Rattansi, A and Skellington, R (eds) (1992), *Racism and
     Antiracism: Inequalities, Opportunities, and Policies*, London, Sage.
Bristow, M. (1979), 'Britain's Response to the Ugandan Asian Crisis', *New
     Community*, Vol. 5, pp. 265–79.
Buduk, K. (1996), *Health Needs of Kurdish Refugees in Haringey*, London, New
     River Health Authority.
Buijs, G. (ed.) (1993), *Migrant Women: Crossing Boundaries and Changing
     Identities*, Oxford, Berg.
Calvar, J (1996), *Asylum-Seekers and Refugees in Britain: An Ethnographic
     Approach*, unpublished MSc. dissertation, University of Westminster,
     London.
Carey-Wood, J. (1994), *Meeting Refugees' Needs in Britain: The Role of
     Refugee Specific Initiatives*, London, Unpublished report to the Home
     Office.
Carey-Wood, J., Duke, K., Karn, V., and Marshall, T. (1995), *The Settlement
     of Refugees in Britain*, London, HMSO.
Chung, R.C.Y. and Kagawasinger, M. (1993), 'Predictors of Psychological
     Distress among Southeast-Asian refugees', *Social Science and Medicine*,
     Vol. 36, No. 5, pp. 631–9.
City and Hackney Health Authority (1992), *Health in the City and Hackney*,
     London.
Community Relations Commission (1974), *One Year On: A Report on the
     Resettlement of Refugees from Uganda in Britain*, London, Community
     Relations Commission.
Crawley, H. (1997), *Women as Asylum Seekers: A Legal Handbook*, London,
     Immigration Law Practitioners' Association and Refugee Action.
Dalglish, C. (1989), *Refugees From Vietnam*, Basingstoke, Macmillan.
Duke, K. and Marshall, T. (1995), *Vietnamese Refugees Since 1982*, London,
     HMSO.
Eisenbruch, M. (1991), 'From Post-traumatic Stress Disorder to Cultural
     Bereavement: Diagnosis of Southeast Asian Refugees', *Social Science and
     Medicine*, Vol. 33, No. 6, pp. 673–80.

Esping Anderson, G. (1990), *The Three Worlds of Welfare Capitalism*, Cambridge, Polity.

European Consultation on Refugees and Exiles (1983), *Asylum in Europe: A Handbook for Agencies Assisting Refugees*, 3rd edn, Rotterdam, European Consultation on Refugees and Exiles.

Field, S. (1985), *Resettling Refugees: The Lessons of Research*, London, HMSO.

Forbes Martin, S. (1992), *Refugee Women*, London, Zed Books.

Fuller, K.L. (1993), 'Refugee Mental Health in Aalborg, Denmark: Traumatic Stress and Cross-cultural Treatment Issues', *Nordic Journal of Psychiatry*, Vol. 47, No. 4, pp. 251–6.

Gold, S.J. (1992a), *Refugee Communities: A Comparative Field Study*, California, Sage.

Gold, S.J. (1992b), 'Mental Health and Illness in Vietnamese Refugees', *Western Journal of Medicine*, Vol.157, No. 3, pp. 290–4.

Gregory, J. and Sales, R. (1997), 'Refugee Women in London: The Experience of Somali Women', paper presented to annual conference of *Women's Studies Network*, London, July.

Hale, S. (1993), 'The Reception and Resettlement of Vietnamese Refugees in Britain' in Robinson, V. (ed.), *The International Refugee Crisis: British and Canadian Responses*, Basingstoke, Macmillan.

Hauff, E. and Vaglum, P. (1995), 'Organised Violence and the Stress of Exile: Predictors of Mental Health in a Community Cohort of Vietnamese Refugees 3 Years After Resettlement', *British Journal of Psychiatry*, Vol. 166, pp.360–7.

Home Office (Various Dates), 'Home Office Statistical Bulletin', London, Home Office.

Hoskyns, C. (1996), *Integrating Gender*, London, Verso.

Irish Refugee Council (1997), *Briefing note on reception facilities for newly arrived asylum seekers in Dublin*, Dublin, Irish Refugee Council.

Joly, D. (1996), *Haven or Hell? Asylum Policies and Refugees in Europe*, Basingstoke, Macmillan.

Joly, D. and Cohen, R. (eds) (1989), *Reluctant Hosts: Europe and its Refugees*, Aldershot, Avebury.

Jones, P.R. (1982), *Vietnamese Refugees: A Study of their Reception and Resettlement in the United Kingdom*, Research and Planning Unit Paper 13, London, Home Office.

Kay, D. (1989), 'The Politics of Gender in Exile: Chileans in Glasgow' in Joly, D. and Cohen, R. (eds) *Reluctant Hosts: Europe and its Refugees*, Aldershot, Avebury.

Kaye, D. (1987), *Chileans in Exile: Private Struggles, Public Lives*, Basingstoke, Macmillan.

Kofman, E (1995), 'Citizenship for Some but not for Others', *Political Geography*, Vol. 14, No. 2, pp. 121–38.

Kofman, E. and Sales, R. (1992), 'Towards Fortress Europe?' *Women's Studies International Forum*, Vol. 15, No. 1, pp. 29–39.

Kofman, E. and Sales, R. (1996), 'The Geography of Gender and Welfare in the New Europe', in Garcia Ramon, M. D. and Monk, J. (eds), *South and North: Women's Work and Daily Lives in the European Community*, London, Routledge.

Koser, K. (1996), 'European Migration Report', *New Community*, Vol. 22, No. 1, pp. 151–8.

Levin, M (1981), *What Welcome: Reception and Resettlement of Refugees in Britain*, London, Action Society Trust.

Liebaut F. and Hughes, J. (1997), *Legal and Social Conditions for Asylum Seekers and Refugees in Western European Countries*, Copenhagen, Danish Refugee Council.

London Borough of Waltham Forest (1994), *Survey of Refugee Women*, London, Report from Race Relations and Women's Units.

Marret, V. (1989), *Immigrants Settling in the City*, London, Leicester University Press.

Mghir, R., Freed, W., Raskin, A., and Katon, W. (1995), 'Depression and Post-traumatic Stress Disorder among a Community Sample of Adolescent and Young Adult Afghan Refugees', *Journal of Nervous and Mental Disease*, Vol. 183, No. 1, pp. 24–30.

Milos, R. (1993), *Race After Race Relations*, London, Sage.

Newham Refugee Centre (1996), *Refugees, Torture and the Health Services*, London.

Noh, S., Speechley, M., Kaspar, V. and Wn, Z. (1992), 'Depression in Korean Immigrants in Canada: Method of the Study and Prevalence of Depression', *Journal of Nervous and Mental Disease*, Vol. 180, No. 9, pp. 573–7.

Owers, A. (1994), 'The Age of Internal Controls?', in Spencer, S. (ed.), *Strangers and Citizens: A Positive Approach to Migrants and Refugees*, London, Rivers Oram Press, pp. 264–81.

Rathzel, N. (1991), 'Germany: One Race, One Nation?, *Race and Class*, Vol. 32, No. 3, pp. 31–48.

Refugee Council (Undated), *Refugee and Training: A Positive Policy for the 1990s*, London, Refugee Council.

Refugee Council (1994), *Increase in Refusals since the Asylum Act*, London, Refugee Council, November.

Refugee Council (1995a), *Homelessness and Asylum*, London, Refugee Council.

Refugee Council (1995b), *Briefing for MPs on Second Reading of Asylum and Immigration Bill*, London, Refugee Council.

Refugee Council (1996), *Women Refugees*, London, Refugee Council.

Robinson, V. (ed.) (1993), *The International Refugee Crisis: British and Canadian Responses*, Basingstoke, Macmillan.

Robinson, V. and Hale, S. (1989), *The Geography of Vietnamese Secondary Migration in the UK*, Research Paper 10, Warwick, Centre for Research in Ethnic Relations.

Robles, M.J.S. (1989), 'Refugees from South-East Asia in Spain – The Challenge of Hope' in Joly, D. and Cohen, R. (eds), *Reluctant Hosts: Europe and its Refugees*, Aldershot, Avebury.

Rogg, E.M. (1974), 'The Influence of a Strong Refugee Community on the Economic Adjustment of its Members', *International Migration Review*, Vol. 5, pp. 474–81.

Sales, R. and Gregory, J. (1996), 'Citizenship and European Integration: The Implications for Ethnic Minority Women', *Social Politics*, Vol. 3, Nos. 2/3, pp. 331–50.

Salt, J., Singleton, A. and Hogarth, J. (1994), *Europe's International Migrants: Data Sources, Patterns and Trends*, London, HMSO.

Schwarzer, R., Jerusalem, M. and Hahn, A. (1994), 'Unemployment, Social Support and Health Complaints: A Longitudinal Study of Stress in East-German Refugees', *Journal of Community and Applied Social Psychology*, Vol. 4, No. 1, pp. 31–45.

Silove, D., Tarn, R., Bowles, R., and Reid, J. (1991), 'Psychosocial Needs of Torture Survivors', *Australian and New Zealand Journal of Psychiatry*, Vol. 25, No. 4, pp. 481–90.

Solomos, J. (1993), *Race and Racism in Britain*, Basingstoke, Macmillan.

Soysal, Y.N. (1994), *Limits of Citizenship: Migrants and Postnational Membership in Europe*, Chicago, University of Chicago Press.

Stein, B.N. (1979), 'Occupational Adjustment of Refugees: The Vietnamese in the United States', *International Migration Review*, Vol, 2, No. 1, pp. 25–45.

Stephenson, P.H. (1995), 'Vietnamese refugees in Victoria, BC: An Overview of Immigrant and Health-care in a Medium-sized Canadian Urban Center', *Social Science and Medicine*, Vol. 40, No. 12, pp. 1631–42.

Summerfield, H. (1993), 'Patterns of Adaptation; Somali and Bangladeshi Women in Britain', in Buijs, G. (ed.) *Migrant Women: Crossing Boundaries and Changing Identities*, Oxford, Berg.

Williams, F. (1989), *Social Policy, A Critical Introduction: Issues of Race, Gender and Class*, Cambridge, Polity.

7 Asylum seekers and access to social security: recent developments in The Netherlands, United Kingdom, Germany and Belgium

Paul E. Minderhoud

INTRODUCTION

The regulation of migration, especially of asylum seekers, has become high on the political and policy agenda of Western European countries in recent years. There are many reasons for this which include: the expansion of migration flows initiated by several social, economic and political events; the problems of unemployment and the limited capacity of the various labour markets to absorb immigrants; the issue of inclusion and exclusion of social services in a period which has seen the curtailment of the welfare state and increasing feelings of nationalism and expressions of xenophobia. As a result, the national migration policies in Western Europe have become increasingly restrictive over the last few years (Engbersen *et al.*, 1995: 14). Except for the period just before and after World War II, the legislative activity on immigration has not been so intense in Western Europe as it was in the early 1990s. Never has there been such a consistent approach to revising the regulations and never before have the restrictions been so severe (Marie, 1995: 51).

This chapter will focus on the recent developments concerning the access to social security benefits for refugees and asylum seekers in The Netherlands, the United Kingdom, Germany and Belgium. Although the various social security schemes are not the same, useful comparisons can be made and policy trends can be identified. While recognized refugees have the same rights to social security as native citizens, the situation of asylum seekers or '*de facto*' refugees and displaced persons, who have a temporary protection status, is very different. In this chapter the term 'social security benefits' will be used in general for all contributory and non-contributory benefits. The term 'national assistance benefit' will be used for welfare entitlements, like national assistance in The Netherlands, income support in the United Kingdom, '*Sozialhilfe*' in Germany and social assistance in Belgium.

THE NETHERLANDS: INCREASING EMPHASIS ON EXCLUSION AND ENFORCEMENT

Over the past ten years the Dutch reception policy for asylum seekers has been reformed a great deal. Reception policy has been influenced by a more restrictive admission policy. Until 1985 there was no special regulation on the reception of asylum seekers in The Netherlands. Pending the decision on their request, asylum seekers were lodged in private accommodation such as boarding houses. After registration at the Alien Police, they were entitled to apply for a National Assistance benefit. An increase in the number of asylum seekers, a deteriorating housing situation and an increase in the (social security) costs for a few large cities such as Amsterdam and The Hague, led to action by the central government when large groups of Tamils arrived in The Netherlands in 1985 (Muus, 1996: 38). A special regulation was introduced for this group of asylum seekers. The Tamils were lodged in government-financed boarding houses, receiving food, clothes and a small amount of pocket money. Because of its restrictive character this special regulation quickly became known as the 'Bed, Bath and Bread regulation'.

Modelled on this special regulation for Tamils in 1987 a general reception policy for asylum seekers was introduced by the government and included in the new Regulation on the Reception of Asylum Seekers (ROA, *Regeling Opvang Asielzoekers*). The government officially qualified this regulation as austere but humane. The introduction of this regulation meant that asylum seekers were no longer eligible to apply for a National Assistance benefit.

The contents of the benefits and services, available to asylum seekers, under this new ROA regulation depended on whether or not the asylum seeker was housed in a central accommodation centre or in a decentralized housing facility in a municipality (Puts, 1995: 36). Asylum seekers who were placed in a collective accommodation centre received benefits in kind, pocket money of £7 a week and clothing money of £20 a month. They were also insured for health care. Asylum seekers who stayed in a housing facility of a municipality, while waiting for the decision on their refugee status, received a modest allowance of £150 a month in cash and were also insured for health care. The municipalities were granted government funds for the accommodation of these asylum seekers, for furnishing their homes and for social and cultural activities.

In 1994 a new temporary protection status was introduced, called conditional residence permit. This status was meant for displaced persons (mostly ex-Yugoslavs) and persons who did not get refugee status but could not be expelled on policy grounds. For the reception of these persons a special Act was introduced. Persons with a conditional residence permit are accommodated as soon as possible in decentralized housing facilities in the municipalities and also receive only the same modest allowance of £150 a month. They are excluded from the regular National Assistance benefit system as well. After three years this status may not be prolonged any more and has to be changed to an unconditional residence permit on humanitarian grounds, in case return to the country of origin is still impossible (Muus, 1995: 44).

Since January 1996, newly arrived asylum seekers are no longer eligible for decentralized housing facilities in the municipalities. During their application procedure they have to stay in accommodation centres. Recent figures show that some asylum seekers wait in these centres, for a decision on their application, for as long as two years (*Volkskrant*, 16 May 1997).

Benefit entitlement under the Dutch social security benefits is related to employment and/or residency status. Asylum seekers have no access to the labour market while persons with the new conditional residence permit are allowed to work, without a labour permit, once they are in the third year of their stay. In general, asylum seekers and persons with a conditional residence permit are not seen as full 'residents'. This means that *de facto* these categories have not got any access to social security benefits during their first years in the country. Asylum seekers, persons with a conditional residence permit, as well as illegal aliens are explicitly excluded from a right to National Assistance benefits. Once asylum seekers have either refugee status or an unconditional residence status, they have the same entitlement to social security benefits as Dutch nationals.

Current problems on the expulsion of rejected asylum seekers

A current problem occurring in The Netherlands concerns the expulsion of rejected asylum seekers. Recently, a few municipalities have refused to either evict from their homes or stop the ROA benefit of asylum seekers whose cases have been rejected. The argument for this refusal is that these asylum seekers will not be expelled effectively to their country of origin and will therefore probably disappear in illegality.

A legal tension has occurred between the government and some municipalities. The government and parliament took the view that the municipalities must evict asylum seekers who have had their cases rejected. However, running concurrently to the government view was a legal judgment made by the court which stated that the municipality in that case was not allowed to proceed to eviction. The judge stated that eviction would lead to inequality in the law, because several other municipalities refused to evict rejected asylum seekers from their houses. According to the Union of Dutch Municipalities this judicial review created a deadlock for municipalities (*Binnenlands Bestuur*, 7 March 1997). This situation concerns a group of approximately 8000 persons. The State Secretary of Justice then announced that so-called mobile assistance teams would be deployed to help municipalities with the eviction of houses and stopping of the ROA benefits. An exception was made for families with children (*Trouw*, 27 March 1997).

Increasing emphasis on exclusion and enforcement

In general, a change in Dutch immigration policy can be noticed, emphasizing the use of restriction of access of immigrants to several public services as a policy instrument. In mid-1998 a Dutch Act will be implemented which will make the entitlement to a whole range of public services, including all social security benefits for aliens, conditional on their residence status. Only legal aid, emergency health care and education until the age of 18 years remain accessible to all immigrants, including illegal immigrants.

In recent years there has been a development in Dutch social security policy which emphasizes enforcement. 'Pursuit of enforcement' has become a leading term, frequently used by the government to defend the introduction of new measures in this area. In the context of this pursuit of enforcement policy, a few measures can be mentioned that will affect asylum seekers and refugees in particular.

In 1996 some far-reaching measures were introduced to check all the data of persons who claim child benefits for children who live abroad. For instance, all parents who have children living abroad have to identify themselves, in person, at the administration agencies concerned every three months. This rule applies also for Dutch citizens and for citizens of the European Union, but will affect particularly citizens from outside the European Union, which includes many refugees. Moreover, strict requirements on the legalization and verification of official records, like marriage and birth certificates, were also introduced and which some refugees are not able to fulfil.

Another recent proposal made by the government concerns the restrictions on the current export possibilities of social security benefits (Tweede Kamer (TK) 1995–1996, 17050, nr 199). In the Dutch social security system, the current principle of personality will be replaced by the principle of territoriality. According to this proposal the export of benefits will only be possible to countries with which a social security treaty is concluded and in which sufficient guarantees are given for enforcement. This means that there will be little change on the export possibilities of social security benefits for citizens from, for instance, the European Union. But for refugees who come from countries that (almost) never have concluded such a treaty, this will mean that they will lose their benefit if they return to their home country.

In summary, there is a tendency to limit the access to social security benefits to persons who stay in The Netherlands on a permanent basis.

UNITED KINGDOM: DISTINCTION BETWEEN 'AT-PORT' AND 'IN-COUNTRY' APPLICANTS

Recognized refugees are treated like British citizens and have the same rights to welfare benefits and employment as any other British citizen. The situation for asylum seekers is very different. There are no accommodation centres for asylum seekers and no reception and resettlement programmes. Prior to 1996, asylum seekers were entitled to 90 per cent of the means tested benefit income support. However, in February 1996, a new regulation came into force which ruled that asylum seekers who did not seek asylum at the port of entry immediately on arrival in the UK would no longer be entitled to social security benefits. Moreover, asylum seekers who were appealing against a Home Office decision on their case would no longer be entitled to social security during the appeals process. The then Social Security Secretary, Peter Lilley, defended the changes by arguing that:

> Seventy per cent of those who claim asylum do not arrive as refugees but come to the UK as visitors, tourists or on the understanding they will maintain themselves and will not have access to benefits. If they subsequently claim asylum, that not only prolongs their stay but also gives the right to claim benefits, at the taxpayer's expense. The number of asylum claims has escalated, partly because of the availability of benefits. The proportion of applicants found to have a valid claim to refugee status has fallen from 32 per cent to 4 per cent between 1984 and 1994. (Department of Social Security Press Release, 3 December 95).

The government used a comparison of the refusal rates of in-country (80 per cent) and port (70 per cent) applications as part of their justification for denying benefits to the former group and as evidence that their claims were less credible. According to Feria (1996: 93) the real reason is that those who claim at ports are easier to remove than those who claim subsequently within the country. The British Refugee Council (1996: 5) indicated that there are clearly many reasons why asylum seekers might not make their applications as soon as they set foot in the UK. They may be scared and ignorant of the procedures. Arriving in a confused and frightened state, language difficulties or fear of officialdom may all be insuperable barriers to making any kind of approach to the authorities at the port of entry.

The proposals for this new regulation provoked a lot of very indignant reactions of church organizations and various pressure groups concerned with the rights of refugees and other migrants. They argued that these changes would force asylum seekers into poverty and homelessness and would effectively remove their right to legal appeal. According to Carter,

> The immediate impact of benefit withdrawal has been to cause intense hardship. Many people are moving between friends, relatives, casual acquaintances, church groups, community organizations, voluntary advice agencies and statutory authorities in a desperate attempt to secure food, clothing and shelter (1996: 15).

This situation was intensified by the fact that asylum seekers are not allowed to apply for a work permit until they have been living in the UK for six months. Furthermore, the process of obtaining a work permit can take more than six months which means that asylum seekers have no leglitimate access to money during the early part of their stay.

On 21 June 1996, the Court of Appeal ruled that the government had acted illegally when it introduced social security regulations which stripped welfare benefits from people who had applied for asylum within Britain, or who were appealing against the refusal of their application (*NLJ Practitioner*, 5 July 1996: 985). The right to these benefits had to be reinstated. A few days later, though, the Social Security Secretary announced that the government would use the new Asylum and Immigration Bill, that was pending in Parliament at that moment, as a vehicle to reintroduce the welfare cuts.

A report, *The Tablet*, produced by Social and Pastoral Action, showed the impact of the withdrawal of benefits on asylum seekers in just a few months. It was estimated that the benefit cuts had, since their introduction in February, affected more than 13 000 people. According to the report:

> the loss of benefits leaves thousands of asylum seekers both destitute and homeless without any income to meet their basic subsistence needs, or access to housing. Having fled situations of violence or persecution, many asylum seekers arrive in the UK with literally no belongings or money. Many people are struggling to feed and clothe themselves on a day-to-day basis.

In July 1996 a new Asylum and Immigration Act came into force. The changes of this Act included the restriction of the rights of appeal for rejected asylum seekers and the penalization through fines of employers who employ people without the correct documentation. It is expected that this will have a large impact on the willingness of employers to hire asylum seekers, a group with already disproportionally high levels of unemployment (see Bloch, Chapter 10). The Act also introduced new immigration offences for those involved in assisting illegal immigrants and asylum applicants to enter the UK (Harvey, 1996: 187). The government used this Act to introduce an amendment (new clause 11) to remove entitlement to benefits from:

- any asylum seeker who applies for refugee status in-country regardless of whether they have a well-founded fear of persecution or not;
- any asylum seeker who exercises their right of appeal against a refusal of refugee status.

The government had to overturn a House of Lords' defeat to its plans to curb asylum seekers' rights. MPs voted by 295 to 274 to throw out a Lords' amendment to the Asylum and Immigration Act which gave asylum seekers an extra three days in which they could apply for refugee status. Asylum seekers now have to apply immediately on arrival in Britain if they want to secure benefits. This move will save the Treasury an estimated £80 million a year (*The Times*, 16 July 1996; *Migration News*, September 1996).

Problems are shifted to the local authorities

From August 1996, homeless asylum seekers lost their entitlement to local authority housing under the homelessness legislation (Refugee Council, Update on the social security regulations, September 1996). However, in October 1996, the situation changed when the High Court ruled that local authorities had a duty under the 1948 National Assistance Act to provide services such as shelter, warmth and food to asylum seekers with no other means of support. In his closing remarks the judge stated:

> I do not regard this conclusion as in any way frustrating the will of Parliament in enacting the 1996 Act. I find it impossible to believe that Parliament intended that an asylum seeker, who was lawfully here and who could not lawfully be removed from the country, should be left destitute, starving and at risk of grave illness and even death because he could find no-one to provide him with the bare necessities of life. But if Parliament really did intend that in no circumstances should any assistance (other than hospital care) be available to those asylum seekers, it must say so in terms. If it did, it would almost certainly put itself in breach of the European Convention on Human Rights and of the Geneva Convention.

This judgment meant that local authorities had to make payments for accommodation and food to destitute asylum seekers. The Association of Directors of Social Services (ADSS) warned that some directors might have to consider closing residential care homes and halting discharges of elderly people from hospitals if they had to cover the costs involved for asylum seekers (Refugee Council Update, October 1996). The housing chairman of Westminster Council said that the number of asylum seekers asking for help had grown daily since the High Court ruling of October. He is quoted as saying:

> We had only eight asylum seekers then but now there are well in excess of 1000 and it is costing us more than £50 000 a week to look

after them. They are using 65 per cent of all the temporary accomodation we have. (*The Times*, 14 February 1997).

On 17 February 1997 the Court of Appeal ruled that asylum seekers who are disallowed state benefits must still be given food and shelter by local authorities. With this judgment the Court dismissed an appeal by the London boroughs of Westminster, Lambeth, Hammersmith and Fulham against the High Court decision of 8 October 1996. Among the asylum seekers who brought the case was a Romanian who arrived aboard a lorry in July 1996, had slept rough under Waterloo Bridge and had nowhere to live, no money and spoke no English and an Algerian who also arrived in July 1996 and slept rough in Hyde Park. In their judgment, the judges stated: 'The plight of asylum seekers who are in the position of the respondents obviously can and should provoke deep sympathy. Their plight is indeed horrendous' (*The Times*, 18 February 1997).

The judgment marks the temporary end of the juridical struggle on this subject. However, judicial review proceedings offer only a supervisory role and the courts can do little when confronted with a determined government (Harvey, 1997: 72). It remains to be seen what the policy of the new Labour government on this important issue will be.

GERMANY: EXTENSION OF THE BENEFIT IN KIND SYSTEM

Germany has received more refugees than any other country in West Europe. More than 300 000 recognized refugees, together with 130 000 family members, currently live in Germany. In addition, the country shelters about 350 000 asylum seekers and a group of 500 000 so-called '*de facto*' refugees, most of them rejected asylum seekers who are allowed to stay in Germany on legal and humanitarian grounds. Furthermore, up to 320 000 Bosnian refugees were until recently permitted to stay in Germany on a temporary basis (UNHCR figures, 1997). The support of all these refugees and asylum seekers has placed a considerable burden on the German economy, especially in the light of the German reunification.

With the aim of reducing the number of asylum applications, new asylum legislation came into force on 1 July 1993. The legislation established a list of so-called 'safe third countries', which included all immediate neighbours of Germany, and a list of so-called 'safe countries of origin'. This legislation made it possible to return asylum seekers who transit safe third countries back to those countries immediately. Related to this new asylum legislation, in November 1993 the legislation on National Assistance benefits for asylum seekers was changed. The insurance of subsistence for asylum seekers was taken out of the federal National Assistance Act (*Bundessozialhilfegesetz*) and regulated in a newly created, so-called Asylum Seekers Benefits Act (*Asylbewerberleistungsgesetz*). Under this new Act asylum seekers are only entitled to welfare benefits 'in kind' rather than cash payments during the first year of their stay. In addition to accommodation, asylum seekers receive a food parcel every week, some clothing and £30 a month for personal requirements. Only in extraordinary situations a benefit in money is possible, but the amount of this benefit is 20 per cent lower than the level of a National Assistance benefit paid to other members of the community. For asylum seekers, who have not been given a final decision on their application within 12 months, access to the regular benefits of the National Assistance Act becomes available. Medical and dental treatment for asylum seekers is only available in cases of acute illness or pain.

The federal government states, in its 1995 annual report, that the introduction of this special Asylum Seekers Benefit Act was a necessary and a practical instrument to guarantee sufficient care for asylum seekers. According to the government, the reduction of the benefits has led to a reduction in the number of people seeking asylum in Germany (Broschüren 'Online': Jahresbericht der Bundesregierung, 1995).

At the end of 1995, the federal government announced the intention to extend the scope of the Asylum Seekers Benefit Act to all aliens whose stay is only temporary in Germany. Another proposal was to leave asylum seekers, who waited for more than 12 months for a decision, under the regime of the Asylum Seekers Benefit Act. One of the coalition parties of the government, the Christian Social Union (CSU), went so far as to call for cuts in the payments to Bosnian refugees and asylum seekers in Germany, in January 1996, in order to safeguard the German economy. Asylum seekers and Bosnian refugees in Germany are estimated to cost the state and local governments between £6 billion and £8 billion per year (*Migration News*, February 1996).

The government's proposals to change the Asylum Seekers Benefit Act were rejected in May 1996 by the Bundesrat (that is, the German Upper House), which is dominated by a majority of the Social Democratic Party. Therefore the intended savings of £0.5 billion for

1996 did not materialize (*Die Welt*, 25 May 1996). After much debate an agreement was reached between government parties and the Social Democratic Party, in April 1997, to extend the scope of the Asylum Seekers Benefit Act to civil war refugees (Bosnians) and asylum seekers for the first three years of their stay in Germany. During the first three years, civil war refugees and asylum seekers will receive only benefits in kind. The discussion on this subject was strongly influenced by the fact that the German economy was not growing and there was a concern that Germany could not meet the criteria of the Maastricht Treaty for joining the European Monetary Union (*Berliner Zeitung*, 17 April 1997).

As in the United Kingdom, recognized refugees (*Flüchtlinge und Asylberechtigte*) have the same access to German social security benefits, including the National Assistance benefits (*Sozialhilfe*) as German citizens (Eichenhofer, 1996: 68). They have full access to the labour market, while this access is limited for asylum seekers.

Different reactions and practical problems

The introduction of the Asylum Seekers Benefits Act has led to very different reactions and several practical problems at local government level. Among some municipalities, mostly under a Social Democratic Party and/or Green Party local authority there was great resistance to this new Act. They refused to provide benefits in kind and gave asylum seekers their benefit in cash, because they held the opinion that a provision in kind would be unworthy. Some other municipalities as well as some German states (*Länder*), like Bavaria and Baden-Württemberg, immediately applied the Act and extended it to other categories of refugees such as asylum seekers who had already been in Germany for a year and *de facto* refugees who were housed in collective accommodation centres and were not included in the Act (Scholl and Schieffer, 1994: 132). This practice has led to several lawsuits, in which it was decided that this extension of the persons covered in general is unlawful (Evangelische Kirche Deutschland, 1995).

The new Act was severely criticized by various organizations, among them the churches. A church leader remarked that this new Act would reinforce the social exclusion of asylum seekers (Evangelische Kirche Deutschland, 1995). An accidental effect of this law was that the access to legal aid for asylum seekers diminished, because they did not have any money to contribute in the costs of an attorney to assail a negative decision on their asylum application. By this, the Act contributes to a further restriction of the legal protection of asylum seekers.

BELGIUM: A NEWLY STRUCTURED ASYLUM PROCEDURE

In the beginning of 1997 the reception procedure for asylum seekers in Belgium was changed in an attempt to give more structure to the asylum procedure. The reception of candidate refugees, as asylum seekers are called in Belgium, is now similar to the Dutch system. The current application procedure in Belgium is divided into two phases. After entering the country candidate refugees are first placed in a reception centre where they are provided with benefits in kind, similar to the Dutch regulation described above. Within three to four months a decision is made about their eligibility to proceed to the second stage of the asylum procedure. Candidate refugees, who are admitted to that second phase – which happens only in 30 per cent of the first applications – are housed in a municipality, assigned by the central government. Then they become entitled to a kind of benefit in cash, called social services. The assigned municipality is responsible for the payment of the benefits, but it can claim the money back from the central government. Before 1997 the situation was less clear. Candidate refugees were free, at least on paper, to choose their place of residence. Some of them stayed in regional reception centres, managed by the Belgian Red Cross, some of them received no assistance and were not accommodated in a reception centre and the largest group stayed in a municipality (Ramakers, 1997: 111).

In Belgium the right to contributory social security benefits is related to employment. Entitlement to non-contributory benefits is in principle only reserved for Belgian citizens. This entitlement is extended to several other nationals as a result of international treaties (Jorens, 1995: 442). As in The Netherlands, Britain and Germany, in Belgium the position of recognized refugees concerning the access to the social security system differs strongly from the position of candidate refugees (Poppe, 1996: 43). Recognized refugees can make a direct appeal to the Geneva Convention and can, based on Articles 17 and 24 of the treaty, command the same rights as Belgian citizens with regard to both contributory and non-contributory benefits. Moreover, recognized refugees have full access to the Belgian labour market.

Candidate refugees do not have the possibility of a direct appeal to the Geneva Convention, because it is not yet decided whether they fulfill the definition of 'refugee'. When they are declared admissible to the asylum procedure, they have a so-called 'provisional' access to the labour market. If they have a job they are, in principle, entitled to all contributory social security benefits such as child benefit and disability benefits. Special problems occur, however, in the case of unemployment benefits. The government department, which is responsible for the provision of unemployment benefits, refuses systematically to pay these benefits to candidate refugees. In order to be eligible for unemployment benefit, one has to have worked for a certain period of time. If this period of time is built up by a candidate refugee, it is only taken into account, when he/she has become a recognized refugee and not when he/she is still a candidate refugee when they become unemployed. According to Poppe (1996: 36) the Belgian jurisprudence is divided on the legitimacy of this issue. Candidate refugees who are employed have to wait for half a year and candidate refugees who are not employed have to wait for a year before they can appeal to the Belgian Health Care Insurance (OCIV, 1997: 95).

Candidate refugees have no right to the non-contributory national assistance benefits, called social assistance. They are, however, as already mentioned, entitled to a benefit, called social services. This entitlement is legally based on Article 1 of the Act on Public Centre for Social Services.

> Every person has the right to social services. It is the goal to enable everyone to lead a life which meets with the requirements of human dignity (Poppe, 1996: 40).

Based on jurisprudence the amount of social services is at subsistence level, which is increased with a sum of money replacing family allowances and with money for the subscription fee to join the Health Care Insurance. These social services are implemented by the local Public Centre for Social Services. In the past some of these Public Centres systematically paid a lower amount of money to candidate refugees than was indicated by the jurisprudence. This attitude is formally allowed because of the legal autonomy of these local centres but is in general not accepted by the Belgian jurisprudence (Adriaens, 1996: 210).

In recent years some Belgian municipalities have refused to accept and help newly arriving asylum seekers and refugees arguing that they had taken in enough candidate refugees already. In order to help alleviate this problem, the federal government introduced a new reception scheme, which distributes candidate refugees over the various municipalities. To make this distribution policy more effective candidate refugees are only entitled to a benefit, paid by the Public Centre for Social Services, of the town they are assigned to. Although candidate refugees are formally still free to settle where they want, that freedom is cramped in practice by this new distribution policy.

Since 1992 the Public Centres for Social Services are not allowed to provide any assistance to illegal aliens, including to finally rejected asylum seekers, who have received a definite order to leave the country. An exception is made for the assistance, strictly necessary to allow the person in question to leave Belgian territory. This assistance has to end at the latest a month from the day the order to leave Belgium was issued (Stokx, 1996: 55). As in other countries in Western Europe the duty to provide assistance has over the last few years been made subsidiary to a more restrictive asylum policy.

USING ACCESS TO SOCIAL SECURITY AS AN INSTRUMENT OF ASYLUM POLICY

In general, governments use three different kinds of legal instruments to regulate migration. The first type of instrument are concerned with the right to stay in a country. These types of instruments regulate the right of entrance and stay, as well as the forced expulsion of immigrants. These instruments contain measures such as visa requirements, pre-flight checks, border control, internal police checks, detention and the issuing of some kind of residence permit. The second kind of instruments are concerned with the inclusion and exclusion of certain categories of immigrants from access to the labour market or to services of the welfare state. The third type of instruments consist of the creation of special facilities, offered by the government, to make the entrance or the departure of immigrants more attractive, for instance, housing facilities, tax facilities, affirmative action, education, and on the other hand, emigration facilities and premiums on departure (Groenendijk and Minderhoud, 1992).

Although governments still use the instruments of the first type extensively, several developments make the use of this type of instrument less attractive and more difficult. Due to the globalization of the trade in goods and services, for instance, large international companies and multinationals have gained more power to decide which economic activity is conducted in what country. International cooperation in Europe has greatly diminished the significance of national borders and nationality (Sassen, 1996: 17). Because of the internally divided political opinions on the treatment of immigrants, the use of methods of coercion like detention and deportation on a large scale is not attractive. In the past few years different governments have been making more and more use of the second type of legal instruments, such as limiting the access of different categories of immigrants to various public services.

Developments on the access of asylum seekers to benefits described in this chapter, reflects this current trend in immigration policy. In all four countries there is a tendency to keep asylum seekers out of the regular social security system and to reduce their welfare entitlements. The main reason for these measures is to discourage people to seek refuge. However, this reason is almost never mentioned explicitly by the government. In the various countries the government defends the necessity for these measures out of financial reasons or as a means to enable a clearer distinction between 'genuine' and 'bogus' refugees.

There are a number of similarities in the way that countries receive asylum seekers which have been identified. First, asylum seekers are a relatively easy target for the introduction of these measures because they receive little popular support and solidarity from the populations of the asylum countries. This is especially the case in times of economic recession and in situations where there are large flows of asylum seekers. Secondly, there is the position taken by the judiciary. In all the countries described in this chapter, government policy on this issue is corrected by judicial review. Judges act as guardians of certain basic values. Thirdly, due to the restrictive policy of the central governments of these countries some of the main problems are shifted to the local authorities. In several situations, it is the local government that has to feed and shelter the asylum seekers, that is confronted with the limits of the expulsion system or that has to deal with the tensions arising at the arrival of asylum seekers in the local community.

The use of access to social security as an instrument of immigration policy can be explained as a result of the tension between immigration control and human rights. Currently, it appears that liberal democracies are not able to control and regulate immigration and refugees flows in an effective way without violating the basic principles of human rights (Calavita, 1995). It may be that controlling the movement of the economically destitute and politically persecuted requires measures antithetical to basic constitutional and human rights. Therefore, governments choose the limitation of access to social security benefits as an instrument. The current attempts, seen primarily in the United Kingdom and Germany, to restrict the welfare entitlements of asylum applicants, raises the fundamental question as to whether some basic values of society are endangered. The danger exists that through this development the balance between respecting basic human rights and effectively excluding asylum seekers is weighted too much at the expense of basic rights.

In this context it should be noted that in March 1997 the European Commission drafted a proposal to establish minimum standards in areas such as housing, social welfare and employment rights for displaced persons in the 15 EU member states (COM(97) def. 97/0081 CNS). This plan was drafted to respond to future cases such as the Bosnians. Many EU member states gave some form of temporary protection to Bosnians, but the absence of an EU agreement meant that most of the Bosnians were sheltered in Germany and that Bosnians faced quite different regulations in the different EU states. The proposal of the European Commission aimed to establish minimum rights on access to the labour market, education, social welfare, housing and conditions for family reunification (*Migration News*, April 1997).

REFERENCES

Adriaens, D. (1996), 'Het OCMW en de vreemdelingen: Nood breekt wet'?, in Foblets, M.C., Hubeau, B. and Talhaoui, F. (eds), *Migratie-en Migrantenrecht: Recente ontwikkelingen II*, Brugge, Die Keure.

Broschüren 'Online': Jahresbericht des Bundesregierung, Bonn, 1995.

Calavita, K. (1995), 'US Immigration Policy: Contradictions, Myths and Backlash', paper presented at the workshop *Regulation of Migration*, University of Nijmegen, 14–15 December.

Carter, M. (1996), *Poverty and Prejudice: A Preliminary Report on the Withdrawal of Benefit Entitlement and the Impact of the Asylum and Immigration Bill*, London, Refugee Council and Commission for Racial Equality.

Eichenhofer, E. (1996), 'Die sozialrechtliche Stellung von Ausländern aus Nicht-EWR- und Nicht-Abkommensstaaten', in *Zeitschrift für Ausländerrecht und Ausländerpolitik*, pp. 62–70.

Elderman, E. (1997), *Oriëntatie in het vluchtelingenrecht*, Utrecht, Nederlands Centrum Buitenlanders.

Engbersen, G., van der Leun, J. and Willems, P. (1995), *Over de verwevenheid van Illegaliteit en Criminaliteit*, Utrecht, Onderzoekschool AWSB.

Evangelische Kirche Deutschland (1995), *Asylsuchende und Flüchtelinge: Zweiter Bericht zur Praxis des Asylverfahrens und des Schutzes vor Abschiebung*, Hannover.

Feria, M. (1996), Commentaries on the Social Security (Persons from Abroad) (Miscellaneous 1996 Amendments) Regulations 1996, *Immigration and Nationality Law and Practice*, Vol. 10. No. 3, pp. 91–100.

148   *Refugees, Citizenship and Social Policy in Europe*

Groenendijk, C.A. and Minderhoud, P.E. (1992), 'Sturing van migratie in Nederland en Europa na 1992: Effecten en dilemma's' in *Migratie, Arbeidsmarkt en Sociale Zekerheid*, SER-rapport, Den Haag.

Harvey, C. (1996), 'The United Kingdom's New Asylum and Immigration Bill', *International Journal of Refugee Law*, Vol. 8, No. 1/2, pp. 184–7.

Harvey, C. (1997), 'Restructuring Asylum: Recent Trends in United Kingdom Asylum Law and Policy', *International Journal of Refugee Law*, Vol. 9, No. 1, pp. 60–73.

Jorens, Y. (1995), 'De rechtspositie van vreemdelingen in het Belgische sociale zekerheidsrecht', in Feyter, K. de, Foblets, M.C. and Hubeau, B. (eds), *Migratie- en Migrantenrecht: Recente ontwikkelingen*, Brugge, Die Keure.

Marie, C.V. (1995), *The EC Member States and Immigration in 1993: Closed Borders, Stringent Attitudes*, Luxembourg, Office for Official Publications of the European Commission.

Muus, Ph.J. (1996), *Migration, Immigrants and Policy in The Netherlands*, SOPEMI-report Netherlands 1995, Amsterdam: University of Amsterdam.

OCIV (Overlegcentrum voor Integratie van Vluchtelingen), (1997), *Vluchtelingenonthaal in de Praktijk: Juridische wegwijzer*, Brussels, OCIV.

Poppe, I. (1996), 'De sociale zekerheid en de (kandidaat) vluchteling', in Instituut voor Sociaal Recht (ed.), *Vreemdelingen en Sociale Zekerheid*, Gent, Mys & Breesch.

Puts, J.H.L. (1995), *Asielzoekers Tussen Rijk en Gemeenten: Onderhandelingen over de huisvesting van migranten*, Den Haag, VNG-uitgeverij.

Ramakers, J. (1997), 'The Challenges of Refugee Protection in Belgium', in Muus, Ph.J. (ed.), *Exclusion and Inclusion of Refugees in Contemporary Europe*, Utrecht, ERCOMER.

Refugee Council (1996), *Welcome to the UK: The Impact of the Removal of Benefits from Asylum Seekers*, London, Refugee Council.

Sassen, S. (1996), *Transnational Economies and National Migration Policies*, Instituut voor Migratie en Etnische Studies IMES-publication, Amsterdam, University of Amsterdam.

Scholl, H. and Schieffer, M. (1994), 'Überlegungen zu einer Novellierung des Asylbewerberleistungsgesetzes', in *Zeitschrift für Ausländerrecht und Ausländerpolitik*, pp. 131–6.

Stokx, R. (1996), 'De sociale zekerheid en de illegaal', in Instituut voor Sociaal Recht (ed.), *Vreemdelingen en Sociale Zekerheid*, Gent, Mys and Breesch.

8 Unaccompanied refugee children: legal framework and local application in Britain[1]

Louise Williamson

In response to various political upheavals, wars and disasters this century, many thousands of unaccompanied refugee children have been resettled in Britain (Ressler *et al.*, 1988; Williamson, 1995). Some children (or members of their families) have been politically active and risk persecution; others are sent abroad by their families in order to avoid military conscription, bombardment or civil unrest (Ayotte and Lown, 1992). Such children usually arrive in this country quite independently of any organized scheme, either completely alone or with adult travelling companions. They may then apply for asylum at the port of entry when they pass through Immigration or after they have entered the country. The Home Office recorded 404 such applications in 1994, 585 in 1995 and (provisionally) 606 in 1996, with children coming from over 50 countries.

Somewhat surprisingly, perhaps, little attention is given to this vulnerable group of refugees. There is growing recognition that the majority of the world's refugees and displaced people, estimated at perhaps 35–40 million, are women and children, at least half of the total being children. It is less well known that between 3–5 per cent of these – in other words, hundreds of thousands in any refugee movement – are unaccompanied refugee children (Williamson and Moser, 1987: 9). The term 'unaccompanied refugee child' encompasses the following definitions: 'Unaccompanied' relates to

> those who are separated from both parents and are not being cared for by an adult who, by law or custom, has responsibility to do so (UNHCR, 1994: 121).

149

According to the 1989 UN Convention on the Rights of the Child (CRC), a 'child' is: 'every human being below the age of eighteen years...' (Article 1). 'Refugee' is often used quite loosely, referring to those who have fled to safety either within their own country or over a national border. However, according to the 1951 UN Convention Relating to the Status of Refugees (Geneva Convention), the definition of refugee encompasses only those seeking asylum deemed to have a 'well-founded fear of persecution' (that is, excluding war, famine or environmental degradation). In this chapter, the term 'refugee' includes asylum-seeking children waiting for their asylum claim to be dealt with, as well as those children whose claims for asylum have already been determined and who have either been granted refugee status or exceptional leave to remain, for example, because war makes it unsafe for them to return to their country of origin.

LEGAL FRAMEWORK

Relevant international law for unaccompanied refugee children includes the Geneva Convention and the 1967 Protocol (both incorporated into UK domestic law), the 1989 CRC (ratified by the UK in 1991) and instruments relating to inter-country adoption and the protection of children (not yet ratified by the UK).

The Geneva Convention applies the same definition of a refugee to all, regardless of age, although an associated Recommendation concerns the prioritization of 'protection of refugees who are minors, in particular unaccompanied children ...' (Section IV B(2)). Forty years later, however, Article 22 of the CRC is very specific concerning refugee children:

> States Parties shall take appropriate measures to ensure that a child who is seeking refugee status or who is considered a refugee ... shall, whether unaccompanied or accompanied by his or her parents or by any other person, receive appropriate protection and humanitarian assistance...

Once an unaccompanied asylum-seeking child has arrived at a British port of entry and has been given leave to enter the country by an Immigration Officer, they become subject to all domestic laws. Of particular importance is legislation concerning immigration and welfare;[2] the important subject of educational provision is covered in the chapter by Duke, Sales and Gregory (Chapter 6).

Immigration law relating to unaccompanied refugee children, like that relating to adult asylum seekers in the UK, is contained in the 1993 Asylum and Immigration Appeals Act and associated Rules, and the 1996 Asylum and Immigration Act and associated case law. The Immigration Service has the right to detain asylum seekers when seeking entry to the country, and this does not exclude children who might lack documentation or whose stories are not accepted. Since its inception in 1994, the Refugee Council's Panel of Advisers for Unaccompanied Refugee Children has worked with over 60 young people under the age of 18 years detained in adult detention centres or prisons, some for many months, in direct contravention of Article 37 of the CRC.[3] Of particular relevance is the Immigration Rule on child asylum seekers (Nos 350–352 of HC 395, 1993). This relates to the conduct of interviews if these are deemed necessary (allowing for breaks), the assessment of children's asylum claims (giving more weight to objective factors of risk than a child's understanding of their risk of persecution) and that priority is to be accorded their cases.

The Children Act 1989 provides the foundation for family and child care law in England and Wales within an overall framework of certain key concepts applicable to all children; some have particular relevance to unaccompanied refugee children. For example, 'paramount consideration' of the child's welfare (Section 1(1)) supports the view that child care considerations should come before those of immigration policy and that each refugee child should be treated as an individual. Any plans should be shaped by the child's ascertainable wishes and feelings (Section 1(3)). This may involve the use of interpreters familiar with the work of social services, who can explain to the child the role of the various authorities and the nature of the choices open to them.

Echoing the CRC, the Children Act states that 'due consideration' must be given to a child's religious persuasion, racial origin, and cultural and linguistic background (Section 74(6)). This is of enormous importance if refugee children who have already lost their closest family, friends, cultural milieu and homeland are not to suffer the further loss of their heritage and, indeed, their identity. Another underlying principle is that children are usually best cared for by their own families. It is stressed that local authorities should work in partnership with parents and the child's wider family. For unaccompanied refugee children, this should involve attempts to trace the children's parents or family members in this country and abroad – they may have travelled here unbeknown to the children – following advice as to whether this may jeopardize a family's safety if tracing attempts are to be made in their country of origin.

General provisions of the Children Act clearly cover children who are unaccompanied refugees. Local authorities have a duty to provide accommodation for any child in their area if there is no-one who has parental responsibility for them, or they are lost and abandoned (Section 20(1)). Any child thus 'accommodated' by a local authority, not in communication with someone with parental responsibility for them, has the right to have an 'independent visitor' appointed to advise, befriend, and if necessary advocate for them (Schedule 2 para. 17). There are also duties and powers in respect of after-care to ensure that a safety net is in place for all those young people no longer looked after by local authorities, of whom refugee young people must surely be among the most vulnerable. Finally, local authorities have powers to provide accommodation for young people between the ages of 16 and 21 if they consider that to do so will safeguard and promote their welfare and if not to do so would 'seriously prejudice' their welfare.

LOCAL APPLICATION

The Immigration and Nationality Directorate of the Home Office set up an Unaccompanied Children's Module in 1995. This small team deals with all asylum claims of unaccompanied children in the UK, and some training – albeit limited – is a prerequisite for all immigration officers dealing with children's cases. Although there are concerns about the low number of unaccompanied children granted refugee status or exceptional leave to remain (just over 20 per cent on average in 1995 and 1996), the Module has ensured greater consistency and increased sensitivity to children's needs. Much unnecessary delay has been eliminated from the asylum determination process for children – although this may still take up to a year. It can thus be said that children's asylum claims are now dealt with in a fairly consistent, and centrally organized, manner by the Module. Improvements in the handling of children's appeals, already afforded priority listing (in practice, still involving waits of 12 months), are currently being instituted by the Chief Adjudicator.

Surprisingly little recent research has been carried out into the particular welfare needs of unaccompanied refugee children and how these are met. The first survey giving an overall picture of the situation in the UK was carried out in 1989 (Cordell, 1992) and the second in 1990 (Finlay), both of which identified wide variations in response to children on the part of different social services departments. Some showed a marked reluctance to accept responsibility for children presenting as unaccompanied refugees, who were subsequently passed from borough to borough before finally being received into care. There was almost no knowledge of how many children might be cared for by members of their communities in informal arrangements; however, the Refugee Council's contacts with refugee community groups suggested that this practice might be quite widespread, and that without adequate support, such arrangements were likely to break down. Until 1991, no statistics were collated centrally on numbers of unaccompanied refugee children and, even then, they related simply to asylum applications, and not to provision of care – either by which authority or type of assistance provided. There was a common assumption that the majority of children were looked after by Hillingdon (because of the location of Heathrow Airport) and certain authorities in central London with good transport links to the airport or with refugee community organizations in contact with children. This view had perhaps been reinforced by one-off central government grants in the fiscal year 1992–93 to just two local authorities – Hillingdon, and Kensington and Chelsea – to meet part of their expenditure in relation to unaccompanied refugee children.

The Association of Directors of Social Services gave backing to a two-stage study by the author designed to ascertain the extent and nature of provision. The first stage was a questionnaire survey of service provision for unaccompanied refugee children in the 32 London boroughs, City of London, Essex and West Sussex (Autumn 1992). The second involved in-depth interviews with service users, providers and policy makers in four representative local authorities, chosen to reflect a mix of inner and outer London boroughs looking after high and low numbers of children respectively.

LONDON-WIDE SURVEY, 1992–93[4]

The questionnaire was devised to determine the numbers of unaccompanied refugee children receiving services from social services departments, any relevant policies and what the services were. Questionnaires were sent to 35 social services departments at the end of July 1992. By January 1993, responses had been received from 28, including the four authorities later selected for the in-depth study.

Of the 28 authorities, 16 had adopted a cross-departmental approach to the planning and delivery of services to refugees, although only one authority corporately produced information for refugees about services available. There was an almost total lack of knowledge among social services departments as to the size of the refugee population in their respective authorities. Very few regularly collated information about the unaccompanied refugee children for whom they cared, and almost none were aware of informal caring arrangements for children which they might wish to monitor or support actively.

Ten respondents reported that they cared for no unaccompanied refugee children; the total number of children accommodated by the remaining 18 was 341.[5] Of these, national origin was given in less than 50 per cent of cases. The question thus arose as to how appropriate services could be provided or planned for children whose nationality was apparently unknown. In addition, 66 children were living with relatives and receiving some form of support from their social services department; at least 13 were living with older siblings.

Some social services departments had made considerable efforts to meet the needs of the unaccompanied refugee children in an appropriate and culturally sensitive manner. However, there were worrying gaps in provision in other authorities, especially regarding the low number of 'same culture/religion/language' matched placements as opposed to 'same race' placements.[6] There was very little evidence that respondents understood the nature of their statutory duties concerning the appointment of independent visitors to children. Few departments appeared to have considered pressing questions of family tracing or (if possible) reunion. Arrangements for translation/interpretation were often made ad hoc. Almost no training was given either to interpreters or to staff who used them. Given the likely nature of these children's experiences, the very small number who had been referred for counselling was surprising. Only one respondent specifically mentioned assistance given to unaccompanied refugee children with their application for asylum.

FOUR IN-DEPTH STUDIES

The aim of the four in-depth studies of local authorities was to provide detailed analysis of their responses to the questionnaire and any subsequent changes, how local authority policy affecting refugee children was made and external influences and constraints on service provision. The first was carried out between October 1993 and May 1994 (in 'Arnbridge'); the second, between April and September 1994 (in 'Barton'); the third, between October 1994 and May 1995 (in 'Crosslow'); and the fourth, between September 1995 and January 1996 (in 'Denham').

The authorities were selected to include two outer and two inner London boroughs with small and large numbers of asylum seekers and refugees respectively settled within their boundaries; one outer (Barton) and one inner borough (Crosslow) were accommodating relatively low numbers of unaccompanied refugee children (both 7 per cent of the total number of looked-after children), and one outer (Arnbridge) and one inner borough (Denham) were accommodating relatively high numbers of unaccompanied refugee children (50 per cent and 33 per cent of the total number of looked-after children respectively). An average of 44 people were interviewed in each authority, including policy-makers, service providers, carers, young people (of whom 23 were interviewed in all) and representatives of refugee community organizations.

A snapshot picture of provision in the four authorities follows, the first of which is 'Arnbridge', a borough in outer London, where the social services department had accommodated a high number of unaccompanied children. Good general provision for looked-after children existed. Social workers were experienced and there was low staff turnover. The need for specialized provision for unaccompanied refugees had been identified as an issue in 1990; a senior (third tier) operations officer given designated responsibility for this group of children was committed to the provision of appropriate services for unaccompanied refugee children and creative in approaching the task. Social workers were encouraged to develop their skills in working with this client group. Detailed statistics were collated and services developed to cater for children's linguistic, cultural and religious needs (refugee foster carers and specialist residential provision). Adequate funding was made available for interpreting and additional educational assistance was provided by means of a grant from the Department for Education and Employment. Close links were developed with refugee communities in inner London for the purposes of tracing relatives and friends, recruiting foster carers and independent visitors and encouraging children's attendance at cultural events. Communities were not, however, involved in planning services in any meaningful way although some refugee staff were recruited who played a crucial role in the development of appropriate services.

Detailed practice guidance was being developed by staff in field, residential and fostering settings. The view was clearly expressed that looking after refugee young people had positive spin-offs for other young people in care because they tended to be articulate and challenged staff's stereotypes about the capabilities of children in care. However, after care services were generally undeveloped, with a lack of move-on accommodation and long waits for young people to move out of expensive and sometimes inappropriate residential care.

The cost of services to unaccompanied children was high, and was met by savings and reserves. Although budget cuts had been made by the Conservative administration, these were presented as necessary due to the poor housekeeping of the previous administration which pre-dated the high number of children arriving from 1990. The Director of Social Services was personally active in supporting the case for appropriate services to refugee children and kept the sympathetic leader of the Council well informed. Political control changed from Conservative back to Labour during the study, but there was no change in the fundamental commitment to meeting the borough's statutory duties to unaccompanied refugee children and providing them with high quality services; they were never used as a political football in relation to expenditure debates.

The second authority was 'Barton', in outer London, with a low number of unaccompanied children looked after by the social services department. There was a growing awareness of the needs of refugees in general in the borough, prompted by a very active local council for racial equality. Key officers responded proactively in the Chief Executive's, Housing, and Education Departments as well as the Health Authority. Increasing consultation with refugee community groups had occurred. They were welcome to attend a Council Community Liaison Forum.

Services for looked-after children were well resourced and of high quality. Social work teams were stable, and consisted of experienced, well-motivated staff. Interpreting services were available with no funding constraints. Numbers of unaccompanied refugee children looked after were low, and had largely resulted from the breakdown of informal caring arrangements. Many social workers lacked experience in working with children from minority ethnic groups, but attempts were made to find refugee children placements matched for 'same race'. Among social workers there was considerable ignorance about refugees in general, and of such issues as children's asylum claims, family tracing, matching of interpreters, independent visitors, etc. However, due to increased concerns about the adequacy of departmental response to refugee children's needs – especially psychological – it had recently been agreed that refugee children were to be given particular attention in the multi-disciplinary children's planning process led by Social Services; this had been warmly supported by health and education colleagues. It also supported the comment of front-line Social Services staff that their views and concerns were generally taken seriously by managers.

The borough was firmly under Conservative control and was not experiencing significant financial difficulties. In any event, expenditure on refugee children was not high, although the educational needs of minority ethnic children had been on the political agenda and quality of local educational provision was a matter of civic pride. Described as a borough where elected members took a clear policy lead generally on the advice of officers, there appeared to be a relationship of considerable trust between Committee Chairs and senior officers with little day-to-day involvement by the former.

The third borough was 'Crosslow'. In inner London, and accommodating a low number of unaccompanied children, social services for looked-after children in general, children in need and child protection were severely stretched; concerns about the latter had been expressed in a recent inspection. Social work teams had many vacancies, morale was reportedly low and many workers were newly qualified and inexperienced. Many cases of children looked after were unallocated, and statutory reviews were often not held within the required timescales. Levels of deprivation throughout the borough had been high for many years and large numbers of refugees and asylum seekers had recently moved into the borough. There was a lively voluntary sector, with well-established as well as emerging refugee community organizations. There had been a tradition for some years of productive consultation between refugee communities and the Chief Executive's, Housing, and Education Departments. Research into the needs of refugees had been commissioned by the Council and Health Authority but this had not focused on the needs of refugee children or the particular provision of the social services department. Several refugee community representatives admitted that children were often low on their agendas because of other more pressing needs. Given the prevalence of refugee communities in the borough, social workers interviewed showed a surprising ignorance of refugee issues.

Although many of the children looked after were from minority ethnic groups, there was no detailed monitoring of the appropriateness of services as regards language, religion and culture which did not appear to be regarded as important as 'race'. Not surprisingly therefore, no statistics were kept on refugee children. All young people interviewed strongly criticized the suitability of their placements (none of which had taken into account the above three factors) and lack of social work support. They expressed considerable feelings of loss, loneliness and isolation. Almost no attention had been paid to their immigration status, educational or psychological needs, independent visitors or possibilities of family tracing. Where foster carers had made particular efforts to meet the needs of refugee children placed with them, this was entirely on their own initiative.

The borough was Labour controlled and although committed to anti-racist policies, some senior officers reported that any apparent prioritization of the needs of 'newly arrived' refugees at the perceived cost of other longer-established minority ethnic groups was a very sensitive issue and one which they wished to avoid. Where possible, it was thought better to target the needs of 'minority ethnic communities' in general, among which would be refugee communities. There were severe overall financial constraints for the authority, and although the Director of Social Services was personally very committed to providing a good service to refugee children, the need to concentrate on raising standards in child protection services and staffing difficulties generally meant that this did not translate into any sense of urgency at middle-management or basic-grade levels; there were just too many other priorities.

'Denham', an inner London borough accommodating a high number of unaccompanied children, was the fourth authority. Like Arnbridge, good general provision for looked after children existed and the Council was well resourced albeit with pockets of high deprivation in the borough. A thriving voluntary sector complemented Council services. Although several well-established refugee community organizations provided valued direct services to refugee children and young people, they were not generally regarded as suitable partners by the social services department regarding consultation about service provision for unaccompanied refugee children; some concern was expressed that this might lead to more referrals of children to the borough. Social workers were experienced, committed and there was low staff turnover. The need for specialized provision for unaccompanied refugees was identified as an issue in 1990 and a senior (third tier) operations officer was given designated responsibility. However, after some specialist provision had been made (a children's home and subsequently fostering and outreach teams), the lead officer did not play an active role in this respect. The majority of refugee children looked after were placed with refugee carers to whom good support services were offered.

Apart from the provision of carers with the same language as the children, there was little recognition of the particular needs of refugee children such as immigration status, psychological and educational support, family tracing and independent visitors. Given the numbers of refugee children looked after, it was surprising that no specific statistics were available, practice guidance had not been developed, and there was a general complacency about the adequacy of children's placements – cultural and religious needs were not always met, and some children were placed with people of opposing political views to those of their parents. Some middle managers were very sceptical about the majority of children's asylum claims to be refugees and there was resentment that lack of funding from central government resulted in reduced resources for local children and families. No attempt was made to formulate good practice in working with children whose claims and appeals were refused. Although otherwise described as a department where the views of front-line staff were welcomed and acted upon, there was no internal forum for discussion about these issues where differing perspectives of social workers and managers could be aired.

The borough was firmly in Conservative control, with an ethos of Member-led policy-making. Expenditure on refugee children had been financed by savings in Social Services spending and Council reserves. Elected Members and senior officers were involved in an ongoing campaign to persuade the government to reimburse expenditure for what was clearly seen as a national responsibility.[7] While committed to fulfilling statutory duties, Members did not want their policies to exert any 'pull factor' in attracting refugee children to the borough, and had approved a more rigorous means of assessing children on referral. Most senior and middle managers welcomed this 'robust' approach; front-line staff and community representatives were concerned at the effect of more intrusive questioning on newly arrived, vulnerable children.

LIKELY DETERMINANTS OF A LOCAL VARIATION

Before the in-depth studies were begun, a number of possibly significant factors were identified. These included political control, presence or absence of well-established refugee communities and their involvement in policy-making, numbers of refugee children being looked-after (having a possible bearing on both financial considerations[8] as well as staff's expertise), the pre-existing level of deprivation/financial constraints, presence or absence of lead officers for race equality/refugees/ children's rights, and the quality of provision for looked-after children in general and children from minority ethnic groups.

Preliminary analysis suggests that no single factor was a significant determinant of policy or variations in service provision. If good services for minority ethnic children or looked after children existed generally, then refugee children also benefited. However, a commitment to race equality, adequate resources and effective management were not on their own sufficient for relevant policies or appropriate services: the range of particular needs of unaccompanied refugee children was likely to go unrecognized in policy or service provision unless:

- a lead officer was appointed for them who was active in ensuring their changing needs were addressed and that staff had the skills and knowledge to do so, and/or
- there was good communication between basic grade and middle manager levels, and/or
- the children were made the particular focus of a planning group.

Good provision was enhanced where refugee communities were active and enabled to contribute to the policy process, but this in turn was enhanced if they themselves had identified children as a priority. Very few interviewees had any appreciation of asylum-seeking children having certain rights.

KEY ISSUES IN PROVISION

While the UK has signed and ratified the Convention on the Rights of the Child, legislation is not scrutinized to ensure it is compatible with the CRC. The Asylum and Immigration Act is a case in point, with its provision to deprive certain asylum-seeking families of Income Support and all asylum-seeking families of Child Benefit. It is, in fact, a discretionary matter for local authorities and other service providers to adopt the CRC; disappointingly few have done so. In the London-wide questionnaire survey, only eight respondents (less than 25 per cent) had lead officers in Social Services with a responsibility to ensure departmental policies reflected the principles of the CRC with its emphasis on the rights of refugee children. Only one of the four authorities studied in-depth had a lead officer familiar with the CRC (Crosslow); newly appointed, they had only just begun an audit of departmental policies to ensure these reflected the spirit and provisions of the Convention and recognized that a huge task lay ahead. The CRC is clearly not being used either in an overarching or practical, day-to-day manner to inform policy-making and service provision.

Where unaccompanied children are concerned, with no adults to protect their interests, this is regrettable. The Children Act unfortunately did not close the loophole in previous child care law concerning the question of parental responsibility for refugee children where contact cannot be made with their parents. The most obvious difficulty arising from this is when consent to medical treatment is needed. However, it is also potentially very serious in cases where a child's asylum claim is refused and no-one is there to represent the child's interests. It is in the local authority's financial interests to ensure the child's return to their country of origin and this could open the way for finance-led (or at least finance-influenced) rather than needs-led decision-making in the child's best interests.

There are shortcomings in other areas of practice due to this particular vulnerability of unaccompanied children and the lack of any firm commitment to their rights. In recognition of the lack of specialized knowledge about, and training for, working with unaccompanied refugee children, draft practice guidelines were drawn up by the Social Services Inspectorate (SSI) of the Department of Health to be published in 1991 in conjunction with the other volumes of guidance accompanying the Children Act. Regrettably there was a delay in publication of several years despite consistent pressure from the voluntary sector. The Training Pack and Practice Guide on Unaccompanied Asylum-seeking Children was finally published by the SSI in May 1995. Although still relevant, the practice guidance has no 'teeth' and cannot be enforced by the SSI. This encourages local authorities to view good practice with unaccompanied refugee children as an option, not a requirement. The guidance does not address three important issues: first, the serious difficulties caused by the 1996 Asylum and Immigration Act where certain asylum seekers are not entitled to claim welfare benefits; second, the implications for family reunion of the UK reservation to the CRC on immigration; and third, the question of who decides what should happen when a child's asylum claim has been refused and there are no further grounds for appeal.

SIXTEEN AND SEVENTEEN YEAR OLDS

As has been outlined in an earlier chapter, those who seek asylum in-country or who receive a negative decision on their application are no longer entitled to Income Support and related benefits, such as certain education and training courses. Permission to work is never granted until a minimum of six months after making their claim. This affects 16 and 17 year olds whose welfare is not deemed to be seriously preju-diced if they are not accommodated under Section 20 by Social Services, and who are not therefore looked-after by foster carers or in a children's home. If unable to work, they are only likely to receive financial support from Social Services under Section 17 of the Children Act as being children 'in need'. This generally includes payment of rent and an allowance for food, but not the same level of social work assist-ance afforded those accommodated under Section 20. The Act also affects those young people who have left care and who then receive a negative determination of their claim. Although entitled to after care support, this may be very limited if they have moved away from the authority who originally had responsibility for them and is unlikely to include financial help. This means that an increasing number of teenagers are only entitled to the extremely limited assistance offered to destitute asylum seekers by social services departments under the 1948 National Assistance Act. The serious impact on asylum seekers' quality of life, physical and mental health of this inadequate approach has been documented (Mercorios *et al.*, 1997).

FAMILY REUNION

The UK government entered a number of reservations when ratifying the Convention, including one concerning immigration and family reunion, reserving the right to:

> apply such legislation, in so far as it relates to the entry into, stay in and departure from the United Kingdom of those who do not have the right... to enter and remain in the United Kingdom... as it may deem necessary from time to time (Lansdown and Newell, 1994: 245).

This would appear to contravene underlying principles of the Convention, such as the child's best interests and the right of family reunification, as well as those underlying the 1989 Children Act in domestic legislation. The UN Committee on the Rights of the Child made a number of concluding observations in 1995 on the UK Government's report of progress on implementation of the CRC. Among other things, the Committee recommended:

> that a review be undertaken of the nationality and immigration laws and procedures to ensure their conformity with the principles and provisions of the Convention. (UN Committee on the Rights of the Child, 1995: Para. 5.46)

CHILDREN'S RETURN

Such a review would be particularly helpful in the issue of children's return. Of course there are cases where a return is made voluntarily, in non-controversial circumstances. However, in cases where a child's claim has been refused and they do not wish to return, immigration law is assumed to have precedence over the welfare paramountcy principle of child care law, regardless of the views of any social services department involved. Although the Home Office has given assurances that no child under 18 will be deported unless suitable care arrangements exist in their country of origin, the adequacy of assessments of such arrangements is questionable when they may be made by British Embassy officials rather than personnel trained in child care. The role of Social Services in such cases is not clearly defined and increasingly, final decisions are being made when young people are over 18 years – that is, beyond the point at which Social Services are usually involved or the above undertaking of the Home Office holds good.

PLANNING SERVICES

There has certainly been no ongoing interdepartmental focus on the situation of refugee children at central government level, although children generally have, of course, been the subject of attention. The Department of Health issued a circular in 1992 (LAC(92)18) outlining its expectations of Children's Services Plans,[9] making clear that they should be the product of consultation between local authorities (including local education authorities), health authorities, voluntary organizations, the private sector and other appropriate agencies. The first plans were to be drawn up for the period 1994–97. Further requirements for inter-agency co-ordination in planning service delivery are specified in the 1993 Education Act (Section 166) and the Children Act (Section 27 regarding day care services for children under 8 years).

Local authorities conduct this planning in different ways. Many have chosen to form multi-disciplinary task groups focusing on different age groups and/or children with particular needs, for example, children with disabilities or children who are looked after by the local authority. The measures outlined above should constitute adequate planning systems to ensure that the specific needs of unaccompanied refugee children – as any other children – are properly addressed and met. In only a few instances have refugee children been the subject of such a focus. In the past this has not been made easy by the lack of basic information about the population of unaccompanied refugee children – or indeed, of any refugee communities – and the absence of a lead officer on the issue. For example, as at December 1992, only 14 of the 28 social services departments responding to the questionnaire survey had a lead officer for refugee children. Since the SSI (London Region) began convening the 'Network on Children and Families from Abroad' in 1995, all social services departments in London have designated such a lead officer and improvement might have been expected. However, some social services departments are still unclear how many children and young people looked after are refugees, whether unaccompanied or otherwise. In 1996, the Network drew up an agreed format for monitoring unaccompanied refugee children and the services provided them, and it is to be hoped that this will lead to a clearer picture of the population and distribution of children throughout London. Another encouraging development is that the Association of London Government recently published a 'Strategy for London's Children' stressing the importance of services to asylum-seeking and refugee children and families.

Nevertheless, even if local services were designed entirely appropriately following extensive consultation with refugee community organizations and young people, their eventual delivery is subject to constraints imposed by central government, both in terms of broad policy and finance. The negative impact of national asylum policy on unaccompanied children and young people clearly demonstrates this, as well as indicating the way in which the rights of children as outlined in the 1989 Convention fail to be taken into consideration by policy makers. There are relatively few authorities in the country as a whole which provide services to unaccompanied refugee children, thereby fulfilling a national responsibility under the Geneva Convention; as such, despite the moral force of their argument for financial reimbursement and the considerable cost involved in caring for even small numbers of children, they have not had a great deal of bargaining power. A long campaign on the part of a handful of London boroughs and local authority associations has resulted in a cash-limited central government grant for unaccompanied refugee children, but threshold levels are so high that only two or three authorities are ever likely to qualify. There is thus no financial incentive for local authorities to adopt positive policies towards refugee children – rather the reverse.

An additional factor is the lack of effective co-ordination of central government departments where children's concerns are involved. This is not confined to refugee children, but applies to service provision for children generally:

> Children's interests are dealt with by at least 14 government depart-
> ments, each of which is dedicated, quite reasonably, to the pursuit
> of excellence in its own sphere. ... But without carefully designed
> government structures and a commitment to forge the necessary
> connections between these separate responsibilities, the excellence
> the departments pursue may elude them or be thwarted by others'
> policies... Developing a children's perspective throughout gov-
> ernment, and ensuring that the impact of policies on children is
> appropriately considered throughout government demands new
> structures, as well as a new political will. It is significant that central
> government has perceived this in relation to the delivery of local
> services to children. It now needs to practise the strategic planning
> and collaboration between its departments and agencies which it
> preaches to, and to some degree now requires of, local authorities
> (Hodgkin and Newell, 1996: 38).

Unless a thoroughgoing commitment to children's rights informs the strategy of central government, the needs of children in general, and refugee children in particular, will continue to be overlooked. In summary, improved planning mechanisms at local level for children's services do not necessarily lead to better services for refugee children. Their needs may not be recognized, financial considerations may play a part and it is difficult for local authorities to influence central gov-ernment policy which has been hostile to asylum seekers generally, including children. Without a successful lobby at the national or local level, and with refugee community groups and concerned voluntary organizations struggling as they respond to the drastic impact of the Asylum and Immigration Act, it is likely that unaccompanied refugee children and young people will continue to be further marginalized in welfare provision even among other groups of vulnerable children.

NOTES

1.   This chapter was completed in April 1997.
2.   The following section is an abridged version of part of Williamson, 1997.
3.   Article 37 specifies that detention must be 'used only as a measure of last resort and for the shortest appropriate period of time', in separate accommodation from adults, 'and in a manner which takes into account the needs of persons of his or her age.' There is growing evidence of the damaging effect on mental health of detention among adults (e.g. Pourgourides *et al.*, 1996); its effect on children has not been the subject of academic research but is unlikely to be less serious. The practice of detaining children is the subject of an ongoing campaign by the Refugee Council and other organizations.
4.   A brief account of the results of the survey has been published (Williamson, 1993).
5.   Contrary to expectation, several authorities were looking after more than 10 unaccompanied children, namely: Brent (11), Camden (42), Croydon (10), Ealing (15), Hackney (11), Hammersmith and Fulham (23), Haringey (38), Hillingdon (41), Hounslow (19), Kensington and Chelsea (50), Lambeth (47), Newham (13) and Westminster (14). West Sussex County Council, where Gatwick is situated, was looking after 11 children.
6.   'Race' was often as imprecise as 'black' or 'Asian', so a Somali child placed with an Afro-Caribbean carer or an Afghani with an Indian carer might be seen as appropriate.
7.   A government grant has been payable from 1996–97 for unaccompanied refugee children, but the threshold is very high and few social services departments qualify.
8.   While numbers of unaccompanied refugee children in Britain remain relatively small in global terms, the cost to a local authority of caring for such a child is nevertheless significant – around £10 000 p.a. for foster care or £45 000 p.a. in a children's home at 1996–7 costs.
9.   This was one of the recommendations of the Utting report, *Children in the Public Care*, following the 'Pindown' scandal in Staffordshire children's homes.

REFERENCES

Ayotte, W. and Lown, J. (1992), *Children or Refugees?: A Survey of West European Policies on Unaccompanied Refugee Children*, London, Children's Legal Centre.

Cordell, G. (1992), *Towards a Coherent Policy Response to the Needs of Unaccompanied Refugee Children*, M. Phil Social Work Thesis, London, University of West London (Brunel) and the Tavistock Clinic, February.

Department of Health Social Services Inspectorate (1995), *Unaccompanied Asylum-seeking Children: A Training Pack*, (with Practice Guide), London, HMSO, May.

Finlay, R. (1990), *Unaccompanied Refugee Children: A Monitoring Report*, London, Refugee Council, December.

Hodgkin, R. and Newell, P. (1996), *Effective Government Structures for Children*, London, Calouste Gulbenkian Foundation.

Lansdown, G. and Newell, P. (eds) (1994), *UK Agenda for Children*, London, Children's Rights Development Unit.

Mercorios, D., Rees, R. and Young, M. (1997), *Just Existence*, London, Refugee Council.

Pourgourides, C., Sashidharan, S.P. and Bracken, P.J. (1996), *A Second Exile: The Mental Health Implications of Detention of Asylum Seekers in the United Kingdom*, Academic Unit Northern Birmingham Mental Health Trust/Department of Education University of Bradford, Bradford.

Ressler, E.M., Boothby, N. and Steinbock, D.J. (1988), *Unaccompanied Children*, New York and Oxford, Oxford University Press.

Williamson, J. and Moser, A. (1987), *Unaccompanied Children in Emergencies: A Field Guide for their Care and Protection*, Geneva, International Social Service.

Williamson, L. (1993), 'Alone in a Strange Land', *Community Care*, 11 November, pp. 26–7.

Williamson, L. (1995), 'A Safe Haven? The Development of British Policy concerning Unaccompanied Refugee Children 1933–93', *Immigrants and Minorities*, Vol. 14, No. 1, pp. 47–66.

Williamson, L. (1998), 'Unaccompanied but not Unsupported', in Jones, C. and Rutter, J. (eds), *Mapping the Field: New Initiatives in Refugee Education*, Stoke-on-Trent, Trentham Books.

UN Committee on the Rights of the Child (1995), *Concluding Observations on the Report of the UK Government*, Geneva, UN Committee on the Rights of the Child.

United Nations High Commissioner for Refugees (1994), *Refugee Children: Guidelines on Protection and Care*, Geneva, UNHCR.

Utting,W. (1991), *Children in the Public Care*, London, HMSO.

9 Age in Exile:[1] Europe's older refugees and exiles

Helena Scott[2] and Claudio Bolzman

A refugee will remain a refugee, even 50 years on.

(Jagucki, 1991)

AN INTRODUCTION

Research into the prevalence and specific living circumstances of older people living in exile,[3] as displaced people or from organized refugee groups, is not widely served, or indeed recognized.

Older refugees and exiles are not a single homogenous group for they occupy a diversity of social and economic backgrounds, hold different religious beliefs and have originated from many different and far reaching continents and countries. Forced migration, often imposing arduous, harsh and life threatening routes into exile, can be recalled with imposing clarity and while the differences may be more of detail rather than major fact, it is an important feature that no two personal biographies can be viewed as quite the same (Scott and Kernberg, 1992).

According to UNHCR, there were 18 million refugees in the world in 1993, that is, people who had to leave their home because of political persecution and violence and seek asylum in another country for a period of unpredictable duration. In general terms, the availability of reliable statistics on refugees and exiles is wholly problematic as data collection may be flawed in its methodology, or/and influenced by how individual countries make decisions and of the overall view they wish to project (Minority Rights Group, 1990). How data is measured and collated, that is, the range and type of variables used, can also greatly affect the outcome. For example, some countries may record only the head of the family (who is recognized as a refugee) while others take every member into account (Minority Rights Group, 1990). From

UNHCR 1983 figures when there was a world projection of 10 million or so refugees, it was speculated that 3 per cent, that is some 300 000 refugees, were over the age of 60 years. What is certain is that the proportion of older people within refugee populations is not a static phenomenon. It should not, however, be simply a matter of statistical data, however accurate or inaccurate, but a qualitative reflection of a series of factors of when, for example, exile took place, at what stage in that person or group's life and its duration.

For these reasons, it is important to differentiate between those people who grew old as refugees, for example, Central and East Europeans,[4] whose settlement in Europe began from the late 1940s onwards (originally estimated at about 150 000, the Poles are believed to be the largest surviving group of older refugees and exiles (Scott, 1997; Scott and Kernberg, 1992; British Refugee Council, 1988), and those who were, albeit quite small numerically, already considered old when becoming exiles in the early 1970s, like the Chileans.[5] It was relatively easy to find information about those who have grown old after becoming refugees, exiles or displaced persons than those who were already old at the point of forced migration.

UNDERSTANDING EXILE

The Ageing Perspective

In every case exile represents a radical severance with the country of origin resulting in loss of the primary social and economic resources that structured everyday life. And for every migrant, but in particular for refugees and exiles, the arrival in a new country that is culturally different proposes encounters with unexpected phenomena that introduces, amongst other things, personal anonymity, loss of language and loneliness (Bolzman, 1994).

These conditions are felt particularly by older people who are, in general, less flexible than younger people in adapting to new situations. Cultural shock hits hard those people without much prior knowledge or experience of urban life in industrialized societies as seen by the many older Vietnamese boat people who sought exile in Europe and North America (Allard, 1987; Ahmed, Tims and Kolker, 1981). Mental stress and anguish tend to increase when refugees and exiles are separated from their ethnic community in the country of exile which was the case for refugees from South East Asia in Europe and North America (Simon-Barouh, 1984; Montero, 1979). Again, older people feel the effects of separation more intensely than younger people.

These feelings of loss are particularly acute when refugees and exiles perceive their situation in the country of exile as permanent; when they realize that they may never see their country of origin again. The Latinoamerican refugees and Central and East Europeans offer a good example of this because exile, for them, was at the beginning of a transitory situation as they had hoped that the political situation within their own countries would be overturned and that they would return within a few years. This sentiment was voiced by Francisco, a Chilean refugee who, as a former trade union leader was imprisoned and then expelled by the military junta. He arrived in Switzerland in 1976 when he was 52 years old. He said:

> My wife and children were not feeling good at the beginning. The fight for our country, for our people, was very important and met with strong conviction. It allowed us to feel more quiet, to be always together, to build up a more organized life in exile, to think always about our country, about the return (Bolzman, 1996: 143).

But exile is a dynamic situation. The perception of the situation changes not only with time but also within the socio-historical context. When older Chilean refugees realized that exile would be a lasting reality and that they could not return to their country of origin, they were left with profound feelings of emptiness. Like Ismael, a Chilean, now retired, who said:

> If I were conservative, passive, I would be very happy in Switzerland. But if you like to do things, to participate, in this country there is nothing to do (Bolzman, 1996: 192).

They felt that there was no place for them in the country of exile other than their ethnic community; that there was no place for older people with political ideals.

Scott (1998), in her study of Polish exiles in Scotland considered the implications of long-term exile not just in its political context but rather as a displacement of lost youth and the lifetime struggle of personal reconciliation of exile:

> For those surviving members of the Polish Armed forces who had been forced into involuntary exile the jubilant celebrations of the fiftieth anniversary of VE Day in May 1995 in Great Britain, were

met with ambivalence. For them, those who were once so young and full of hope, there began in 1945 a point of no return. What was thought a temporary period of exile became as we can now testify, a permanent exile that has spanned more than fifty years. For these men and women who represent a generation of Central and East Europeans displaced in their youth by the ravages of war, the VE Day celebrations were ultimately a silent commemoration of their lost families, friends, comrades and last, but not least, their ojczyna (homeland) (1998: 2).

Kalemkarayan and Ohanian (1996) in their recent survey of some 500 older Armenian people living in the London Borough of Hounslow, the majority of whom had been born in Turkey (occupied Western Armenia) or in the Middle East, believe that the experience of persecution leaves an indelible mark which becomes further engrained when the greater part of one's life has been lived under various colonial or totalitarian regimes, as in Syria, Iran or Lebanon. They suggest that older people, in particular, have not only had the greater experience of one form or another of persecution, but their survival presents an additional set of concerns:

The experience of surviving the systematic destruction of their nation in Ottoman Turkey and living as refugees in societies where freedom of speech/ expression was denied for many years, continues to haunt and influence the way Armenian older people perceive the world and society, even in today's more liberal/ multicultural Britain (1996: 2).

What seems clear is that for the first generation of refugees, the feeling of identification with their country of origin remains strong, even after a long residence in the country of exile. This is supported by Leser and Seeberg (1991) who in their study of Hungarian refugees, now settled in Switzerland for 35 years, noted that there was a rebirth of identification with the country of origin and with the idea of return, but only after the end of the cold war.

In a somewhat similar vein, Polish respondents reflected upon their early years of exile as being met with hostility, in particular by the mining trade unions which perceived their political stance solely in terms of anti-communist behaviour. Therefore, Polish exiles and to a large extent, their children, developed a tendency towards conformity in terms of education and work, with Polish language and culture becoming an introverted practice.

Again, like Leser and Seeberg (1992) the coming down of the iron curtain, symbolic not only in terms of victory over political terror and repression, but in opening up the eastern part of Europe kept under dark cover for more than four decades, instilled in the younger generation a positive feeling about their origin and ethnic identity and from it came an interest in the country of their parent's origin. Some older Polish respondents living in Scotland, did act and return to Poland, but some found the transition after more than half a century too difficult and returned with deeper disappointment, if not a sense of utter failure.

Others took the easy route by revisiting Polish organizations and associations formed shortly after exile in the late 1940s and early 1950s. For many, this return was bound up with guilt about long periods of absence, often presented as work related or family orientated. It is certainly true that many Poles were self-employed, choosing this as an alternative to confrontation and direct discrimination in the hard-core industries. Long hours endured in labour and the geographical distance to Polish centres were all too often barriers to full participation in community life, but in retirement the need for Polish familiarity and company is seen as essential. It could be argued that the self-realization of ageing bears a close correlation to death and dying, and that this stage of a person's life holds greater invitation towards a reaffirmation of ethnic identity and roots of origin, in all its symbolism and ritual (Scott, 1997).

WOMEN

Research studies of women refugees and exiles appear to be limited and those of older women remain negligible. While this is not the place to speculate on why this may be the case, it is nonetheless important to recognize and acknowledge that women, and in this instance, older women, occupy the same legitimacy as men in discussions of forced migration and exile. Scott (1997) believes that women, particularly in exile communities post-dating the Second World War, were obscured by what was seen as largely a male orientated migration dominated by the armed forces, as in the example of Central and East European groups. Women, who had themselves served in the armed forces and in resistance movements, women who had worked as secret agents and who had experienced torture and inhuman treatment in labour and concentration camps are too often overlooked and limited reference is made of their contribution to the war effort and/or little is known of their own secret war.

Within this context, and whether political oppression takes the form of physical or mental torture or brutality, it applies equally to men and women but there still remains, relatively speaking, a silence around the specific forms that this may have taken and which is gender defined. Frelick (1992), in his discussion of how refugees are defined refers to research undertaken by McCallin (1991) in which of the 110 Central American women interviewed, 85 per cent had had at least one traumatizing event and that an average women had had 3.3 experiences of, for example, rape or injury, bombings and gunfire, threats, interrogation and house searches: 24 of the women in the sample had been present at a murder. The implications of these experiences, as shown by McCallin (1991) of the Central American women, leads to a poorly sustained quality of life even in a safe country because the haunting memories result in continuous mental health problems such as anxiety, tension etc. A failure to recognize these and other health problems and the lack of appropriate counselling or support services, meant that women carry these burdens of psychological stress (often with physical consequences) for many, many years. Kmita-Dawson, former team leader of the Transcultural Health Unit at Lynfield Mount Hospital, Bradford, UK, encountered a range of psychosomatic conditions and mental illnesses amongst older women clients who had experienced sexual abuse and rape during the Second World War (Kmita-Dawson, 1990). Clients, often believing that they had been the only ones to go through such an experience, had continued to live with shame and guilt for nearly five decades.

Bolzman (1993) in his study of women in political exile uses the dichotomy of the private versus public sphere in order to distinguish between three kinds of women:

- activist women – those who were politically engaged in their home country and fled direct persecution;
- participative women – those who were interested in public life and who found themselves in exile due to indirect violence. Often they had arrived with their husbands who were in direct danger;
- private women – who were not interested in events outside of their family but had found themselves in exile due to indirect violence but without really understanding the reasons why.

For activist women what is of primary importance in exile is the need to overcome psychological and, sometimes, the physical consequences of political repression in their country of origin. Learning the language of the country of exile and having the opportunity to find a public role remain ongoing goals because as activist women get older, it is shown to be easier for them to engage in social and political activities because they have had previous experience of public life. For participative women, the main concern is to find a balance between public life (work, community involvement etc.) and private life (family). These goals are difficult to obtain in the first years of exile as the main problems are families fragmented by loss or distance and in terms of professional status there is often a lack of recognition of professional qualifications. If they can overcome these problems then getting older in the country of exile can be lived as a positive experience particularly if participative women discover that there can be more opportunities for women there. For private women, the central focus is the family and importance is placed upon keeping it together in the belief that life in exile is evaluated in relation to the family. Private women believe that they derive their personal value through their family role which, if viewed positively, leads to their evaluating exile in similar terms. This is particularly difficult when families are often incomplete and extended kinships lost, resulting in women feeling isolated. The situation improves in time with the appearance of grandchildren, and as private women become grandparents extended families can once again be built up and the women's roles once again become established.

Bolzman (1993) believes that the majority of women in exile belong to the last two categories, that is, participative women and private women. Hurna (1997) supports this observation because as a Polish exile herself, and now as chair of the Polish Women's Association (*Zwiasek Polek*), an association formed in 1947, she has both her own experience to hand as well as that of her exiled women friends. She stresses the underlying struggles for women in rebuilding their own lives and that of their families when she says:

> The beginnings were very difficult. I must stress the great courage of women struggling in alien surroundings, working hard to raise young families and often looking after elderly relatives, building homes from scratch. Language was a great problem, which had to be overcome somehow. A great number of women had to combine home responsibilities with outside work to supplement the family income – some had to learn a new trade or profession, occasionally with great success.

The Polish Women's Association (Edinburgh) now celebrates fifty years of working together with women. It is remarkable that a voluntary association, based entirely on self-help initiative, has kept its momentum for all this time. These women, as supported by Hurna (1997), have maintained their ideals of supporting the cause in Poland especially in terms of fundraising for medical support to individuals and their families as well as offering continued care and support to members of the Polish community in lifetime exile. Careful at all times, and especially during the years of communist rule, the women never compromised their political ideals. Many are now widows, and the association has always been welcoming of Scottish women, those who were married to Polish ex-servicemen. Custom and ritual, for long established exiled groups, has been maintained in line with traditional practice and while numbers fade the tenacity of the women to keep together keeps that spirit of bonding in exile as real as if it were yesterday.

FAMILY LIFE

Redefinition and reconstitution

Minority ethnic groups are often characterized by their traditional extended family networks which are based on a solidarity between the generations. Family support by younger members to older members is perceived as the hallmark of its anchor, stability and continuity. This concept of family is carried forward from the country of origin by individuals and groups, in all its widest interpretations, but as forced migration creates not only fragmentation but also permanent loss of close family members, the redefinition and reconstitution of families becomes particularly challenging when these previously held concepts are actually put to the test in the country of exile. This is particularly true where different value sets are used to describe the concept of family and different inter-familial practices are employed. Consequently, the family as a close network of blood relatives takes on a new meaning, and the need to reaffirm an identity for those now forming the core of that family unit becomes a primary task.

Scott (1997) considers how non-blood kinship has developed amongst older Poles, many of whom arrived as single individuals and married from within their ethnic groups, and the small numbers who married outside of it. In this context, she argues, extended 'family networks' are created through affiliations between exiles and realized through a series of symbolic adoptions, for example, importance is given to godparents under catholic rite. This specific affiliation, like blood kinship, raises expectations about inter-generational support and also provides maintenance and semblance to the reconstituted family. Bolzman, Fibbi and Vial (1997) see the family network in terms of a 'reservoir' where resources, be they material, spiritual, symbolic etc., are gathered and used as and when required. In an ideal situation this form of ongoing inter-generational support takes place spontaneously and without pre-conditions being set. But within exile groups, forced migration upsets that equilibrium and families have to learn how to adjust and cope with their new found situation and all its ramifications.

For many older people in exile, the cultural value attached to age diminishes because older people in industrialized societies, in general, are perceived as non-economically viable and therefore dependent. Status afforded to an older person – that which is acquired through life experience, knowledge and wisdom – is not held with the same high esteem as in the country of origin. The respect and honour attributed to a person on account of his or her age is often displaced in favour of the younger generation. Braito (1988) in her study of older Polish people in the UK considers age from a cultural perspective when she says:

> As they age in a culture in which age is less valued than perhaps in their country of origin, they may experience greater status loss and react negatively to ageing in an environment different from their youthful expectations. Things that were appropriate in their own culture are not acceptable in the host environment (1988: 7).

Older people are therefore faced with cultural differences, particularly within the redefined and reconstituted family, and their expectations of being central to that core unit do conflict in exile. For example, many Chilean refugees fear being alone in their old age. They dream of going back to Chile where they know that support from their family and social network would be forthcoming. Although some older Chileans are in good health or/and have relatives in Switzerland and maintain an active participation in voluntary associations and community activities, there is a significant number of older people who experience a definite loss of specific role or engagement which leads to low self-esteem and the dependency factor (Bolzman, 1996).

Conditions of loneliness become a reality for older people and even if the family is strong and supportive life in exile is often fraught with social and economic difficulties which places pressures upon the younger members. Older people, often caught within the cycle of poverty do become dependent on their children for, amongst other things, the basics of daily living. This is the case of Silvia, an older Chilean woman, who needs her children to remain at home with her in order to help to pay the rent of the flat:

> The problem is that the children want to leave the house ... They are already too old as one of them is married and wants to live alone with her husband. That is my problem. I feel somehow guilty to try to keep them here because of my low income. I am used to living with my family. To live without family here is like to be sent to die in an older person's home: that is the way they do it here ... (Bolzman, 1996: 221–2).

The role of the family remains important to older people. The economic side of care, as shown above, is relevant but what remains at the core is the need for reassurance that in old age and, as inter-familial dependency grows, children will continue to play a role in offering and giving support to older members. How different societies offer care for older people varies greatly, and for older refugees and exiles the image of living out their lives in residential or nursing homes in anonymity is particularly stressful and, in the main, contrary to their expectations. Younger members do play important roles in care provision for older members particularly in health or welfare contexts. But, as will be discussed later, exile communities are put under considerable pressure to maintain that care and support.

HEALTH

Older refugees and exiles share many common aspects with other older people from minority ethnic groups in that there is often a lower quality of life which is accompanied by poor physical and mental health. While this can be attributed to low status employment in that depression and loss of self esteem, for example, can be found amongst refugees and exiles who have had to take employment which belies their skills, it is bound up with a whole set of psycho-social conditions imposed through forced migration. For the majority, the reality of that forced migration persists in their memories, and remains as complex in its political content as it is in terms of that person's response to it (Scott, 1997: Bowling, 1990; Braito, 1988). In later life, trauma and its many concomitants can re-emerge and take the form of different mental conditions, such as depression, anxiety, neurosis and, in particular, what is termed the 'Polish Disease' – paranoia (Bram, 1983). Braito (1988) supports this when she considers how forced migration impacted on the Poles following the Second World War:

> Refugee paranoia is also a problem. Such groups as Poles or Ukrainians were separated from their homeland by war, locked in concentration camps, and utilized as forced labour. They are refugees and displaced persons. The experience itself may create health problems. Additionally, behaviours developed to deal with these experiences may have contributed to survival but are a problem in a new and different environment (1988: 10).

For older refugees and exiles their forced migration, while in itself traumatic and life-threatening, was but one controlling aspect of their future lives. For example, making the transition from a largely agrarian background to a highly industrialized and urban environment proposes numerous challenges in adjustment and acculturation, and for older people the extent of resettlement is determined by having to learn to compromise cultural values and norms which often remain in conflict. Faced with the reality that the return home may not be possible in the short term, if at all, initial optimism is replaced with despair, longing and homesickness. Having to face up to and live in the knowledge that you were a single survivor while others perished continues to produce endless guilt which, for refugees and exiles, can never be quite reconciled in their lifetime. While time is considered a great healer and offers distance to personal tragedy it seems there is to be little respite from their earlier experiences which as they grow older become, if anything, more accentuated and real.

Kmita-Dawson (1990) provides a good example of this when she draws a parallel between the war generation of Poles divided between Poland and the UK following the Second World War. She says:

> From my experience, the Poles in Poland mention the war far less frequently than the Poles in Britain. The latter always talk about how difficult their lives were during and after the war and how their survival in 'top gear' (survival syndrome) after traumas had exhausted and often annihilated them. Many of them are still stateless and angry with the results of the Second World War and what happened to them (1990: 205).

The Second World War had a particularly devastating effect on Jewish people through Nazi persecution and extermination which gives a harrowing example of post-event trauma expressed through interminable personal suffering and grief for loss of family and friends. Davidson (1983) in looking at Jewish survivors of this period considers how in later life older people face what now lies ahead of them. She says:

> Old age brings with it the loss of gratifications, of supports and the inescapable necessity to face one's past. There is often a 'flooding back' of memories which are extremely traumatic and the old survivor has once again 'to look at' the unfinished mourning and grieving, and to face his own death with images of dehumanized death. The death which the old refugee and the old traumatized survivor is facing may not be the death which the majority of us think of – natural death, death from disease or accident but the dehumanized death of the concentration camps, death in the gas chambers, death from torture or simply from loss of the desire to live (1983: 26).

It is therefore not surprising that mental illness is one of the most frequently reported health conditions amongst older refugees and exiles. As already discussed in the section on women refugees, forced migration often commits the individual and group to inhuman conditions and experiences which require professional intervention, clinical awareness and sensitivity of that person's experience and the skills and competence to treat it. It is only relatively recently that we have come to understand psychological trauma and how this can affect individuals in the long term.

Scott (1997), in interviewing older Polish people, found a number of people who expressed irrational anxiety about their neighbours who they felt were trying to poison them, neighbours who had broken into their homes while they had been on holiday and used their electricity and neighbours who were conspiring against them etc. Bowling (1990) referred to one woman who had been in forced labour on a German farm and imprisoned in a labour camp:

> God I haven't suffered there [in Germany] half as much, because I had plenty of people in Germany who would have protected me if anybody had really wanted to hurt me ... the real suffering only lasted five years, and here is for over seven years now I been suffering (1990: 8).

In referring to her suffering brought on by neighbours she claimed different acts of violation against her. For example:

> They do all sorts of things to me – sticking hot needles and nails into my body and giving me electric shocks ... when I was having a

bath, they made a hole where the bath was, they would pipe there gas ... Now they don't have to come round here any more, they're doing it by witchcraft (1990: 8).

For today's older people, that learning and understanding may have come too late to be of any longer term benefit but notwithstanding this, there is a desperate need to consider how mental health conditions are diagnosed and treated amongst older refugees and exiles. Dementia, as one condition affecting mainly an older population, needs to fully take into account the personal biographies and life experiences of the patients and consider how therapeutic resources might be best mobilized. Mental health support for refugees and exiles has now attained some recognition, particularly in the case of torture victims whose physical injuries are clearly defined but mental welfare still remains decidedly an area that proposes the greater challenge. Too often older refugees and exiles are misunderstood in terms of the nature of their condition and their response to outward help. Labelling, as a social phenomenon, becomes a common practice amongst professionals in mental health especially when there is a failure on their part to correlate today's behaviour with yesterday's experience. For example, symptoms of paranoia and persecution may perhaps not be so unusual if they are understood in the context of that person's own biography and how they endured forced migration.

SELF-HELP AND COMMUNITY DEVELOPMENT

Many scholars agree with the fact that for refugees and exiles their ethnic community is very important to them, particularly in the early stages of exile when contacts with the local population are difficult. Refugees and exiles are themselves the stimulus for much self-help and support, whether it is material, social, psychologicial or cultural: what remains important is how the community responds to need. As Oerster (1986) pointed out in the case of Tibetans in Switzerland, self-help initiatives were made much easier when refugees and exiles were settled in close proximity to each other.

Scott (1997) in her study of the Polish community in Scotland found amongst the respondents a firm belief in the importance of self-help as a survival strategy; its strength having been sustained for more than fifty years of exile. Many Poles felt that self-help had been, and still is, the only way forward because of the hostilities directed towards them following the end of the Second World War when it was thought that they would return. Polish exiles formed numerous organizations and associations in the late 1940s and early 1950s to represent various interests ranging from religious and community activity to schooling for children. While the ideological basis of exile was held intact, it was through these self-help initiatives that the Polish community was able to discreetly maintain its ethnic identity and give cohesion to what could very easily have become a fragmented group of exiles.

Understandably, in the early stages of exile, groups are cautious about public engagement particularly if this can be construed as political agitation and also because any overt community action might jeopardize their current status and conditions of asylum. But the fact remains that there is an important value in refugees and exiles taking control of their own lives while in exile (and when in permanent settlement), and it is from their solidarity that lessons are to be learned about minority ethnic support, particularly when it comes to long-term care of older people.

The Poles, one of the longest surviving refugee groups, recognized this from a very early stage when they set about establishing the first residential home and sheltered housing scheme in Penrhos in North Wales in 1949. The Polish Housing Society, a registered charity, formed Penrhos in order to care for ex-servicemen and women who had fought in the Second World War and who had as a result suffered disabilities and had no families to look after them. To this day, although now subsidized by the government, older people with differing degrees of need feel a common basis of acceptance and understanding of what their life has meant in exile. The fact that Polish is spoken daily and that care staff are Polish-speaking and Welsh promotes a well-being amongst the residents. The Jewish community is a further example of a remarkable self-help initiative with the setting up of various nursing homes and sheltered housing, largely funded through private means. Tankel (1997) gives examples of self-help dating back to the 1840s when Jewish welfare organizations were introduced and in Scotland, the sheltered housing at Giffnock set up in the late 1980s and early 1990s, is a fine example of ethnic cohesion at work.

Numerous day clubs and day centres have been formed in the UK around specific refugee groups. In London, voluntary associations for the Chilean, Vietnamese, Armenian, Somalia, Russian and Latvian groups, for example, continue to operate on a daily basis offering immediate support to older people. Many of these initiatives are run for and by older people. In Edinburgh, Ognisko – the Polish Lunch and Social Club formed over three years ago – goes from strength to strength with a stable membership of 25 people. Members not only have to organize the lunch club but other less able members are dependent on transport to and from the centre by older people.

In Switzerland, Chilean refugees became concerned with self-help when they realized that exile was not a transitory phenomena. From that point on, they created different associations in order to respond to the different anticipated needs of community members. More recently they have opened a weekly social centre where older persons are particularly welcomed and actively involved in different activities. The Chilean community has also strongly mobilized its resources to obtain the signature of a Social Security agreement between Swiss and Chilean governments, which is the first of this kind between a 'Third World' country and Switzerland. This agreement is very important for older community members as it allows them to return to Chile, if they wish, while continuing to receive an old age pension from the Swiss government. So, now they have, from the financial point of view, a real opportunity to decide if they want to stay in Switzerland in their old age or return to Chile.

CONCLUSION

There is little research on the subject of older refugees and exiles in Europe. For those older refugees and exiles who have survived from as early as the mid 1940s, there is little in the way of recognition and acknowledgement of their needs as a specific category under the different minority ethnic groups. Having lived in exile for the best part of their lives they have not only contributed a wealth of knowledge and experience of what it means to grow old in a second country – thereby informing social gerontologists, social and cultural anthropologists about ethnic community identity – but they have contributed economically to the country of exile through their labours. Their experiences, firstly as active refugees and exiles and thereafter as members of ethnic minority groups, should be considered in old age especially when making assessments in health and social welfare. What may be considered today as paranoid behaviour may well have a logical basis grounded in early experiences as young refugees and exiles but which is all too often overlooked. We mark annually the contribution to war veterans and their important contribution to our freedom and democracy, but yet we infrequently mark the many thousands of people living in permanent exile across the world not through choice but forced circumstance.

Reference was made earlier to how no two personal biographies can be the same (Scott and Kernberg, 1992). It is vital to recognize not only the collective history of a group of people displaced by forced migration, but the individual's story is also essential for they have been the victims of collective violence.

Alienation has been a central concern of this paper, how refugees and exiles settle, often permanently, in their country of exile is important not only for their well-being but how that society responds to victims of forced migration is equally important. Being part of that society means having the opportunity to share in its social, cultural and economic history, and therefore how older refugees and exiles are represented in what is for them a painful and living memory, is the all pervading question.

NOTES

1.   Age in Exile was the name given to a European conference on older refugees held in The Netherlands in 1988. It was the first one of its kind to project interest into older people. Regrettably, there has been no follow up on a Europe-wide basis since then.

2.   I wish to dedicate this chapter to my mother, Jadwiga Teresa Wiczlic (nee Laniszewska, born 1916 in Poland, died in Scotland, 26 September 1997) whose personal experience of exile and internment in forced labour during the Second World War was integral to my learning and understanding of ageing in exile.

3.   McCronin (1992) suggests that, 'The term older refers to refugees aged 50 years and over. Older refugees have to cope with the traumatic experiences of the past that have led to their flight as well as the trauma of ageing.' Finlay and Reynolds (1987) support this perception of when is old when they say: 'The standard definition of the elderly as being those over retirement age is not always suitable for members of refugee communities. In common with other different cultures they may have been used to different lifestyles and experiences and to economic disadvantages. Many will have been through traumatic experiences and losses in the course of their escape and subsequent exile. These factors can all have the effect of ageing people earlier.'

4.   The Second World War resulted in the resettlement of significant numbers of Central and East European across Europe. These included Lithuanians, Latvians, Estonians, Ukrainians, Yugoslavs, Czechs and Russians. The Poles constituted the largest single group

with approximately 150 000 (including those who had been displaced persons or recruited through the Ministry of Labour's European Volunteer Workers' Schemes from Germany in the early 1950s) and as they were largely members of the Polish Armed forces they were mostly men (see Sword, 1989).

The Ukrainians settled within the UK between 1946 and 1950. Many had been members of the Polish, Canadian or US Armed Forces while others had arrived as displaced people from Germany, Austria and Italy recruited to work in designated industries through the European Volunteer Workers Scheme. In 1951 it was estimated that some 46 000 Ukrainians were settled in the UK (see Petyshun, 1980).

5.   The Chilean exile began after the Military Putsch of September 1973. It is estimated that about one million people left the country escaping from direct or indirect political persecution. As it was a massive flight, people of all social conditions and ages were concerned with migration. The number of Chilean refugees in Western Europe was approximately 100 000. Switzerland and Great Britain have both received between 4000 and 5000.

REFERENCES

Ahmed, P.I., Tims, F. and Kolker, A. (1981), 'After the Fall: Indochinese Refugees in the United States' in Cohelo, G.V. and Ahmed, P.I. (eds), *Uprooting and Development: Dilemmas of Coping with Modernisation*, New York, Plenum Press.

Allard, D. (1987), *L'insertion Socio-Culturelle des Réfugiés Vietnamiens, Mémoire de licence*, Genèva, Département de Sociologie, Université de Genève.

Baker, R. (ed.) (1983), *The Psychosocial Problems of Refugees,* London, British Refugee Council.

Bolzman, C. (1993), 'La place des femmes dans une migration politique. L'exemple des exilées Chiliennes en Suisse', in Preiiwerk, I. and Sauvain, C. (eds), *Vers un ailleurs prometteur ... Paris-Genève*, Presses Universitaires de France Institut Universitaire d'Etudes du Developpement.

Bolzman, C. (1994), 'Stages and Modes of Incorporation of Exiles in Switzerland: the Example of Chilean Refugees', *Innovation*, Vol. 7, No. 3, pp. 321–33.

Bolzman, C. (1996), *Sociologie de l'exil: Une approche dynamique,* Zurich, Seismo.

Bolzman, C., Fibbi, R. and Vial, M. (1997), 'Family Network and Family Support of Older Migrants in Switzerland: An Asset for Later Life'? Paper presented at the *European Conference on Older Migrants and Refugees* in Helsingoor, 21–23 March.

Bowling, B. (1990), *The Development, Co-ordination and Provision of Services to Elderly People from the Ethnic Minorities: A Report on Four*

Innovatory Projects, Age Concern Institute of Gerontology, London, King's College.

Braito, R. (1988), 'The Polish Immigrant Experience and its relevance for Quality of Life Issues Among the Elderly' Paper presented at the Annual Meeting of the British Sociological Association, Edinburgh, Scotland, March 28–31.

Bram, G. (1983), 'Breakdown in Elderly Polish Refugees' in Baker, R. (ed.) (1983), *The Psychosocial problems of Refugees,* British Refugee Council.

British Refugee Council; (1988), Age in Exile: A Report on Elderly Exiles in the United Kingdom, presented at the 'Age in Exile: An International Conference on Elderly Refugees in Europe' Leeuwenhorst Congress Centre, Noordwijkerhout, The Netherlands, 25–27 1988 November.

Davidson, S. (1983), 'Psychosocial Aspects of Holocaust Trauma in the Life Cycle of Survivor Refugees and their Families' in Baker, R. (ed.) *The Psychosocial Problems of Refugees,* London, British Refugee Council.

Finlay, R. and Reynolds, J. (1987), *Social Work and Refugees: A Handbook on Working with People in Exile in the UK*, London, National Extention College/ Refugee Action.

Frelick, B. (1992), *Call Them What They Are – Refugees*, World Refugee Survey 1992, US Committee for Refugees.

Hurna, I. (1997), Zwiasek Polek: Polish Women's Association in Scott, H. (ed.) *Ageing in Multicultural Europe: Making the Challenge – Setting the Agenda*, Papers presented for the Age Concern Scotland Scottish European Symposium for the European Year of Older People and Solidarity between Generations, 15–16 December 1993.

Jagucki, W. (1991), 'The Polish Experience: 50 Years On', unpublished paper presented at the Age Concern Scotland national seminar, *Ageing in a Second Homeland: An Introduction to Transcultural Health Issues for Older Older People from Black and Minority Ethnic Groups*, September.

Kalpmkaryan, E. and Ohanian, M. (1996), *Survey Report of Armpnian Older People Living in Houston*, London, Portee for Armenian Information and Advice.

Kmita-Dawson, M. (1990), 'The Effect of the Second World War on the Mental Health of the Polish Immigrants in Britain' in Brunon H. (ed.) *Mental Health in a Changing World,* Warsaw, The Polish Society for Mental Health.

Leser, M. and Seeberg, B. (1992), *Alter und Migration. Eine empirische Untersuchung an ungarischen Migranten in Basel*, Basel, Bad Kissingen.

McCallin, M. (1991), *The Psychosocial Consequences of Violent Displacement: The Experience of Central American Refugee Women in Washington*, DC, New York, International Catholic Child Bureau, 1991 quoted in Frelick, B. 'Call Them What They Are – Refugees' in McCrohan, P. (ed.) (1992) *The Psychosocial Needs of Elderly Refugees Living in Lambeth and the Neighbouring Boroughs, and the Degree to which those Needs are Met by Statutory and Voluntary Agencies. A Report of the Elderly Project of the Refugee Support Centre*, London, October.

Minority Eights Group (1990), *Refugees in Europe, A Minority Rights Group Report*, London, Minority Rights Group.

Montero, D. (1979), 'The Vietnamese Refugees in America: Toward a Theory of Spontaneous International Migration', *International Migration Review*, Vol. 13, No. 4, pp. 624–48.

Oerster, K. (1986), *Les réfugiés en Suisse. Aspects de l'intégration*, Lucerne, Caritas.

Petyshin, R. (1980), 'Britain's Ukranian Community: A Study of the Political Dimension in Ethnic Community Development', unpublished PhD thesis, University of Bristol.

Refugee Action (1987), *Last Refuge: Elderly People from Vietnam in the UK*, Derby, Refugee Action.

Refugee Council (1990), *Age in Exile: A British Response*, Report from a Conference on the Needs of Elderly Refugees, London, Refugee Council.

Scott, H. (1997), (ed.) 'Ageing in Multicultural Europe: Making the Challenge – Setting the Agenda', paper presented for the Age Concern Scotland Scottish European Symposium for the European Year of Older People and Solidarity between Generations, 15–16 December 1993.

Scott, H. (1998), Invisible and Involuntary Exiles: A Generation of the Polish Community in Scotland, Draft M.Phil thesis, University of Edinburgh.

Scott, H. and Kernberg, T. (1992), 'Invisible and Involuntary Exiles: Older People from Eastern Europe in Scotland', paper presented to the Age Concern Scotland national conference, Growing Old in Multicultural Scotland: Agenda for Action, University of Strathclyde, April.

Simon-Barouh, I. (1984), 'L'accueil des réfugiés d'äsie du sud-est à Rennes', *Pluriel*, No. 28, pp. 23–55.

Sword, K. with Davies, N. and Ciechanowski, J. (1989), *The Formation of the Polish Community in Great Britain 1939–1950*, London School of Slavonic and East Europe Studies, University of London.

Tankel, J. (1997), 'The Glasgow Jewish Housing Association', in Scott, H. (ed.) *Ageing in Multicultural Europe: Making the Challenge – Setting the Agenda*.

Valters, J. (1992), *Elderly Refugee Project: Report on the Third Six Months*, September 1991–March 1992 Sheffield, Northern Refugee Centre.

10 Refugees in the job market: a case of unused skills in the British economy

Alice Bloch

This chapter will document previous research which shows the importance of employment for refugee settlement, the position of refugees in the labour market and some of the barriers that refugees might experience in gaining access to employment. It will then present data from a survey of 180 refugees, from the Somali, Tamil and Zairian communities in the London Borough of Newham, to show the position of refugees in the labour market (Bloch, 1996). This chapter will show the high levels of unemployment experienced by refugees in Britain, in spite of the range of skills and high levels of academic qualifications that many refugees bring with them from their country of origin.

BACKGROUND

The importance of employment as a means through which the settlement of refugees can occur has been highlighted by many researchers (Robinson, 1986; Srinivasan, 1994; Joly, 1996). Finnan (1981) argues that refugees who are working and economically independent adjust more easily to the host society than those who are unemployed or dependent on benefits for extended periods of time. Knox (1997) highlights the importance of employment by stating that:

> In many ways, for refugees, employment is the key to successful integration because it leads to interaction with British people, the chance to learn English, the ability to support oneself and rebuild a future, as well as a chance to regain self esteem and confidence (1997: 31).

However, refugees remain the most underemployed group in Britain. Estimates about the levels of unemployment among refugees vary although the Refugee Council (1992) estimated that 70 per cent of refugees in London were unemployed. A survey of 263 refugees carried out by the Home Office in conjunction with researchers from Salford University found that 56 per cent of those interviewed had never been in paid employment while 30 per cent had only had sporadic employment careers in Britain. That is, they had been in a series of temporary jobs or had moved between unskilled jobs spending most of their time out of work (Home Office Research and Planning Unit, 1993).

Sivanandan (1990) refers to the unskilled and sporadic work which tends to be carried out by asylum seekers and undocumented workers. He points to jobs like fast-food assistants, petrol-pump attendants, porters and security guards in private security firms and argues that they tend, increasingly, to be carried out by people from Colombia, Chile, Turkey, Sudan, Sri Lanka, Eritrea and Iran. He states that these workers:

> with no rights to housing or medical care, and under the constant threat of deportation...are forced to accept wages and conditions which no indigenous worker, black or white, would accept (1990: 156).

The research by the Home Office also found that as few as 14 per cent of refugees had been in employment for most of their time in Britain. At the time of the survey only 27 per cent of those considered economically active were in paid employment (Carey-Wood *et al.*, 1995). People who were employed had been in Britain longer than those who were unemployed, spoke good English on arrival to Britain, felt settled in the community and were more likely to be living in the Southeast than were others.

One of the problems faced by refugees in the UK labour market is that they are 'functionally overqualified'. According to Bravo:

> they are too well qualified for lower grade posts, have too little work or professional experience for higher-management posts, and feel that they are too far along in their career path to switch careers. Frequently their language skills are not commensurate with their qualifications (1993: 3).

This is compounded by the fact that, for some refugees, the qualifications obtained in their country of origin may not be recognized in Britain. For example, Gambell reported a case of an asylum seeker from Iraq who was a qualified dentist from the University of Baghdad. According to Gambell:

> She has been told by the British Dental Council that she must requalify or complete a dental course in order to practice in the United Kingdom. She has been considered for a University place but as an asylum seeker she would have to pay overseas student fees, and does not qualify for a grant (1993: 34).

This case also illustrates the wider problem faced by refugees as a result of government legislation; asylum seekers are not entitled to grants for study for their first three years of residence and because the majority of asylum seekers are under 40 years of age, this will seriously affect their retraining opportunities and their employment prospects (HMSO, 1995).

In addition to the problems of being overqualified and the lack of recognition for qualifications obtained overseas, there are a range of other difficulties that refugees may experience in gaining employment (Marshall, 1989). First, some refugees, especially those from rural areas like Kurdish refugees, may not have the sort of skills and experience that are relevant to the UK economy and this will hinder job prospects. Secondly, around 60 per cent of all jobs are filled without advertising, that is through personal contacts or internal promotions. Rates of unemployment are so high among refugees that using personal contacts is not going to be an effective strategy for getting a job. Thirdly, refugees may lack information about where to look for jobs, the best ways to fill in application forms and how to handle the interview situation in Britain. Fourthly, employers require references and these can be very difficult for refugees to supply to prospective employers. The fifth difficulty faced by refugees is their propensity to see themselves as guests rather than settled in the host community. This can result in an orientation towards people from their own country rather than the host society. With regard to refugees from Iraq, Al-Rasheed states that:

> This prohibits people from having access to local information networks regarding job opportunities. Lack of social relations with the host society also entails lack of knowledge about how the occupations are organized here, potential gaps in the market which might be exploited, and a general feel about how businesses work in this country (1992: 543).

Finally, employment record is the most important selection criteria for employees and so refugees lose out because they have no employment history in Britain (Marshall, 1989). According to Marshall:

> refugees lose out because their qualifications and experience are not recognized in this country. In addition they have a gap in their work history just because they are refugees and have faced huge upheavals (1989: 14).

Refugee women may face particular difficulties gaining access to the labour market, especially as they are less likely to be proficient in English than their male counterparts. Research carried out by the Home Office found that 44 per cent of men said their English language was good compared to 28 per cent of women. On arrival to Britain a quarter of the men interviewed had no English language skills compared to a third of women (Carey-Wood *et al.*, 1995). Moreover, research has found that the difficulties that women might face in gaining access to the labour market are compounded by lack of child care provision, transportation difficulties and the impact of social isolation that results from staying at home and looking after children (Bach and Carroll-Seguin, 1986).

EMPLOYMENT BEFORE COMING TO BRITAIN

Before coming to Britain, most refugees were either economically active or studying. Figure 10.1 compares the main activity of refugees before coming to Britain with their main activity at the time of the survey.

The main difference in activity in the homeland compared to Britain is the reduction in the proportion of respondents who were working or students and the increase in the proportion who were unemployed. As many as 46 per cent of respondents described themselves as unemployed at the time of the survey although there were very significant differences by community, with Tamils more likely to be in employment than were others.

Before coming to the UK refugees had been employed in a diverse range of jobs although nearly one in five had been teachers in their country of origin. There was a gender difference in the types of jobs that respondents had done prior to coming to Britain. Men were more likely than were women to be working as teachers, engineers or shopkeepers. Women were much more likely than men to be working as cashiers, market traders, secretaries or typists.

Figure 10.1 Main activity before coming to Britain and main activity in Britain

Percentages
Base number (before): 180
Base number (in Britain): 178

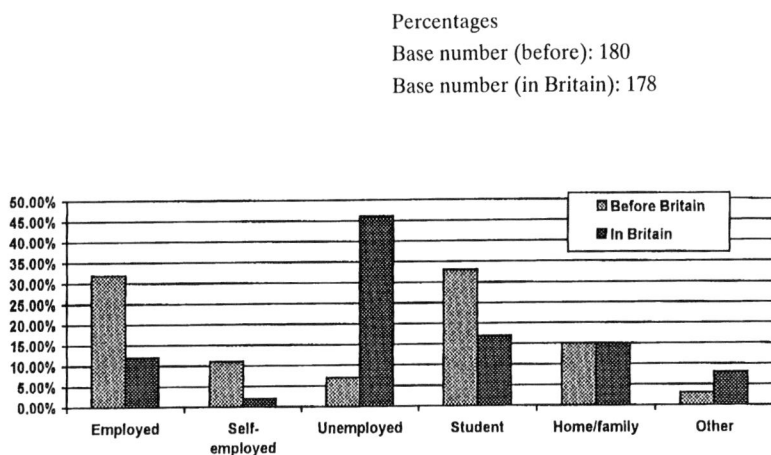

Source: Bloch (1996), Figure 17, p. 44.

As many as 20 per cent of respondents who were working before coming to the UK, had been employed in their last job for more than 10 years. Thirteen per cent had been employed for 5 years but less than 10 years, 20 per cent had been employed for two years but less than five and 10 per cent had been employed for two years or less.

Clearly refugees living in Newham came to the UK with diverse skills and labour market experience. Moreover, as the next section will show, they were a very well qualified group.

EDUCATION AND QUALIFICATIONS

Levels of education and qualifications obtained by refugees, before arriving in the host society, are known to affect adaptation to the new society, including labour market participation (Bach and Carroll-Seguin, 1986). According to Desbarats:

In clarifying the role of various determinants of adaptation, growing agreement has emerged concerning the importance of some pre-migration characteristics such as education and training (1986: 410).

Respondents were asked what their highest level of education, if any, was on arrival to Britain. Table 10.1 shows that as many as 22 per cent had attended university but that there were clear differences in educational background by sex and country of origin. Zairians tended to be the most educated group while the majority of Somali women had received no formal education.

Three-quarters of all respondents had a qualification on arrival in the UK. Table 10.2 shows that nearly a quarter of all respondents had either a degree or a postgraduate qualification before applying for asylum and this is similar to the findings of a national Home Office study of refugee settlement (Carey-Wood *et al.*, 1995). People who described themselves as having 'other' qualifications tended to have vocational and trade qualifications such as building, carpentry, hairdressing, dressmaking and welding. People with professional qualifications had a range of skills which included a computer scientist, a few mechanical engineers and someone with a Masters in Business Administration (MBA).

Clearly refugees are a very well-qualified group. In fact, they were better qualified on arrival to the UK than were others in the community. Figure 10.2 shows that, in the London East Training and Enterprise Council (LETEC) area, people from refugee communities have arrived in Britain with higher levels of academic qualifications than those achieved by people from minority ethnic communities as a whole and their white counterparts.

Table 10.1   Highest level of education by country of origin and sex

Frequencies
Base Number: 176

	Somali		Tamil		Zairian		Total
							%
	Male	Fem	Male	Fem	Male	Fem	
University	11	1	4	7	12	4	22
Further education	2	–	7	3	15	5	19
Secondary education	12	4	19	17	6	18	43
Primary education	2	1	1	–	–	–	2
None	3	22	–	–	–	–	14
Total number	30	28	31	27	33	27	176

Source: Bloch (1997), Table 45, p. 217.

Table 10.2   Highest level of qualification on arrival to the UK

Base number: 134

	Percentages
'O' levels	19
'A' levels	17
General certificate of education*	2
Diploma/Baccalaureate*	22
Degree	11
Postgraduate	4
Professional qualifications	6
Teacher training	5
Secretarial	2
Other	12
* 'A' level equivalents	

Source: Bloch, (1996), Table 13, p. 34.

Figure 10.2   Highest academic qualifications

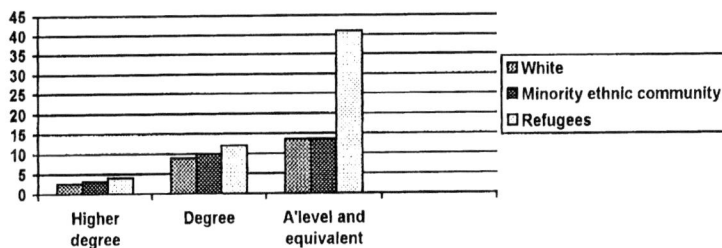

Source: Data for white and minority ethnic community populations from LETEC (1995).

One of the difficulties faced by refugees is that some qualifications obtained outside of the UK are not recognized or are not directly transferable (Gambell, 1993). Less than a quarter of those who had qualifications on arrival in Britain (23 per cent) said that their qualifications were recognized in the UK. In addition to qualifications not being recognized, some refugees leave their homeland without certificates so even if their qualifications could be converted to their

UK equivalents, they did not have the evidence to enable the conversion to take place.

LABOUR MARKET PARTICIPATION IN BRITAIN

As Figure 10.1 showed, 14 per cent of respondents were working, either as employees or were self-employed at the time of the survey while 46 per cent described themselves as unemployed. Respondents who were working tended to be from Sri Lanka (18 out of 25) while those who described themselves as unemployed were most likely to be from Zaire (44 out of 83).

There were a number of factors which affected the propensity of refugees to be in employment. First, a greater proportion of men were employed than were women (53 per cent and 39 per cent respectively). Secondly, length of residence was also important. A third of those who arrived in Britain before 1990 were working compared to one in ten who arrived between 1991 and 1994 and less than one in ten who arrived in 1995 or later. Thirdly, immigration status also influenced labour market participation. Those with refugee status or exceptional leave to remain were more likely to be working than people on temporary admission or those who were appealing against a Home Office decision on their case. Finally, refugees who felt settled in Britain and saw it as their home, were slightly more likely to be working (two in ten) then those who did not see Britain as their home (one in ten) which verifies the importance of employment as a factor affecting settlement.

Levels of unemployment were higher among refugees than they were among people from other ethnic communities. Table 10.3 shows the different rates of unemployment, in Newham, by ethnic group.

Table 10.4 shows the type of jobs that those who were employed were engaged in. Those who were working in Britain were employed in low level jobs, in spite of the skills and experience that refugees bring with them. There was also a lack of diversity of employment. Lack of diversity of employment among refugees has also been demonstrated by research carried out among Vietnamese refugees in Manchester where over half of those in employment were employed in the catering industry (Girbash, 1991).

Refugees in employment tended to work unsociable hours, that is before 8.30 in the morning and after 6.30 at night (eight in ten). Eight in ten worked in the evening or at night, eight in ten worked regularly

Table 10.3   Total percentage unemployed in Newham by ethnic group

Total population: 212 170

	Levels of unemployment
White	15.4
Black Caribbean	18.2
Black African	39.6
Black (Other)	22.9
Indian	18.9
Pakistani	35.4
Bangladeshi	42.8
Chinese	21.1
Other Asian	23.3
Other	25.1
All (percentages)	19.3

Source: 1991 Census.

Table 10.4   Current employment in the UK

Base number: 25

	Frequencies
Security work	2
Shop work/cashier (including petrol stations)	9
Factory: packing/machine operator	4
Administration	3
Other*	7

* Jobs classified as 'Other' include: sorting at the post office, civil engineer, self-employed printer, self-employed English language teacher and community worker.

Source: Bloch (1996), Figure 19, p. 47.

at the weekends, that is two or more weekends in every month. Moreover, job turnover was high among refugees who tended not to have been in their current jobs for very long. Three in ten had been in their current job for less than a year, five in ten had been in their current job for one year but less than three years and only two in ten had been in their job for three years or longer.

Refugees were also working in jobs which, on the whole, showed little relation to their previous employment and did not utilize their skills and experience. Table 10.5 shows present and previous employment among refugees who were working in Britain at the time of the survey and who were also working before leaving their country of origin.

The employment patterns of refugees differed from those of the community at large. While 52 per cent of men of working age and 36 per cent of women of working age were employed full-time (Rix, 1996), eight in ten refugees were in full-time employment. Moreover, only 2 per cent of refugees in Newham were self-employed compared with a national average of 13 per cent and a Newham average of 9 per cent among men and 2 per cent among women (Sly, 1995; Rix, 1996). Finally, more than half of the refugees who were in employment were employed in temporary positions compared with 22 per cent of refugees nationally and 6 per cent of the population at large (Carey-Wood *et al.*, 1995).

Respondents were asked how many hours a week they worked on average, and what their take-home pay was per week, after any deductions for tax, national insurance and pensions. The data in Table 10.6 shows that refugees were working very long hours for very low pay.

All the part-time workers worked for 20 hours a week or less each week and they all earned less than £200 a week. All of the full-time

Table 10.5   Current job and job before leaving country of origin

Frequencies
Base number: 11

Last job in country of origin	Current job
Clerical	Security guard
Army Colonel	Security guard
Clerical	Administration
Teacher	English language teacher
Farmer	Packer in factory
Clerical	Administration
Personnel manager	Administration
Marketing executive	Voluntary sector outreach worker
Teacher	Shop work
Cashier	Shop work
Mechanical engineer	Shop work

Source: Bloch (1997), Table 46, p. 236.

Table 10.6   Number of hours worked by take-home pay

	20 or fewer hours	36 but less than 50 hours*	50 hours or more	Total
Take-home pay				
Less than £50	1	–	–	1
£50 but less than £75	2	–	–	2
£75 but less than £100	1	–	–	1
£100 but less than £125	1	–	–	1
£125 but less than £150	1	5	–	6
£150 but less than £200	–	3	5	8
£200 but less than £250	–	1	2	3
£250 but less than £300	–	–	1	1
Total column	6	9	8	23

* No respondents worked between 20 and 36 hours.

Source: Bloch (1996), Table 20, p. 48.

Table 10.7   Average hourly earnings of the workforce, in pence

	1990	1991	1992	1993	1994	1995	% change
Barking and Dagenham	674	758	828	886	879	907	34.6
Havering	652	736	800	814	843	868	33.1
Newham	684	757	839	870	856	860	25.7
Redbridge	701	743	823	850	865	889	26.8
Tower Hamlets	865	980	1066	1168	1280	1257	45.3
Waltham Forest	606	712	755	711	785	830	40.0
London East	718	808	887	994	994	1005	40.0

Source: New Earnings Survey reported in LETEC (1996).

workers worked for 36 hours a week or more and most were paid less than £200 per week.

Refugees were earning less money than people from other ethnic groups in Newham. When the weekly rates of pay were transferred to hourly rates, most refugees earned less than £4 an hour. Table 10.7 shows that this was much less than the average hourly pay in Newham and across East London.

There are wage differentials among different ethnic groups. Data from the 1994 Labour Force Survey, and analyzed by Sly (1995), shows that average hourly pay among those in full time work was £7.44 among the white population and £6.82 among ethnic minority communities. People from the Pakistani and Bangladeshi communities tend to be less well paid than people from other ethnic groups, averaging £5.15 and hour, but this is still more than the average pay commanded by refugees (Sly, 1995).

ATTITUDES TOWARDS CURRENT EMPLOYMENT

Refugees who were working were asked whether they were satisfied with their job: around half said that they were either very satisfied or satisfied. Three in ten were neither satisfied nor dissatisfied and two in ten were dissatisfied or very dissatisfied. Among those who were working, as many as seven in ten were looking for a different job. Table 10.8 shows the reasons why those who were in employment were looking for a different jobs.

Pay and the fact that respondents saw their current job as a fill in were the main reasons why people were looking for different jobs, suggesting that those who were working felt that they should be doing something more commensurate with their qualifications and/or experience. Linked to this, seven in ten felt that there was another sort of job that would be more suitable for them than the one they were currently doing. The sorts

Table 10.8   All the reasons why those in employment are looking for a different job

Base number: 17

	Frequencies
Present job just a fill in until I find something I want	12
Pay unsatisfactory	12
Journey unsatisfactory	3
Wants to work longer hours	3
Present job may end	2
Wants to work shorter hours	1
Not my profession	1
Harassment	1
Other (not specified)	1

Source: Bloch (1996), Table 20, p. 48.

of jobs that people felt would be more suitable were linked to their previous employment experience and skills and included: accountancy, civil engineering, finance/banking, mechanics, teaching, hairdressing, farming and clerical work.

The length of time spent looking for more suitable work ranged from six months to eight years. Eleven people had applied for what they considered to be a more suitable job, but only four had been interviewed and only one had been offered a job. One respondent, who had not been offered a job noted that in interview situations, he was always asked for work experience in the UK but had been unable to gain access to such experience.

Table 10.9 shows that perceived barriers to more suitable jobs revolved mostly around racial discrimination and discrimination against refugees.

Table 10.9 Numbers of those working, stating different barriers as preventing them from getting a more suitable job

	Frequencies Base number: 16*	
	All barriers	Main barrier
Barriers		
Racial discrimination	11	4
Lack of experience	9	2
Discrimination against refugees	9	1
Little work available	7	2
English literacy skills	6	1
Wages too low	5	–
English language skills	3	2
Relevant vocational skills	3	–
Lack of information	3	–
Child care problems	2	1
Sex discrimination	2	–
Lack of self-confidence	1	1
Accent	1	1
Non-recognition of experience/ qualifications	1	1
Culture	1	–
Total	64	16

* Respondents were asked to state all the barriers then the main barrier.

Source: Bloch (1996), Table 22, p. 50.

LABOUR MARKET ASPIRATIONS

More than half (51 per cent) of respondents who were not working said that they were looking for paid work, while 49 per cent were not looking for paid work. Figure 10.3 shows the reasons why some respondents were not looking for paid work.

The reasons given for not looking for work in the 'other' category were lack of English language skills (three respondents) and immigration restrictions (one respondent).

Respondents who were currently seeking employment, were asked what sort of job they were looking for. In some cases respondents gave more than one type of job and their responses are shown in Table 10.10.

Differences in labour market aspirations emerged by sex and country of origin. Of the 15 respondents who said that they wanted 'any job', two thirds were Zairian. Tamils were more likely than were others to want a job in the retail, service or garment industries, six in ten Tamils who wanted a job. Zairians were more likely than were others to want a job in cleaning or security work, nearly four in ten of Zairians who wanted a job.

Figure 10.3   Reasons for not looking for paid employment

Base number: 71

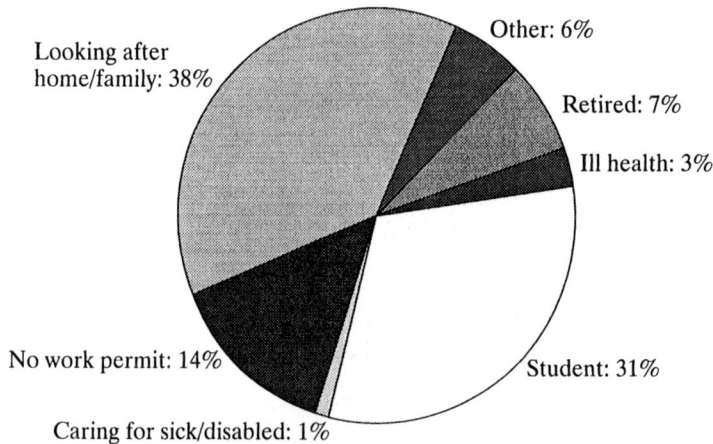

Source: Bloch (1996), Figure 20, p. 52.

Table 10.10 Number looking for different types of employment

Base number: 76

	Frequencies
Cleaning/security	19
Clerical/office/finance	18
Retail/service/garment	18
Any job	15
Teaching	8
Other*	7
Child care/nursery	2
Driving	2
IT/technical	1

* 'Other' included: carpentry, electrician and interpreting.

Source: Bloch (1996), Table 24, p. 54.

Table 10.11 Type of work wanted by qualifications on arrival to Britain

Frequencies
Base number: 76

	'O' levels	'A' level or equiv.	Degree	Postgraduate	Teacher training	Other
Any job	1	7	3	–	–	2
Clerical/office/ finance	2	7	3	2	2	2
Retail/service/ garment	5	3	3	–	1	3
IT/New Technology	–	1	–	–	–	–
Teaching	1	–	1	1	4	1
Security/ cleaning	2	9	–	–	–	5
Driving	–	1	–	–	–	1
Child care/nursery	–	2	–	–	–	–
Other	2	3	–	–	–	–

Source: Bloch (1996), Table 25, p. 54.

The sort of employment that refugees were seeking did not always reflect their skills and experience. For instance, teachers were looking for jobs in retail and service industries or in security. Table 10.11 shows the qualifications that respondents who were looking for work at the time of the survey had on arrival to Britain and reinforces the fact that people were seeking jobs which were not commensurate with their qualifications.

Interviews with refugees suggests that the reasons why people were going for low skill jobs was because new arrivals were told, based on the experiences of other refugees, that unskilled or low skilled jobs were the only ones they could get. Other research has also indicated that refugees may be reluctant to make an economic investment in Britain as they do not see it as a permanent move (Al-Rasheed, 1992).

UNUSED SKILLS AND BARRIERS TO EMPLOYMENT AMONG THOSE SEEKING WORK

Those looking for employment were asked if they had any skills that they had been unable to use in a paid job in Britain: two thirds (52 out of 78) said that they had. The skills that respondents identified as remaining unused reflected their employment experience, prior to coming to Britain. For example, one respondent with teaching skills described his own situation in the following way:

> I have nearly 25 years of experience, 15 years teaching and 10 years as a school principle, but without British training I cannot get into teaching.

Fifteen people had experience in retail and service industries which had been unused in Britain, 13 had teaching skills, 11 respondents had clerical and office skills, nine had trade skills which included electricians, carpenters and mechanics, two had skills in law and five had other skills including accountancy, computing and civil engineering.

In order to understand the difficulties that refugees felt they faced getting into the labour market, those who were looking for work were asked what barriers they faced, if any in gaining employment. Figure 10.4 shows the responses.

Respondents from Zaire were more likely than others to identify racial discrimination or discrimination against refugees as the main barrier to employment. Of those who said that discrimination against refugees or racial discrimination was the main barrier to employment, seven in ten were from Zaire.

The longer people had been in the country the more likely it was that they would specify discrimination, either racial or specifically against refugees, as the main barrier to employment. Nine in ten of the respondents who said racial discrimination or discrimination

Figure 10.4   Barriers to employment

Frequencies
Base number: 78

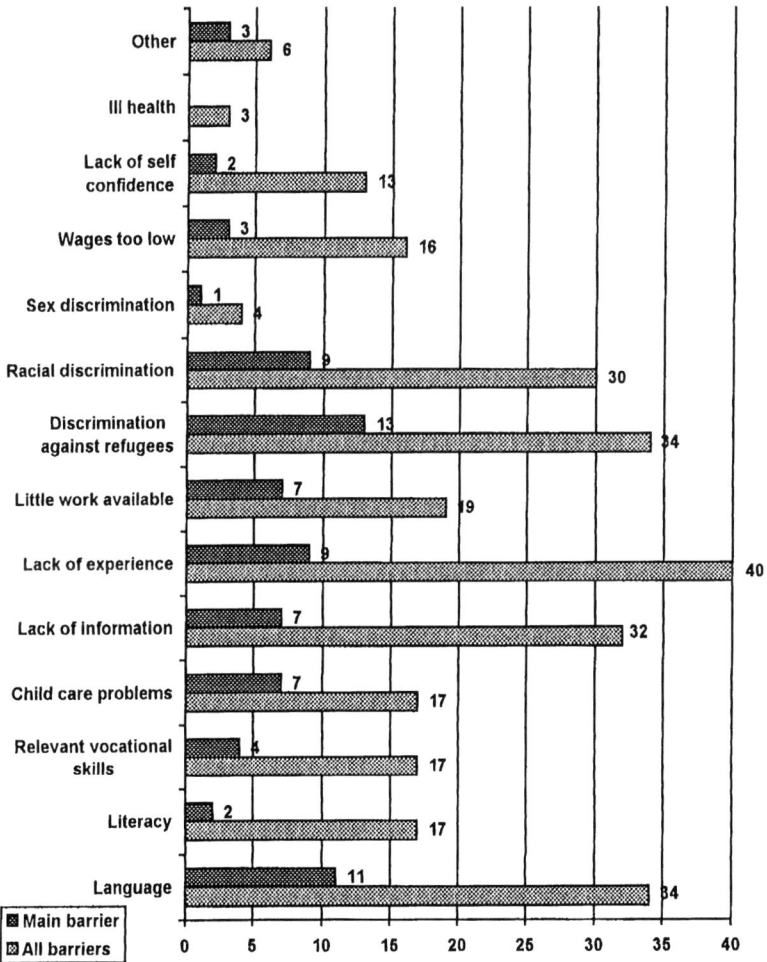

Source: Bloch (1996), Figure 24, p. 60.

against refugees was the main barrier had been in Britain since 1992 or before. Finally more men than women stated that discrimination was the main factor preventing access to the labour market; the proportions were seven in ten and three in ten respectively.

Nearly half of those who identified barriers to employment mentioned a lack of information. Those who had arrived before 1993 were less likely to see a lack of information as a barrier to employment; three in ten of those who arrived before 1993 identified a lack of information compared to half of those who arrived in 1993 or later. Country of origin was also important, although this was linked to length of residence. Tamils were less likely than were others to see a lack of information as a barrier to employment. The proportions were one in ten among Tamils compared to half of the Somali and half of the Zairian respondents.

Clearly there was a very negative perception of the sorts of employment opportunities that were available to refugees. Some of the difficulties could be alleviated with targeted resources in the areas of language skills, information, child care and vocational skills.

METHODS OF JOB SEEKING

Methods of job seeking varied between the three communities and this reflects the cultural specificity of job seeking which has been highlighted by other research (Marshall, 1989; 1992). Table 10.12 shows the way in which respondents, who were employed before coming to Britain, found their last job by country of origin.

Mostly respondents had found their job through an advertisement (five in ten). Other ways of finding employment was through family members (more than one in ten), friends (more than one in ten), through promotion (less than one in ten), through a recommendation from their college of study (less than one in ten) and the rest through other means such as applying for a job in person or being a member of an organization already. In contrast, Figure 10.5 shows that people who were either working in Britain or who had worked in Britain in the past tended, for the most part, to find their jobs through friends.

Methods of job seeking varied by community. A comparison of the data in Table 10.12 with the data in Table 10.13 shows the differences in the way in which respondents who were working before coming to Britain and those who were working at the time of the survey found their job.

Table 10.12 Way of finding last job by country of origin

Frequencies
Base number: 53

	Somalia	Sri Lanka	Zaire	Total Frequencies
Advertisement	11	14	3	28
Friends	1	4	3	8
Family	–	2	5	7
Recommendation from college	–	–	4	4
Promotion	–	–	2	2
Other	–	1	3	4
Total	12	21	20	53

Figure 10.5 Ways of finding current job or last job in Britain

Frequencies
Base number: 63

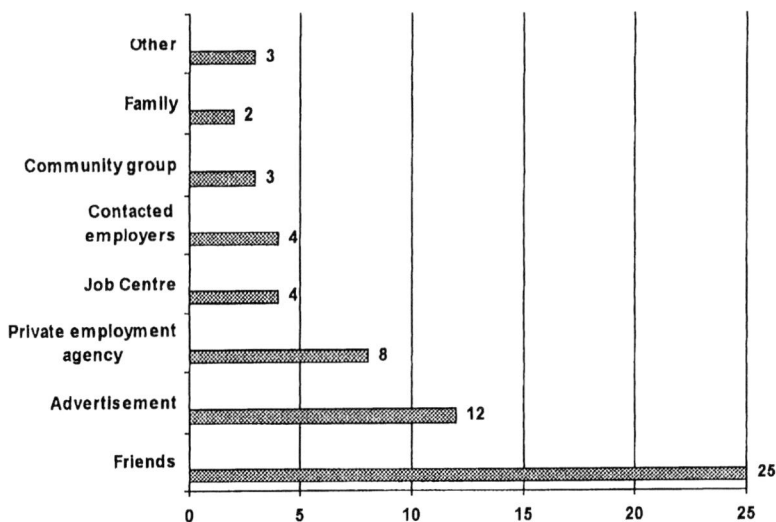

Source: Bloch, (1996), p. 55.

Table 10.13   Way of finding job in Britain by country of origin

Frequencies
Base number: 25

	Somalia	Sri Lanka	Zaire	Total
Friends	1	10	–	11
Family	1	–	–	1
Community group	–	1	–	1
Job Centre	1	–	–	1
Advertisement	1	5	–	6
Private agency	–	–	1	1
Own business	–	1	1	2
Contacted employer	–	–	1	1
Other	–	1	–	1

Source: Bloch (1997), Table 58, p. 235.

Informal contacts were much more important in terms of finding employment in Britain than they had been in the country of origin. More than half of the Tamil respondents who were working had found their job through a friend while a quarter had also found work by responding to an advertisement. Those who spoke English at the level of simple sentences were most dependent on informal contacts for employment while those who spoke English fluently were more likely to find their job by responding to an advertisement. Thus language skills were, in some cases, enabling Tamil refugees to successfully use the more formal job search mechanisms which are available in Britain and, as a result, reduce dependence on the ethnic enclave or community.

Desbarats (1986) noted in research among Sino-Vietnamese refugees that economic self-sufficiency was dependent, in part, on English language skills on arrival to the United States. Those who arrived with high levels of English were more able to adapt economically and were less dependent on the ethnic community as a way of finding employment. This finding is replicated among Tamils in Newham where all of those who spoke no English on arrival, but who were working at the time of the survey, had found their jobs through friends. Thus, the ethnic enclave was providing a stepping-stone for those members of the community who were not sufficiently adapted in

Figure 10.6   Different methods of job seeking by those currently looking for employment

Frequencies
Base number: 78

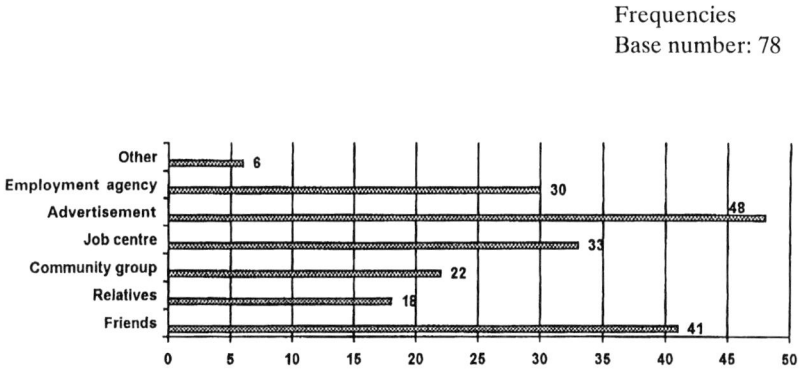

Source: Bloch (1996), Figure 22, p. 56.

terms of language skills to seek employment through the statutory and formal mechanisms which exist.

In order to compare methods of job seeking among those who were looking for work with the methods that had been successful among those who were working at the time of the survey, respondents who were seeking employment were asked where they were looking for a job. Figure 10.6 shows that respondents were seeking employment through a number of different avenues.

Refugees from Somalia were the most likely to seek employment through informal contacts. Eight in ten Somalis looked for work through friends compared to five in ten Tamils and four in ten Zairians. Seven in ten Somalis looked for work through relatives compared to two in ten Tamils and less than one in ten Zairians. Respondents from Somalia were also more likely than others to look for work through their community group. Around three-quarters of Somalis looked for work through their community organization compared to two in ten Zairians and less than one in ten of the Tamil respondents. Even though the Somali community was less likely than others to participate in community activities, Somalis were still using informal networks as a mechanism for trying to gain access to the economic institutions in the host society. This reflects the dependence of Somalis on the voluntary sector for basic information and advice. It is not surprising that Zairians are less likely to use the informal network of friends and family than are others, given their more recent migration and relative lack of social networks.

There was a direct relationship between length of residence and job seeking through friends: the more recent arrivals were more likely to seek employment through friends than were people who had been resident for longer. People who had been resident in the UK for longer looked for jobs through the Job Centre or in newspapers. Six in ten of those who arrived before 1989 used the Job Centre as did half of those who arrived between 1990 and 1992. In contrast only a quarter of those who arrived between 1993 and 1995 had used the Job Centre and one in ten of the most recent arrivals who have been in Britain since 1995. Those who had been in the UK longer were more likely to look for jobs through advertisements in the paper than those who had been resident for less time. People from Sri Lanka were more likely to look for advertisements in the paper (eight in ten) than were those from Zaire (six in ten) and Somalia (four in ten).

Private employment agencies were used more by respondents from Zaire (six in ten) than by respondents from Somalia (three in ten) or Sri Lanka (one in ten). Private agencies were also used more by men than women, nearly half and less than a quarter respectively.

Clearly, people from Somalia were much more dependent on the informal contacts of friends, relatives and community groups for job seeking than were others. This was related, in part, to language skills but also, Somalis were most likely to want information about job seeking and this suggests that they lack information about what avenues are available to them for finding employment. Moreover, it should be stressed that Tamils, who were living most within the ethnic enclave were the most likely to be in employment and have got jobs through formal avenues. The methods used by the Somali community were clearly not successful in terms of finding employment.

CONCLUSION

This chapter has shown that refugees arrive in Britain with high levels of education and employment experience but that their skills and experience remains unused. The small proportion of refugees who are in employment, are employed in low skilled jobs that are not commensurate with their qualifications. Moreover, those who are seeking employment are looking for jobs which do not use their skills and demonstrates that labour market aspirations among refugees are very low.

Refugees face many barriers when trying to obtain employment. Some of the barriers could be alleviated by the direct targeting of resources such as more work experience and more advice and information about methods of job seeking. Indeed, there was an over dependence on informal contacts. Given the high rates of employment among refugees, and the nature of refugee employment, informal networks will not provide refugees with the sorts of employment opportunities which reflect their skills and experience and without such opportunities, barriers to settlement will be very difficult to overcome.

REFERENCES

Al-Rasheed, M. (1992), 'The Iraqi Community in London', *New Community*, Vol. 18, No. 4, pp. 537–50.

Bach, R.L. and Carroll-Seguin, R. (1986), 'Labour Force Participation, Household Composition and Sponsorship among Southeast Asian Refugees', *International Migration Review*, Vol. 20, No. 2, pp. 381–404.

Bloch, A. (1996), *Beating the Barriers: The Employment and Training Needs of Refugees in Newham*, London, London Borough of Newham.

Bloch, A. (1997), 'Refugee Migration and Settlement: A Case Study of the London Borough of Newham', PhD thesis, Goldsmiths College, University of London.

Bravo, M. (1993), *The Special Training Needs of Refugees*, London, Refugee Council.

Carey-Wood, J., Duke, K., Karn, V. and Marshall, T. (1995), *The Settlement of Refugees in Britain*, Home Office Research Study 141, London, HMSO.

Desbarats, J. (1986), 'Ethnic Differences in Adaptation: Sino-Vietnamese Refugees in the United States', *International Migration Review*, Vol. 20, No. 2, pp. 405–27.

Finnan, C.R. (1981), 'Occupational Assimilation of Refugees', *International Migration Review*, Vol. 15, No. 1, pp. 292–309.

Gambell, J. (1993), *Welcome to the UK*, London, National Association of Citizens Advice Bureaux.

Girbash, C. (1991), *Manchester Vietnamese Employment and Training Survey*, The Centre for Employment Research, Manchester, Manchester Polytechnic.

Home Office Research and Planning Unit (1993), *Refugee Resettlement Research Project*, Newsletter No. 4, April 1993, London.

HMSO (1995), 'Asylum Statistics United Kingdom 1994', *Home Office Statistical Bulletin*, HMSO, London.

Joly, D. (1996), *Haven or Hell? Asylum Policies and Refugees in Europe*, Basingstoke, Macmillan.

Knox, K. (1997), *A Credit to the Nation: A study of refugees in the United Kingdom*, London, Refugee Council.

London East Training and Enterprise Council (1995), *Household Survey 1995*, London, LETEC.

London East Training and Enterprise Council (1996), *Economic Bulletin*, Number 3, September 1996, London, LETEC.

Marshall, T (1989), 'Cultural aspects of job hunting', *Refugee Issues*, London, Refugee Council.

Marshall, T. (1992), *Careers Guidance with Refugees*, London, Refugee Training and Employment Centre.

Refugee Council (1992), 'Careers Guidance – When and Where it's needed', *Exile*, No. 64, November 1992, London.

Rix, V. (1996), 'Social and Economic Change in East London' in Butler, T. and Rustin, M. (eds) *Rising in the East: The Regeneration of East London*, London, Lawrence and Wishart.

Robinson, V. (1986), *Transients Settlers and Refugees: Asians in Britain*, Oxford, Clarendon Press.

Sivanandan, A. (1990), *Communities of Resistance: Writings on Black Struggles for Socialism*, London, Verso.

Sly, F. (1995), 'Ethnic Groups and the Labour market: Analyses from the Spring 1994 Labour Force Survey', *Employment Gazette*, June, pp. 251–62, Employment Department, London, HMSO.

Srinivasan, S. (1994), *An Overview of Research into Refugee Groups in Britain During the 1990s*, paper presented at the fourth International Research and Advisory Panel Conference, Oxford, January 1994.

11 Asylum seekers, refugees and the future of citizenship in the European Union

Carl Levy

With the Treaty of Amsterdam, the future of European Union citizenship is directly linked to developments in European refugee and asylum policy. The Treaty on European Union granted European Union citizenship to all citizens of the member states, while one of the chief aims of the Treaty of Amsterdam's Area of Freedom, Security and Justice is to regularize the position of third-country nationals within the European Union and the Single European Market. Refugees and asylum seekers will be directly affected by the harmonization of migration policies and by the future evolution of the still underdeveloped concept of citizenship of the European Union.

This chapter will discuss possible future developments by focusing on four areas of policy. First, the future of refugee and asylum policy is essentially tied to the question of *de facto* refugees. How will the status of 'temporary protection' affect the status of the *de facto* refugee? The wars in former Yugoslavia initiated the widespread usage of temporary protection, but has brought home to the member states the need for burden-sharing or balance of effort. But the Yugoslav tragedy is far from over. The question of the repatriation of Bosnian refugees to their homelands not only casts light on the evolving policy of temporary protection and balance of effort, but the way it is handled may also affect the final settlement in Bosnia itself.

A second set of policies are concerned with solving the root causes of refugee movement. In this respect the creation of an area of Freedom, Security and Justice overlaps with areas of foreign policy address by Common Foreign and Security Policy (CFSP) and by Union trade policy embodied in such international treaties as the Lomé Convention.

A third set of policy concerns address the issue of which institutions in Europe are best placed to help shape the future of asylum and refugee policy. Although the European Union has assimilated most of the European Free Trade Area (EFTA) and the European Economic Area (EEA), and it plans to expand to Eastern Europe and Cyprus early in the next century, this process will take years. It is not at all clear if the United Nation Office of the High Commissioner for Refugees (UNHCR), the Council of Europe and the Organization for Security and Cooperation in Europe (OSCE) might not end up playing a similarly important or greater role than they had already displayed in the early 1990s. In any case, new European Union policy under the First Pillar will take years to become law due to the fact that most legislation will be passed under the unanimity rule. In the meantime there may well be contradictions between the Area of Freedom, Security and Justice of the 12 member states, the Dublin Convention of the 15 member states and the activities of the UNHCR. Furthermore, the variable opt-outs given to the UK, Ireland and Denmark concerning the Schengen *acquis* is a guarantee for constitutional and legal confusion.

The fourth area of policies is the most important for the future of the European Union and involves the evolving relationship between labour migrants, refugees and asylum seekers, their residential status and EU citizenship.

REFUGEE STATUSES AND THE FUTURE RECEPTION OF ASYLUM SEEKERS IN THE EU

By the early 1990s the search for a new type of system to address the needs of non-Convention refugees was becoming an important policy objective in Europe. Dacyl (1995), for instance, argued for the creation of a regional protection regime in Europe called the Comprehensive European System for the Protection of 'Non-Convention' Refugees (CES). Dacyl (1995) raised key points for future discussion. First, who should receive protection and/or material assistance (Convention as against non-Convention refugees)? Secondly, which type of protection do different statuses afford (asylum, temporary protection or other forms of protection)? Thirdly, who should allocate the duties for protection, the region or the international community? Finally, should this protection be focused in or near the country of origin of the refugee or in the potential host state or states?

Former Yugoslavia was a test-bed for these policy concerns, and indeed remains a crucial model for the evolution of a European response to *de facto* refugees and displaced persons. These measures included the internationalization of the refugee crisis via the United Nations Office of the High Commissioner for Refugees, the creation of 'safe havens', the containment of the refugee crisis in the region and finally the direct intervention of foreign troops and observers to secure a cease-fire and temporary settlement.[1]

The idea of creating a CES was first advanced by the Swedish Minister for Immigration, Birgit Friggebo, on 21 July 1992 at the Geneva conference on the Yugoslav refugee crisis. The UK, France and Spain vetoed the proposals. According to Dacyl:

> a tacit consensus was reached that host States in the future would retain their own distinct administrative procedures with respect to non-Convention refugees (1995: 593).

This was associated with the growth of temporary protection. However the practice of temporary protection can be traced back to the haven offered by the French and British governments to refugees fleeing the Spanish Civil War after 1936 and has been practised many times since (Thorburn, 1995: 465). The conceptualization first appeared in a UNHCR document in the 1970s in relation to the Vietnamese Boat People crisis (Thorburn, 1995: 467). In the early 1990s the Slovene government argued for the creation of a new definition of 'temporary refugee', namely, the victim of a military engagement and not merely victims of individual persecution (Thorburn, 1995: 474).

In the meantime, the member states of the European Union created their own forms of *de facto* protection through a variety of largely unco-ordinated practices and non-legally binding Conclusions, which have been detailed in Chapter 2. The refugees from the former Yugoslavia, who benefitted from this Conclusion, were not encouraged to integrate in their host country 'but were to be returned to their country of origins as soon as possible' (Joly, 1996: 76). However, temporary protection may have been a device for the member states and others from avoiding their full responsibilities under international law. Unlike the member states, the UNHCR believed that the victims of ethnic cleansing in the former Yugoslavia should have been treated under the Geneva Convention. In other words, temporary protection was advanced as a method of defining away a potentially large group of refugees who otherwise would have been given the far greater entitlements of

Convention status in their host countries. A quick resolution of the conflict was assumed and therefore the swift return of the refugees was predicted. Indeed,

> Already before the negotiations of the peace settlement in Bosnia Herzegovina at the end of 1995, the General Affairs Council of the European Union had stipulated that good will on the part of the countries of origin to accept the return of refugees was to be one of the criteria for the granting of reconstruction aid to the states of former Yugoslavia (Joly, 1996: 78).

By the end of 1996 bilateral readmission agreements between Bosnia-Herzegovina and Germany concerning 200 000 Bosnian refugees in Germany were in force. The first phases of repatriation occurred in the late spring of 1997 and included single adults and married couples without children (*Migration News Sheet*, December 1996: 10–11). It was agreed that 80 000 Bosnians would return voluntarily to Bosnia or face future forced repatriation. However, those going to a third country (the USA, Canada or Australia usually) or those refugees traumatized by the war or in need of medical treatment would be allowed to stay.[2] This was accompanied by a Bosnian Fund established by the German government which allocated DM 750 million for the first five years of reconstruction. However, these agreements were considered too slow for the *Länder*, who through their Council of Interior Ministers, voiced their demands for quicker repatriation. In fact, in order to accelerate procedures 60 per cent of the Bosnians present in Germany would have to have been repatriated to the Serbian territories of the Sprska Republic within the Bosnian Federation (*Migration News Sheet*, April 1997: 8). But the Bavarian government kept up the pressure by deporting some Bosnians directly from their places of work. This heavy-handed policy brought a strong rebuke from Volke Rühle, the Christian Democratic Federal Defence Minister, demanding the halt of any further repatriation directly to the Sprska Republic, as this might endanger the entire peace settlement in Bosnia (*Migration News Sheet*, May 1997: 10).[3]

In any case, the net effect of these episodes in Germany caused over 600 Bosnians to flee from Germany and seek refuge in Sweden. Unlike Germany, Sweden made it clear that for the time being repatriated Bosnians would not be sent into Serb-controlled areas (*Migration News Sheet*, June 1997: 10). While in Austria only 2000 of 10 190 Bosnians were returned home because the rest would not be sent to the Sprska Republic (*Migration News Sheet*, May 1997: 10). Thus these conflicting policies within the European Union and within

Germany itself, not only demonstrated the failure to get to grips with the nature of temporary protection, they also revealed similar 'adhocery' that had characterized the Yugoslav crisis from its beginnings.

The future of temporary protection

Given the past involvement of the Swedes in the Yugoslav crisis, it is not surprising that Anita Gradin, the European Commissioner from Sweden, in charge of refugees and migration in European affairs, proposed a Joint Action for the Temporary Protection of Displaced Persons in March 1997. The aim of this Joint Action was the creation of a framework for common decision-making between the member states for the initiation, prolongation and phasing out of temporary protection regimes, as well as the establishment of a common threshold as regards rights and benefits for persons under temporary protection (*Migration News Sheet*, April 1997: 6). In order to avoid future disorganized responses witnessed in regard to Bosnian or Albanian refugees, Gradin believed that a Joint Action based on Article K.3 of the TEU (although under the Treaty of Amsterdam this could be passed under the provisions of the First Pillar's Area of Peace, Security and Justice) would be seen as a compliment to the 1951 Geneva Convention and put in place when the normal procedures were overwhelmed by a sudden flow of refugees. The temporary protection regime would apply to persons in need of international protection from any third country or any stateless person who has left his or her country of residence and whose safe return under humane conditions is impossible in view of the situation prevailing in that country (*Migration News Sheet*, April 1997: 6).

These conditions include:

1. Persons fleeing from areas affected by civil conflict.
2. Persons who have been expelled or are fleeing from the systematic abuse of human rights due to religious persecution and/or ethnic cleansing.
3. Persons who flee due to reasons specific to their case and are in need of international protection.

According to Gradin's proposal, the Council of Ministers could introduce a temporary regime if no adequate protection could be found in the region. It could be implemented on the initiative of any member state or the Commission, and measures would be adopted through the Council via qualified majority voting. Annual reports, or at least a report six months before the conclusion of a temporary protection regime, by the European Commission to the Council of Ministers and the European Parliament would be required. Repatriation would then be on a voluntary basis with the assistance of the UNHCR and the non-governmental organizations (NGOs).

Beneficiaries of a temporary protection regime would be granted the right of family reunification and the same entitlements as Convention refugees as regards regular renumeration, social security and other working conditions. In the first period temporary accommodation would be offered but later the same housing entitlements given to Convention refugees would also be offered them.

The granting of asylum to the beneficiaries of temporary protection regimes could be delayed as long as the Council of Ministers had not accepted to phase out a temporary protection regime, but would not last more than five years. If there was no decision after five years, then the Council of Ministers would initiate longer term measures for the beneficiaries of temporary protection.

Although Gradin's proposal comes too late to deal with the crises of the 1990s, it might be a firm basis for European policy in the next century. It also reveals the extent to which she has been listening to the criticism of the NGOs who fear the pursuit of an illiberal lowest common denominator at the European level of policy making. Thus a ECRE position paper, slightly earlier than Gradin's proposal (see, Levy, Chapter 2 of this volume), argued that temporary protection could only be used as a temporary stop-gap and did not reduce the need for a supplementary definition of a refugee in Europe. Temporary protection, as Gradin also argued, could only be seen as strictly time-limited status and should not prevent access by applicants to other refugee determination procedures in the host country. Although this demonstrated an encouraging interaction between NGOs and the European Commission, still the future of the definition of temporary protection rested on the acceptance of a European Union system of burden-sharing or balance of effort concerning the reception of those displaced persons and refugees granted this status.

'BALANCE OF EFFORT' (BURDEN-SHARING) AND ROOT CAUSES

Just like temporary protection, burden-sharing came into widespread usage during the Yugoslav crisis. This meant either the sharing of the physical protection of displaced persons and the associated financial costs within the countries in the former Yugoslavia itself, or it could mean 'employing the spreading of either the physical and economic burden throughout the Union' (Thorburn, 1995: 468). However, the concept of burden-sharing can be found much earlier in the Final Act of the 1951 Geneva Convention and was reiterated by the UNHCR in 1986 (Thorburn, 1995: 468). The concept of burden-sharing pre-dates the Yugoslav crisis and is mentioned in a Resolution of the European Parliament in March 1987, and was fleshed out in the Conclusions of the meeting of the Council of Ministers of the European Community in Edinburgh held in November 1992 and at a meeting of the Council of the European Union held in June 1995 (Thorburn, 1995: 475; Joly, 1996: 70).

Since 1991 the Germans had attempted to create a policy in which burden-sharing would be based upon calculating the national burdens of each member state in relation to the size of the population, territory and per capita GDP of the member states, but modified by the amount each member state contributed to peace-keeping forces devoted to a refugee-producing area (Thorburn, 1995: 466). However in 1991 and during the Yugoslav wars, other member states were reluctant to endorse the German proposals.

During the course of the Bosnian war, burden-sharing was very closely linked to the fortunes of temporary protection. The most vulnerable group of displaced persons who seemed the prime candidates for temporary protection were refugees and displaced persons in besieged cities and regions, caught between the crossfire of warring factions. However, those member states reluctant to afford temporary protection could use a moral argument to disguise their less than noble objections to opening their borders, by claiming that the establishment of safe areas (Bihac, Tulza, Zenica, Sarajevo, Mostar and Srebrenica) would counter the use of temporary protection by ethnic cleansers to expedite their policy of cleansing Bosnia of Muslims. However, in this case the concept of safe areas may have been the functional equivalent of *refoulement* because these safe areas were used to prevent displaced persons from seeking protection

for which the responsibility might be said to be not only with those states returning the displaced, but also with those apparently unwilling to share the burden (Thorburn, 1995: 475).

The future of burden-sharing or balance of effort

The unseemly dilemma created by most member states refusing to accept a sufficient number of displaced persons has caused policy makers to address the problems of burden-sharing in the context of the Yugoslav experience. Some indications of the future trend in discussions can be detected in the remarks of Cornelis D. de Jong, formerly the Adviser to the Head of the Justice and Home Affairs Task Force of the European Commission, in the mid-1990s.

In a similar fashion to Gradin he argues for a comprehensive treatment of temporary refugees through the framework of the European Union. The harmonization of refugee and asylum policy in the European Union can only be accomplished through a properly transparent system of burden-sharing because if the member states are not convinced of its reciprocity, footdragging and meaningless compromises will be the chief result. Steps to give aid to member states with little experience of asylum could also be part of a Union policy (de Jong, 1997: 333). This could be capped off with a quota system once the mechanisms for burden-sharing were in place. In such a system each member state would have a set quota which once filled then spilled over to another member state's unfulfilled quota responsibilities (de Jong, 1997: 333).

Another more disturbing approach might combine the 'Yugoslav' policies of containment and safe havens with the establishment of European reception centres in the regions of origin of the refugees (de Jong, 1997: 333). In this case 'spontaneous asylum applicants might be required to go to these reception centres, even if they had already entered the territory of the Union' (de Jong, 1997: 333). But, then, if the applicants were refugees under the terms of the Geneva Convention they would be admitted by one of the member states through the quota system. Drawing the worst possible conclusions from the Yugoslav crisis, this proposal would be draconian and probably unworkable.

Prevention: the early warning of refugee crises

The connections between burden-sharing, an early warning system of future possible mass flows of refugees and the root causes approach is noted by de Jong whose suggestions are shaped by the failures of the EU during the Yugoslav wars (Thorburn, 1995: 472). Thus before the Treaty of Amsterdam he argued for closer coordination between the Second Pillar (Common Foreign and Security Policy – CFSP) and the Third Pillar (Justice and Home Affairs) of the European Union. De Jong argues that early warning, preventive diplomacy, peace-making and peace-keeping activities are essentially connected with a coordinated asylum and refugee policy (de Jong, 1996: 159–60).

A European early warning system could be constructed, through foreign embassies and local networks, in potential crisis regions. Although this would work through the framework of CFSP, it would also impinge upon ministers responsible for immigration and therefore since the Treaty of Amsterdam, this new institutional arrangement could be placed within the First Pillar of the European Union. The European Commission, in the future, might help coordinate burden-sharing (now balance of effort). If the early warning systems failed to alleviate a refugee-producing crisis in the region, immigration ministers could determine the number of persons each member state could accept for resettlement on its own territory (de Jong, 1996: 160).

De Jong anticipated the advantages of the Treaty of Amsterdam by arguing that the communitarization of asylum and refugee policy would 'reinforce the Union's flexibility and effectiveness in its external relations' (1997: 335). However, other commentators see a more effective form of early warning functioning around the more inclusive Organization for Security and Co-operation in Europe (OSCE) or the Council of Europe.

Gilbert (1997) points to the successes of the High Commissioner on National Minorities of the OSCE in defusing several refugee-producing crises in Eastern Europe. During 1992 he succeeded in protecting ethnic Greeks in Albania and ethnic Russians/Russian speakers in Estonia. The Vienna and Moscow mechanisms could also possibly prevent a future refugee crises caused by massive violations of human rights. Furthermore, the current War Crimes Tribunal at The Hague dealing with war criminals from Bosnia and elsewhere could help build up confidence for the settlement in the former Yugoslavia (Gilbert, 1997: 217, 223).

Prevention: tackling the root causes of refugee crises

Early warning forms one part of the roots causes approach. However this must be one of the most difficult areas to tackle because long-term policy may have perverse unintended effects. Aid to the Third World may, for instance, initially increase flows of migration to Europe as the traditional patterns of rural life are severely disrupted (Castles, 1993: 21). The liberalization of the global economy may cause climatic and economic refugees on a massive scale. 'Should', Ahmed asks (1997: 184), 'people who are starving to death be given asylum?' In any case, the European Union will have to think very carefully about some aspects of its world trade policy. 'Stopping arms exports to LDCs', Castles argues, 'could be the biggest single step towards cutting the number of asylum seekers' (1993: 33). In any case, current aid programmes are insufficient to prevent migration from 'hotspots' such as the Maghreb. Collinson's recent study demonstrates that while the Moroccan and Tunisian governments will accept the aid from the European Union they are not particularly worried about preventing their 'excess' populations from migrating to the North. In any case, the aid policies to the Maghreb carried out by the Spanish, French and Italian governments are ill-thought out and under-funded (Collinson, 1996: 92–3).

If root causes policies are to be efficient and equitable, and not merely palliatives hiding the harmonization of a restrictive migration policy in the European Union, the member states will have to spend considerable sums of money on aid and seriously question their trading policies with the Third World. While it is true that the Lomé Convention now contains a clause requiring participants to adhere to human rights, in reality domestic pressures on member states of the EU, especially over the long-term viability of their arms industries, means that this aspect of the root causes approach is still largely a rhetorical smokescreen.

INSTITUTIONS AND FUTURE POLICY-MAKING

Europeans may be suffering from a surfeit of institutions devoted to formulating and implementing a pan-European policy for asylum seekers and refugees. There are several candidates who could replace or supplement the role of the European Union. The OSCE might be ideal to deal with future refugee movements. 'As it encompasses states where ethnic tension and nationalistic sentiments run strong' (Thorburn, 1995: 478). However, if, the High Commissioner on National Minorities had some success in the early 1990s in Albania and Estonia, according to Joly, the OSCE Office for Democratic Institutions and Human Rights (ODIHR) has been less active due to 'the lack of political will amongst its members' (1996: 80).

The EU and other institutions

Another useful forum might be the Council of Europe since it now includes Croatia and the Russian Federation (Thorburn, 1995: 479). In October 1997, the 40 members of the Council of Europe agreed to extend and reinforce the organization's role in defending human rights in Europe. The European Court of Justice will probably be transformed into a full-blown body and then, in the near future, appoint a human rights mediator, and encourage members, particularly from Eastern Europe, to sign the Council's social charter (*Financial Times*, 10 October 1997: 3). However, so far it has had little effect on the debate over burden-sharing.

Finally the UNHCR has played an absolutely essential role on the ground in Bosnia and elsewhere in the former Yugoslavia and in the intellectual debate shaping asylum and refugee policy during the IGC preceding the Treaty of Amsterdam. But perhaps at the end of the day an earlier suggestion by Christensen and Kjaerum in 1990 (330–3) for the establishment of a new European Refugee Commission encompassing the European Union, the Council of Europe, the OSCE and the UNHCR deserves further consideration by the member states of the European Union as they try to coordinate their refugee and asylum policy in an Area of Freedom, Security and Justice.

The future of 'Schengenland'

Although it is worthwhile to speculate on a new European architecture to address asylum seekers and refugees in a more comprehensive and equitable fashion, there remains the fact within the European Union itself that there are still considerable problems of coordination that may have indeed been worsened by the competing claims of the Treaty of Amsterdam, the Schengen *acquis* and the Dublin Convention.

As shown in Chapter 2 of this volume (Levy), the relationship between the 12 member states who fully accept the Schengen *acquis* and the variously opted-out UK, Ireland and Denmark still needs to be established. There is the equally serious matter of operationalizing the Schengen *acquis* within the EU itself. It seems difficult to reconcile aspects of Schengen, which emphasize promotion of security, with the Treaty of Amsterdam's intention to also underscore the importance of freedom and justice. The incorporation of the Schengen Accords into the EU means the incorporation of the Schengen Information System (renamed the European Information System – EIS) and a second intelligence system called Sirene. Asylum policy will be under the jurisdiction of the European Court of Justice but the EIS will be in the Third Pillar and only marginally affected by the Court. This data control system can be placed into operation through a Joint Action of the Justice and Home Affairs Council operating under Third Pillar rules, but it does not need to be ratified by national parliaments of the member states. In the end, therefore, the EIS will have little Union or national vetting (Norton-Taylor, 1997).

There is the further issue of whether or not Schengen will be considered effective by its very signatories. Before the acceptance of Italy into the Schengen Accords, the State President of Bavaria (much to the annoyance of Chancellor Kohl) expressed his scepticism over the effectiveness of Italian border controls (*Migration News Sheet*, August 1997: 2). Since Italy has few legal means of enforcing the deportation of illegal immigrants caught coming over its borders, most detainees are issued a deportation order and then set free.

Whether or not this will create a flood of illegal migrants with easy access to Austria or Germany remains to be seen, but the controversy over Kurdish asylum seekers in Italy in December 1997 and January 1998 highlighting the general lack of trust between partners is not an auspicious start for greater Schengenland (Traynor and Smith: 1998).

The Dublin Convention: the 'Roma crisis' and the UK

Another serious and immediate challenge may be the implementation of the Dublin Convention. Since the Dublin Convention includes all the member states of the European Union, its operation will foreshadow future harmonization of refugee and asylum policy.

The arrival of Roma refugees in Britain in the autumn of 1997 was one of the first tests of the newly ratified Convention. Not only does this case study reveal the difficulties of using the Dublin Convention, moreover, its very use might in any case undermine the first principles of the Treaty of Amsterdam's Area of Freedom, Security and Justice.

During the election campaign in the spring of 1997, the Labour Party promised to repeal the 1996 Immigration and Asylum Act and restore social security benefits to asylum seekers who claimed asylum from inside the country. But by July 1997 with a Labour government in power, Mike O'Brien, the Home Office minister responsible for immigration, seemed to be backtracking. Although the new government would not leave people destitute, he was uncertain if restoring benefits was the cheapest and most effective way of giving asylum seekers effective aid (Mortimer, 1997a). During the summer of 1997, due to the 1996 Act, local councils were forced to make cuts in their provisions of other services in order to fund assistance for destitute asylum seekers. The Courts had previously ruled that councils were bound under the National Assistance Act of 1948 to protect the lives of its residents, including the cut-off asylum seekers (Meikle, 1997). Under the new Labour government's ruling the local councils – mainly in London which had 95 per cent of all asylum seekers in the UK – were not to be reimbursed for 30 per cent of their costs (Buckby, 1997: 16). In the autumn thousands of asylum seekers were still being denied welfare benefits and asylum seekers were still being sent to safe third countries before their appeals had been heard 'despite earlier promises to retain the right to remain in Britain pending appeal' (Mortimer, 1997b: 11). Furthermore, hundreds of asylum seekers were still being detained in ordinary prisons and hundreds more in detention centres. Fast-track procedures were still in operation despite the promises of the Home Office Secretary, Jack Straw, to change them. Thus a new deal for asylum seekers had yet to materialize and 'the promised land' had eluded the asylum policy makers (Mortimer, 1997b: 11).

It was in this context of some disarray and discouragement that several hundred Roma from the Czech Republic and Slovakia arrived in Dover in October 1997. They were instantly accused by the tabloid press and by implication, O'Brien, of being economic migrants. Reports in the media described mounting pressure on the budget of local social services in Dover and resentment by local residents against the asylum seekers were given wide coverage (Connolly, 1997; Millar, 1997a). But the truth was that the Czech Republic had made them stateless when Slovakia declared its independence in 1993 and in both countries vigilante and state-inspired discrimination and violence made life difficult for Roma communities (*The Guardian*, 1997).

The response by the British government demonstrated how clearly European refugee and asylum policy was still marked by an uncoordinated form of intergovernmentalism. First, Jack Straw announced that asylum claimants would only have five days rather than 28 days to appeal their cases (Buckby, 1997: 16). Secondly, the Dublin Convention was invoked but was difficult to use because of the contesting interpretations of the British and French governments. Once some of the Roma withdrew their claims of asylum after they saw how difficult it would be to receive recognition, the question of how to deport the Roma was foremost in the minds of British ministers. The Czech Republic and Slovakia have relatively easy access to the European Union as their intention is to join the Union as soon as possible. The Roma had been issued valid transit visas with the UK as the destination. France would not allow them to be deported through its territory because it was the UK's responsibility as the country of destination to make sure that the Roma were returned to their home country. Because carrier liability was invoked, not only were the ferry companies fined £2000, they would also have to pay £500 000 for the air fares of the deportees (Millar, 1997b). In the midst of all this haggling, the bigger issues seemed to have been forgotten. The Dublin Convention focused on the mechanism of deportation and the assessment of the cost of the transportation of the deportees, but the spirit of the Area of Freedom, Security and Justice was nowhere to be found. It appears that the uneasy Roma had fled from the Czech Republic and Slovakia after seeing a local television programme extolling the virtues of the British welfare state and in particular the life enjoyed by previous Roma refugees in Dover. There is little secret that many East European states would like to rid themselves of their Roma populations. In this case a form of 'velvet' ethnic cleansing seemed to be the objective. Thus fundamental issues that had characterized the policy debate during the Yugoslav crisis had not gone away, merely the geographical locus of the migration had shifted from the Balkans to East Central Europe.

CITIZENSHIP, LABOUR MIGRATION AND REFUGEES

Asylum seekers and refugees comprise a group of 13 million legally resident third-country nationals and stateless persons in the European Union (*Migration News Sheet*, August 1997: 1).[4] The future statuses of asylum seekers and refugees are bound up with the future statuses of all third-country and stateless residents in the European Union. Ultimately, the future arrangements for the free movement of labour within the European Union and the allied future development in deepening the concept of citizenship of the European Union will affect asylum seekers and refugees.

The closure of the European Union's borders is not an option, as it prepares Eastern Europe for membership. In any case, as in the past, denizens, the reunification of families, refugees and guestworker systems (particularly a revived version in Germany) will sustain the contradictory behaviour of the Union's policy makers (Morris, 1997). One of the most glaring contradictions is the relationship between EU citizenship, the status of resident third-country nationals living in the European Union and the position of refugees.

Since citizenship of the EU is dependent on citizenship of one of the member states, their varying naturalization laws give third-country nationals uneven access to full freedoms throughout the European Union (Guild, 1996). The two key variables to naturalization are the length of wait before the process can begin and the ability to retain dual citizenship (Magleby Sørensen, 1996: 169). However, in an over-arching sense, the member states of the European Union are becoming similar in their naturalization procedures. For if we take the four models of citizenship – imperial, ethnic, republican and multicultural – (Castles and Miller, 1993: 39), then the trend is towards a modified form of ethnic-based citizenship.

Germany is becoming less restrictive and is beginning to allow some leeway within its regime based on *jus sanguinis*, with an acknowledgement that Germany is slowly becoming a multicultural society (Duke, Sales and Gregory, Chapter 6 of this volume). France is weakening its commitment to republican citizenship and *jus soli* and making it more difficult for the children of resident foreigners to adopt French citizenship (Hollifield, 1997: 45). The UK acknowledges itself as a multicultural society and was one of the first European countries to develop policies specifically addressing the problems of racism, but within an immigration policy that virtually only accepts patrials implicitly decided on racial criteria (Schuster and Solomos, Chapter 3 of this volume). Meanwhile Belgium and The Netherlands have eased their naturalization laws (Baldwin-Edwards and Schain, 1994: 11). The proposed new Aliens Bill in Italy would regularize the position of residents in Italy so that after six years they would get the same access to health care and council housing allowed Italian citizens and they would be given the right to vote in local elections (Adler Hellman, 1997: 38).

Even if modified ethnic-based citizenship in most of the member states may be a progressive improvement from the past, the result is that citizenship of the European Union is also indirectly based on an ethnic element. But tens of thousands of Bosnian displaced persons within the European Union had in fact been the victims of the politics of ethnic cleansing which merely took the principle of *jus sanguinis* to its logically bloody conclusions. It is therefore difficult to reconcile ethnic-based citizenship with the high ideals of the Treaty of Amsterdam. The continued sanctioning of this approach not only marginalizes the most marginal group – asylum seekers and refugees – it also inflames the particularism of the ethnic cores of each member state and thereby undermines the political and economic coherence of the European Union itself. As Dave Edye remarks:

> If ethnic cleansing is considered so abhorrent as an idea and practice, then the EU must have another set of values on which a society can be based. If it is not the mono-cultural or mono-ethnic, then it has to be multi-cultural or multi-ethnic, the ideal the Bosnian government was attempting to defend. If we accept the logic of this position then it has implications for the EU in the way, for example, nationality is defined, and immigration and asylum laws are drafted and implemented. Unfortunately, it appears that the most restrictive and exclusive set of rules are in the process of being instituted. However, if a significant number of people living within its borders are denied one of the basic rights of citizenship, then it is difficult to see how a pan-European identity and sense of belonging can be secured and fully developed (1997: 76–7).

Thus, a wider acceptance of the concept of *jus soli* would certainly ease the plight of all resident third-country nationals in the EU, including refugees and asylum seekers. But this will mean that naturalization becomes a normal process throughout the European Union. Citizenship of course entails many entitlements and social citizenship has become an important variable since 1945. In this respect asylum seekers, refugees and migrants may be granted access to the welfare state before they are enfranchised in the national polity. Historically, guestworkers have been recipient of welfare entitlements without having access to the ballot box. But more recently the health of the community has forced some member states of the European Union to grant free social entitlements to *all* residents of their country. Thus in 1997 the regional government of Italy's Veneto region offered free medical treatment to all legal and illegal migrants for fear they endangered the population by carrying infectious diseases (Harper, 1997).

A similar logic of inclusion might solve the current pressures placed on local councils in the UK and The Netherlands (see Chapters 7 and 8 in this volume). The creation of proactive employment and housing programmes, in cooperation with NGOs, would ease the burden recently placed upon local authorities because of their statutory duty under the National Assistance Act of 1948 (see Chapter 8 in this volume).

Refugees and the politics of inclusion

Migrant workers in Europe have enjoyed the fruits of the welfare state, but what has been more difficult is to grant complete civil and political rights to migrants (Duke, Sales and Gregory, Chapter 6 and Minderhoud, Chapter 7 in this volume). The Americans find it relatively easy to grant civil and political rights in a social system with a threadbare welfare state. Nevertheless, this has a direct impact on refugee communities because enfranchised members of refugee communities can lobby the government for more liberal attitudes towards asylum seekers. Similarly, in the UK, even if naturalization for at least the past twenty years has been restricted largely to patrials, the enfranchisement of ethnic minorities has meant that they have now become a significant force within British politics. On the other hand, unmobilized or disenfranchised ethnic minorities in France and Germany respectively allow for a much larger political space for the radical right to use the concept of *jus sanguinis* to mobilize significant minorities of the population around racist agendas (Hollifield, 1992: 204). Thus, easier routes to naturalization would create enfranchised pressure groups for refugee communities and allow for more vigorous contestation of xenophobia at the hustings.

The European Union is at a crossroads, caught between the contradictory logics of inclusion and exclusion, part of 'an increasingly interdependent international system founded on the liberal principles of free trade and human rights.' (Hollifield 1997: 58). And although the contradictions within the Treaty of Amsterdam may push the European Union in an illiberal and self-defeating direction, the Treaty of Amsterdam also announces its intention to combat racism and xenophobia, that has earned the praise of representatives of NGOs defending the rights of migrants (Niessen, 1997).

The contradictory logics of inclusion and exclusion are also at the heart of future success of economic performance and social policy in the European Union. The member states of the European Union will also have to accept a certain amount of permanent and temporary migration to supply the needs of their labour markets in the future (Morris, 1997). Furthermore, the demographic deficit threatening Europe's generous pension provision may only be solved by the immigration of young workers from outside Europe (Thränhardt, 1996).

In this respect the quota systems operated in Australia, Canada and the USA may have to be included in future European policy.

Citizenship of the European Union and the future status of refugees and asylum seekers in the EU

There may still be a wide gulf separating the noble declarations of the Treaty of Amsterdam pledging to combat racism and xenophobia and the likelihood that the EU would institute an American-style immigration quota system. However, recent concrete proposals to facilitate the movement of third-country nationals within the European Union may at least be a step towards bold innovative liberal policies that broaden the concept of European Union citizenship and undermine the demagogic appeals of a Le Pen or a Haider.

In the summer of 1997, Anita Gradin proposed a new Convention to facilitate the movement of third-country nationals in the European Union (*Migration News Sheet*, August 1997: 1–2).[5] Rather than a Recommendation, Resolution or Joint Action in the Third Pillar, only a legally binding Convention would give the proper guarantees throughout the Union, and with the ratification of the Treaty of Amsterdam this could be recast in the form of a Directive. Although under the Treaty's rules (Levy, Chapter 2 in this volume) it would still require unanimous agreement and this would not expedite its passage, once passed it would be under the jurisdiction of the European Court of Justice. Such a Convention (or Directive) would regulate the rules of admission for third-country nationals for employment, self-employment, study, non-gainful residence and family reunification. The main aim of her Convention (or Directive) was the granting to long-term residents in the European Union the same social rights afforded to citizens of the member states by the Treaty on European Union.

Although long-term residents would not be granted the right to vote in European Union elections or stand as MEPs, they would enjoy the full fruits of the Single European Market. Most importantly, long-term residents would be granted residence under the European Union after a five-year sojourn in any member state in which they have been guaranteed a 10-year stay calculated from their first arrival. In this respect, the European Union would become the 'sixteenth member state' for these long-term residents. In other words, this Convention or Directive would grant the functional equivalent of EU economic and social citizenship for long-term residents of the Union. They would be better protected from deportation, and they would be granted the same rights as EU citizens concerning employment, association and social entitlements.

In this respect Gradin's proposal would have a direct effect on Convention refugees. It might also affect the condition of long-term *de facto* refugees who have been given status rather close to full Convention recognition. And by potentially enhancing the position of all third-country nationals in the European Union, it might liberalize popular attitudes towards asylum seekers.

Gradin's proposals are an optimistic and expansive reading of the potentialities of European integration at the end of the twentieth century. A liberal interpretation of citizenship of the European Union would thus be a practical and immediate way to combat the xenophobia and racism that the Treaty of Amsterdam proposed to do. The inclusion of third-country nationals in the Single European Market will be an appropriate way to fulfil the aim of the Treaty of Rome to foster an ever closer union among (all) the peoples of Europe. In any case, without a European polity based upon the respect for human rights, the European Union will be neither economically nor politically successful.

Migrants, refugees and asylum seekers are not the prime danger to the future of Europe. If the European Union is to create a just and equitable Area of Freedom, Security and Justice it must not endorse the arguments of the zero-sum nationalists who have aroused the worst ghosts of Europe's past. The Single European Market has not created a vast flood of poor Southern citizens of the European Union directed towards the richer North. Nor would the liberalization of refugee and migration law in the Union instantly produce a flood of applicants at its borders from the East or South (Thränhardt, 1996). No, migration is not the prime danger to Europe. Rather this threat is found amongst the political merchants who peddle doomsday scenarios that besmirch the liberal democratic values underlying the last fifty years of European integration.

NOTES

1. The intervention of Italian and other troops in Albania in 1997 is based on a similar logic.
2. It was estimated that up to April 1997, 25 000 to 50 000 Bosnians refugees had repatriated (*Migration News Sheet*, April 1997: 8).

3.   The Federal government itself was far from blameless. The UNHCR warned the Foreign Minister, Klaus Kinkel, that further repatriation of Bosnians to Serb-controlled areas of Bosnia might destabilize the entire peace settlement (*Migration News Sheet*, June 1997: 8–9).
4.   They are perhaps over one million undocumented persons in the European Union.
5.   She had first suggested the Convention on 24 April 1995.

REFERENCES

Adler Hellman, J. (1997), 'Immigrant "Space" in Italy: When an Emigrant Sending Becomes an Immigrant Receiving Society', *Modern Italy*, Vol. 2, Nos. 1/2, pp. 34–51.

Ahmed, I. (1997), 'Exit, Voice and Citizenship', in Hammar, T., Brochmann, G., Tomas, K. and Faist, T. (eds), *International Migration, Immobility and Development: Multidisciplinary Perspectives*, Oxford, Berg, pp. 159–85.

Baldwin-Edwards, M. and Schain, M.A. (1994), 'The Politics of Immigration: Introduction', *West European Politics*, Vol. 17, No. 2, pp. 1–16.

Buckby, S. (1997), 'Tighter Controls on Asylum Seekers', *Financial Times*, 28 October, p. 16.

Castles, S. (1993), 'Migration and Minorities in Europe. Perspectives for the 1990s: Eleven Hypotheses', in Wrench, J. and Solomos, J. (eds), *Racism and Migration in Western Europe*, Oxford, Berg, pp. 17–34.

Castles, S. and Miller, M. (1993), *The Age of Migration. International Population Movements in the Modern World*, Basingstoke, Macmillan.

Christensen, A.P. and Kjaerum, M. (1990), 'Refugees and Our Role in the European House', *International Journal of Refugee Law*, Vol. 2, Special Issue, pp. 323–33.

Collinson, S. (1996), *Shore to Shore. The Politics of Migration in Euro-Maghreb Relations*, London, Royal Institute of International Affairs.

Connolly, K. (1997), 'Sun, Seaside and Singing for TV's Romany Exiles', *The Guardian*, 21 October, p. 4.

Dacyl, J.W. (1995), 'Europe Needs a New Protection System for 'Non-Convention' Refugees', *International Journal of Refugee Law*, Vol. 7, No. 4, pp. 579–95.

de Jong, C.D. (1996), 'Elements for a More Effective European Union Response to Situations of Mass Influx', *International Journal of Refugee Law*, Vol. 8, Nos. 1/2, pp. 156–68.

de Jong, C.D. (1997), 'European Immigration Policies in the Twenty-First Century', in Uÿarer, E.M. and Puchala, D.J. (eds), *Immigration into Western Societies: Problems and Policies*, London, Pinter, pp. 323–37.

Edye, D. (1997), 'Citizenship in the European Union: The Post-Maastricht Scenario', in Symes, V., Levy, C. and Littlewood, J. (eds), *The Future of Europe: Problems and Issues for the Twenty-First Century*, Basingstoke, Macmillan, pp. 63–80.

Gilbert, G. (1997), 'The Best "Early Warning" is Prevention: Refugee Flows and European Responses', *International Journal of Refugee Law*, Vol. 9, No. 2, pp. 207–28.

The Guardian, (Leader) (1997), 'A Clear Case of Discrimination. Vaclav Havel Must Explain Why His Romanies Are Leaving', *The Guardian*, 21 October, p.12.

Guild, E. (1996), 'The Legal Framework of Citizenship in the European Union', in Cesarani, D. and Fulbrook, M. (eds), *Citizenship, Nationality and Migration in Europe*, London, Routledge, pp. 30–54.

Harper, J. (1997), 'Health Care Free for Illegal Immigrants', *The Guardian*, 23 September, p. 10.

Hollifield, J.F. (1992), *Immigrants, Markets and States: The Political Economy of Postwar Europe*, Cambridge, MA, Harvard University Press.

Hollifield, J.F. (1997), 'Immigration and Integration in Western Europe: A Comparative Analysis', in Uÿarer, E.M. and Puchala, D.J. (eds), *Immigration into Western Societies: Problems and Issues*, London, Pinter, pp. 28–69.

Joly, D.(1996), *Haven or Hell? Asylum Policies and Refugees in Europe*, Basingstoke, Macmillan.

Magleby Sørensen, J. (1996), *The Exclusive European Citizenship: The Case for Refugees and Immigrants in the European Union*, Aldershot, Avebury.

Meikle, J. (1997), 'Asylum Seekers' Support System Near Collapse', *The Guardian*, 14 June, p. 12.

Millar, S. (1997a), 'Hard Times for the Gypsies', *The Guardian*, 21 October, p. 4.

Millar, S. (1997b), 'Carriers Face £ 1/2 m Bill for Gypsies', *The Guardian*, 4 November, p. 4.

Morris, L. (1997), 'A Cluster of Contradictions: The Politics of Migration in the European Union', *Sociology*, Vol. 31, No. 2, pp. 241–59.

Mortimer, E. (1997a), 'Ministers Backs Tough Line on Refugees', *Financial Times*, 10 July, p. 4.

Mortimer, E. (1997b), 'Promised Land Eludes Asylum Policymakers', *Financial Times,* 21 October, p. 11.

Niessen, J. (1997), 'The Treaty of Amsterdam and its Clauses on Immigration, Asylum and Anti-Discrimination', Brussels, Migration Policy Group, June 26.

Norton-Taylor, R. (1997), 'Watch on Suspect Citizens', *The Guardian*, 22 July, p. 2.

Thorburn, J.E. (1995), 'Transcending Boundaries: Temporary Protection and Burden-sharing in Europe', *International Journal of Refugee Law*, Vol. 7, No. 3, pp. 459–80.

Thränhandt, D. (1996), 'European Migration from East to West: Present Patterns and Future Directions', *New Community*, Vol. 22, pp. 227–42

Traynor, I. and Smith, H. (1998), 'EU Passport-Free Regime Buckles', *The Guardian*, 6 January, p. 9.

Index